Love from Blodwen

Love *from* Blodwen

MARGARET WYLES

seren

Seren is the book imprint of
Poetry Wales Press Ltd
Nolton Street, Bridgend, Wales
www.seren-books.com

ISBN 1-85411-359-3

A CIP record for this title is available from
the British Library.

The publisher works with the financial assistance
of the Welsh Books Council.

Printed in Great Britain by CPD (Wales), Ebbw Vale
Cover painting by W. Wyles.

Part One

September 1932 to September 1939

Chapter One

F'annwyl Miriam,

Here's some news for you now, you'll have a real shock! Haydn and I have decided to leave the South as soon as I'm strong enough, after the baby's born. He's not half well, and the old business is worrying him to death. So many poor people, and he just can't bear to refuse them food. Women with babies in the shawl, and plenty more round their feet. Bad debts at the back of the ledger are overtaking the paying ones at the front. We tried not to give credit, but what can you do when all the other shops give it? The Depression is getting worse and Haydn's father doesn't help, poking his nose in every five minutes with his extravagant schemes. I feel we must get away before it's really desperate. We thought it would be best to find a little shop where money isn't everything. Martha heard of this place near you and we are coming to see it. It's a house, shop and Post Office, with enough land for a few cows and pigs. The rent is very reasonable, and we can move in early spring. It sounds ideal, don't you think? Write and tell me, I expect you know it.

Miriam fach, can we stay one night with you? We hope to come down a week next Thursday, and back early Friday. Mamgu Poli will look after the shop, and Trefor is driving us down. He'll stay at Hafod, of course, and we'll bring plenty of food, so don't worry about that.

If we like the place, Poli's giving us a bedroom suite for the baby's room. She says she knows for certain we're going to live there, you know Poli and her signs. She ordered it to be made last week, lovely satin pine with a brown marble washstand. She's bought the water jug and basin already, blue, and very pretty too. Full speed ahead as usual with Poli, she can't wait to see.

I'm very good indeed, carrying a lot of weight, it's going to be a big baby for sure. Write back quick now, Miriam fach, can't wait to hear from you. It would be lovely to live close again, wouldn't it? Any news at your end? I hope you, your Dat and the children are well.

Love from,
Blodwen.

I was lying on my bedroom floor, in a circle of warmth spreading from the hanging lamp below. Through a gap in the boards, I watched my mother washing her long, black hair and for a while, her graceful movements pushed away the terrors of the dark. The sudden scream of a fox sent me hurtling down the narrow stairs, to be held in a warm, wet hug.

'Nothing to be frightened of, Margaret *fach*, only the old fox crying for his supper. I thought you were fast asleep. Let me dry my hair and I'll tell you another story.'

It was Friday night, bath night for Mam and me. I loved having her all to myself, sitting close together on the *sgiw*, the drops of water from her brush flying into the fire, spitting and hissing. Dad and Col wouldn't be home for ages, leaving plenty of time for a favourite story. I wanted the one about our arrival in the village, when I was a baby.

Mam brought us from the coal-mining valleys of the South, to the peace and beauty of the country, where my father's health would surely improve. Her people, born and bred in Sîr Aberteifi and mostly answering to the name of Davies, lived on both sides of the river from Llanybydder to Aberystwyth. My father's maternal family had its roots in Sîr Gaerfyrddin, so we were going home to the country, *gatre' i'r wlad*. The village was to be a haven for the three of us, a new beginning.

'Now then, what story would you like?'

'The one about coming here in Mamgu Poli's car when I was a baby.'

'Again?'

'Yes, again.'

'All right then. When you were a very little baby, Daddy and I brought you over the big mountains from the South, where Mamgu and Dadcu Davies and Mamgu Poli and Dadcu Jono live. It was a bright, April day when we started off in Mamgu Poli's car, cold, but sunny. Trefor was driving, of course, and Daddy followed us in our old van. Mamgu Poli said it wasn't fit for a new baby. Everyone gave us lots of presents for the house, and Mamgu Poli packed enough food for an army. You were wrapped up safe and sound in a thick, white shawl knitted by your Mamgu Davies. Good thing too, because as we drove over the Beacons it got colder, and I started to vex about the house being damp and miserable. Trefor drove very slowly on those narrow roads. All those twists and turns! The journey seemed endless, but fair play, he never asked me to get out once. We stopped at Sennybridge for dinner, but I was anxious to be here before dark. There were fires to light, food to cook and above all, beds to be aired. Your Uncle Ifor left early with the lorry, to see to the bed frames, first thing. I thought they might have to take out the upstairs windows to get the furniture in, the stairs being so narrow. So much to do before we could go to sleep. It was very cold by then, with the smell of the sea in the air. There were hundreds of primroses in the high hedges and in the woods, you could see the promise of bluebells. Very quiet it was, not just the lack of sound, but another world somehow. Made you hold your breath it did.

'We left the main road and from the top of the hill we saw the village in the valley, green hills all around. Very green it was, I remember, with small fields in patchwork patterns, the hedges dark in- between. The leaves on the willows along the river were all rusty in the sunset. To me, it was the most beautiful sight I'd ever seen. There's a good omen, I thought. Your Mamgu Poli would have agreed with that. Trefor stopped outside the gate of our new home, just as Aunty Miriam opened the door, all smiles. She thought we were never coming. She wanted to see us settled, a bit of a surprise like, and she took us inside to meet everybody. Mrs Emrys, Mrs Morris, Mrs Thomas and Mrs Davies, Tŷ Capel, had all helped make the house ready. The *sgiwiau*, the big table and the Aladdin lamp came with the house, and our rag mats looked grand on the slate floors. A good thing they were mostly red, it showed up a treat.

'Uncle Ifor and the women had worked like Trojans, and the beds were ready with hot bricks in both of them. What a welcome for strangers! It made us feel right at home. Everyone made a fuss of you. Two babies in the village now, you and Rhodri, the only little ones in the place. There was a big fire with a pot of *cawl* bubbling away on the chain, fresh bread, butter and cheese. Aunty Mir had baked Welsh cakes and Mrs Morris brought one of her best trifles, with hundreds and thousands and sugar violets on top, like the ones she makes for you when you're ill in bed. I couldn't help having a little cry, it was all so lovely. Before they went, the women told me the house had been kept aired since the other people left. It's very, very unlucky to let the fire go out, and seeing it was too far for us to bring hot coals from our other house, they'd kept it going. *Yr aelwyd* is the centre of the home and the *pentanfaen* at the back is never to be removed. That's the tradition, isn't it? We still keep the old ways here.

'They said good night, they'd be back tomorrow to help with the rest of the furniture, and scrubbing out the shop, to be on the safe side. After supper, Uncle Ifor left with the lorry driver and Trefor took Aunty Miriam home. We were alone, just the three of us, with you fast asleep on the *sgiw*. We were so happy to be here, I can't tell you how happy. It was a grand start and we knew from then on, everything would be A1. We went to bed and slept like logs. The End.'

'You left out the bit about the pup.'

'Oh, yes, Mrs Davies said that when her corgi had pups, we could have one as a present for you. Dogs and children should be brought up together, then they'll be friends forever. And that's what happened, isn't it, *cariad*? You and Pedro have always been the best of friends. Best little dog in the world. Right then, time for bed now, Daddy and Col will be home before long.'

She sang me to sleep, her voice singsong, my favourite song, my favourite baby song.

'Gee Ceffyl bach yn cario ni' n dau,
Dros y mynydd i hela cnau,
Dŵr yn yr afon a'r cerrig yn slic,
Cwympo ni'n dau,
Wel dyna chi dric'

It was difficult at first being outsiders in such a close community, a remote place even by Welsh standards. My mother, a servant on a large farm from the age of thirteen was well used to country life, but my father, a town dweller, had much to learn. The same self-reliant

families had lived in the village and surrounding farms for generations, keeping old customs and traditions in the natural events of
each day. Family, Chapel, community, work and the turning of the
seasons were the most important elements of their lives. Success was
judged by the amount of food on the table and the whiteness of your
wash. Strangers did not visit, little heed was paid to the changing
world outside, and only in extreme hardship was help sought from
elsewhere. Although there were undercurrents of tension and division, mutual dependence left little room for open discord. They trod
gently with a deep feeling of obligation towards each other, their animals, their land and surroundings. Daily life was similar to that
described by my grandparents with nature as a powerful master and
poverty and adversity never far away. The village was calmly and
impassively behind the times.

Approaching from the coast road, the school and School House
lay at the bottom of a steep hill, separated from the village by the
river. Our home, over the bridge on the valley floor, was the first of
ten small, stone houses built on the left of a gentle incline to the
crossroads. The Chapel and Manse dominated the row of *tai bach*
with the vestry and cemetery alongside. Nain Pritchard, landlady to
most of the village, lived in Caenant, the only house on the right. Her
daughter, Miss Eirlys, was married to a sea-captain, and spent much
of her time with her mother. Evan, the only surviving son, ran a
prosperous farm beyond the crossroads, near the forge and Besi's
cottage. Even there, the trees grew to the east, leaning away from
strong sea winds, laden with rain. It rained and rained.

None of the houses had electricity or sanitation, and water came
from a standpipe at either end of the village. Each lavatory stood as far
from the house as possible. Ours, beyond the pigsty, in a corner covered with ivy, was a place of dread for me. Three holes in a scrubbed
white plank, the smallest graced with a footstool! Not that my feet
remained there for long. The rustle of rats in the rafters and other fidg-
ety noises filled me with terror. Accompanied by my mother in the
daytime, nothing on earth would persuade me to visit after dark.

We lived in a draughty, rambling place with cavernous outbuildings straggling behind the shop into the yard. In the parlour, too

damp for use, my mother's best, leatherette, three-piece suite lurked under sheets for half the year. It retained a distinct hint of mould for the rest of its days. The *gegin fawr*, or big kitchen, was the heart of the house, dominated by a large table covered in the afternoons with a red, plush cloth. My mother cooked on the open fire where pots, ovens, trivets, cranes and racks glowed with black lead. An enormous kettle heated water for bathing and hair washing, once a week. Two *sgiwiau*, settles, stood on either side of the hearth, easily converted into beds by pulling out the base. My father's oak desk occupied most of one wall with Col's chair next to the door. Under colourful rag mats, thick layers of newspaper absorbed moisture from slate floors laid on earth.

The rest of the house, two bedrooms and a recess on the landing, was unheated, except for the warmth of the bread oven in the *gegin fach,* or scullery. A long, deal table and benches took up most of this room, scrubbed daily with white sand by my mother. Was it true that in the old days, the household ate their midday *cawl* from ten hollows in its surface, to save on the washing up? I preferred our wooden bowls and carved spoons any day, keeping china dishes for tea and supper and the best for Sundays, holidays and visitors. Cream, enamel washing bowls and soap dishes stood on a third bench, with towels as stiff as cardboard on the line above. Hams and sides of bacon hung from the beamed ceiling, wrapped in muslin and herbs to keep away fat, black, blue and green flies and their maggoty legacy. The smooth, slate shelves of the dairy at the north end were crowded with bowls, pans and pails of butter, cream and milk. Cheese was always in the making, and jugs of buttermilk cooled near the churn. Painted blue to deter flies with perforated zinc covering the window, it was a gloomy place, smelling strongly of moss. In the storeroom dividing the house from the shop, a heavy door led to the barn, outbuildings and dreaded coalhole.

All the women worked hard to keep their homes spic and span, cleanliness being next to godliness. Floors were swept and scrubbed daily, mats thrashed in the yard, lamps cleaned and trimmed and everything on the hearth black-leaded and polished with a piece of velvet for extra shine. My mother, too busy to be obsessed with the duster, liked the house to look homely and bright, keeping a good fire, plenty of food on the table, and a welcome for all. Nothing better.

Carefully tended gardens were mostly the men's province. The Misses Bowen looked after their own, everything in order like their house, and Besi would never let anyone near her special plants and herbs used for medicines. *Hen* Mr Hopcyn and Mr Rhys were neighbours and the best gardeners in the village. The former, well into his eighties, produced far more than his needs, showering the women with raspberries, strawberries, honey and vegetables in abundance, receiving puddings and jams in return. Not so Mr Rhys, the meanest man in the place. To outshine Mr Hopcyn, he bought seeds from the catalogue, growing unusual things like perfect tomatoes, stringless beans, thin-skinned, long cucumbers and luscious logan-berries. Very tempting for the good cooks in the village, but Mr Rhys never gave away a morsel, always demanding cash on the spot. Even his wife had to pay for every single vegetable! Did she charge her husband for cooking his meals, my mother asked? Mrs Rhys looked shocked. How could Mr Rhys be expected to buy his special seeds without money? Mam would sooner starve than buy anything from Mr Rhys. Potatoes, grown across the road on Caenant's ground, were either paid for in cash, or the villagers gave a day's labour for every row of eighty yards. We picked and bagged them ourselves, to be stored for winter, along with other root crops.

A butcher's van called on Friday providing the Sunday joint, sausages and liver, and sometimes, a horse and cart brought fresh fish from the coast. In early spring, Dad and I often visited Cenarth to buy trout, still caught from coracles at night. On warm days, we walked the river path below steep banks of bluebells, their heavy scent filling the valley. It was an unforgettable sight, the foaming white falls against the intense blue flowers, as far as you could see.

Love from Blodwen

F'annwyl Miriam,

Well, we are beginning to settle in. Everyone has been more than kind in helping. They say they are glad to see the shop going again, and another baby in the village.

My confinement is over at last. I'm feeling very well now, but I don't think I could go through that again, Miriam fach, and the doctor did advise no more children. Anyway, this one is as happy as the day is long, and as fat as mud. Very dark her hair is now, and she's going to have dark eyes too.

The shop is beginning to take shape, all clean and tidy. Haydn has put up more shelves, and sorted out a way to keep the food safe. I've started making butter and cheese to sell. The butter is lovely, we have good milk from Bon, the Jersey, but the cheese is touch and go. Too crumbly yet, but practice makes perfect, I hope. We are going to have our own bacon in time.

The school has asked me if I'd like to make cawl for dinner for some of the children. Mrs Thomas takes several, but she can't manage any more. It would be extra money, and we could do with it. It's a lot of work, though, I'll have to think about it. God knows, Miriam, you have plenty to do yourself. If things go well we might have a gwas to help on the farm. Haydn hasn't taken to that very well. A town boy born and bred, see, not much clem in that direction. His health still isn't good and I'm praying he'll get better soon.

Do you know, I still can't get used to the quiet? I've been in some out of the way places, but this beats the band. It's quiet beyond, except when the children come out of school to play, and then the sound rings through the valley like an explosion. And no traffic, nothing passes through except the post. There is talk of the farmers selling milk to a Milk Marketing Board soon, so there'll be a lorry every day then. But at the moment, our old van is the only thing on four wheels for miles. We're not on the way to anywhere, or on the way back.

I'm getting used to the Aladdin lamps again, but I keep on breaking the mantle. No water in the house is the hardest, I think, but I'm lucky to have the tap straight across the road. I do like it here, and the people are A1. Haydn likes Saturday nights best, when the farmers come down for their tobacco and Woodbines. They tell stories about droving from Tregaron, but I don't know half the time whether to believe them or not.

Well, Miriam, I must go, time for tea before Chapel. It is lovely and peaceful there, with a bit of a clonc afterwards. The singing is much slower than in the South.

I hope you are well, see you a week Thursday.

Love from,
Blodwen.

I once heard my father describe himself as an educated master grocer with a bad chest, who couldn't make money if it grew on trees. Sitting on the Post Office stool, I watched him making blue paper bags for packing sugar. He looked very smart in his collar and tie and starched, white shop-coat, his dark hair glossy with Brilliantine, his shoes highly polished. Dad never wore clogs, not even in the yard. Today, he was happy. He always sang *'Twas on the Isle of Capri* when he was happy. Finishing the song with a flourish, he went down on one knee before me, arms in the air. I clapped hard, pleased to see him so well.

Dad was good at shop work, making sure everything looked clean and inviting, the windows newly dressed every week. He liked pyramids best, built high with tins and packets, all colours of the rainbow. Counters were polished, marble tops thoroughly washed before placing butter, cheese, lard, bacon, blocks of yeast and salt on their cold surfaces. These were packed away every night to prevent contamination by mice. Dad feared contamination, it didn't agree with groceries. The bacon-slicing machine in the corner was a mighty, red and silver monster, its shiny, circular blade swishing through the meat, putting my teeth on edge. I was never allowed to touch it.

New shelving displayed mouse-proof goods, from jars of Bovril, bottles of castor oil and Angers Emulsion to Derbac soap for killing nits, Snowfire cream for chapped hands, which didn't work, and senna pods, which did. A tea chest stood in the corner next to the milk churn and at the end of the counter, a basket of bread, baked daily by my mother. Goods bought to order included yards of cotton and flannelette for bedding, feather-proof ticking for pillows and mattresses, and thick rolls of coloured towelling. Creamy *cartheni*, Welsh wool blankets with plaids or stripes in red and black, were brought on approval from Llandysul mill, along with skeins of wool. The women used every spare moment to knit and crochet countless garments, from formidable underwear to dainty summer gloves for Chapel. Many of our other clothes were made by the Misses Bowen, with special outfits for the *Cymanfa Ganu* at Easter.

The catalogue lay on the counter next to the glass-fronted Post Office desk. We all spent ages looking through the packed pages, waiting excitedly for orders to arrive in fat parcels by post. In the storeroom, the telephone hung lop-sidedly on the wall. Regarding it as an instrument of the Devil, the previous postmaster had refused to touch it, leaving it to ring in vain. My father's readiness to give and receive messages, and his ability to speak English, helped him find a place in his new life. Gradually, the villagers grew accustomed to his mangled version of the Welsh language.

I liked everything about the shop, except the poor dead rabbits hanging next to the door by their neatly crossed legs, their stomachs held open by slivers of stick, showing the liver and kidney. I was glad when they were taken to the railway station in the van, leaving behind a heavy, filling smell and drips of blood in the sawdust.

'Why aren't you playing with Rhodri today?'

'His mam won't let him out with me anymore.'

'Why not?'

'I took him up the school hill in the pushchair this morning and it went off on its own. He fell out at the bottom and bashed his knees and his nose. He was bleeding. He can't play with me now because his mam says I'm too rough. I didn't mean to hurt him.'

'Did you say how sorry you were?'

'Yes, but Mrs Thomas says I'm a real tomboy, dragging him off too far. I'm given too much rein, she says, always disappearing on my own. She thinks we're a funny lot in this house.'

'I expect she does, Snwny, and I'm sure she's right, but that's the way things are. Anyway, there's always your old pal Col to play with, and Ita'll be here before long, it's almost time to cut the hay.'

'I can't wait to see Ita. I'll go and see if they're on the *rhos*.'

'Just a minute. Take this parcel to Mr Morris first.'

Mr Morris was a stonecutter and monumental mason, and the parcel contained books of gold leaf for his lettering. Once used, he gave them to me, the rustly tissue paper a lovely see-through pink. His workshop, next door but one to us, had gravestones stacked outside, waiting to be worked and polished. I watched him delicately brushing gold, like touching a butterfly's wing, into the names of the dead. Wil Morris was a good craftsman, an artist, some said, and even strangers came to buy his headstones. His eyes were exactly the colour of his grey overalls. So were those of his daughter, Ceri, a striking girl with pale yellow hair, paler than any gold leaf. Exceptional, according to my Mamgu Poli. Training to be a nurse, far away in Swansea, Ceri's visits always caused a stir. She no longer wore clothes made by the Misses Bowen, or ordered from the catalogue. Her modern, fashionable outfits were bought from big, posh shops in Swansea, with colours that matched, silky stockings and high-heeled shoes. What an eye-opener for the women, especially the pale green costume, cream frilly blouse and velvet hat with a long feather. Ceri often gave a fashion parade in the shop, walking up and down, twirling around in her pretty colours and swishy materials. Clapping and laughing, the women said the pale stockings were absolutely gorgeous. All except Dilys Rhys. She wasn't smiling and I could see she was jealous. Several years older than Ceri, there was no hope of her having pretty things, her father being such a tight-fisted old miser. A woman's place was in the house according to Mr Rhys, a stern, miserable man with a loud voice. He irritated my mother, who considered meanness a cardinal sin, by pestering Dad to buy needles for his new gramophone, at cost price in the warehouse. Mr Rhys' gramophone was a big surprise for the village. How did he manage to part with the money? We often heard it playing Handel's *Messiah*, but nobody was ever invited into the house to listen in comfort.

Mrs Rhys shunned the fashion shows, insisting that no good would come of prancing about, just you wait and see. There was a lot of wait and see lately, because Ceri had totally abandoned the band of silk around her neck. It was worn by many women and girls in the village, to keep away diseases and stop the Devil going down their throats. Mrs Rhys, in particular, was watching Ceri very closely.

The band was a mystery to me. Although the Chapel preached the Devil's presence around every corner, day and night, we removed it on the first day of June, along with our winter clothing. *Twt, twt*, my mother explained, the old Devil goes on holiday like everybody else! Another thing, why didn't the men wear a band, summer or winter? Siencyn, the cobbler, had the answer. Men were safe because they didn't open their mouths non-stop, talking and *cloncing*. His workshop, built on a platform between our shop and his house, was a place of refuge for Siencyn. There he stayed, at the top of the steps, until the men returned from work. He complained that the village was falling under petticoat rule, the women taking over on the quiet. Things were changing fast, but surely fifteen men could stand up to twelve women? Well, my mother said, men are rocks and women like water, and we all know what water does to rock, given time. Mrs Olwen Guto didn't think so, I'd seen her crying in her garden, her apron over her face, and Mrs Rhys' eyes were always cold, even when the little ones sang *Sua'r Gwynt* for Christmas.

The *Ladi Llwyd*, the Grey Lady, was sad in a different way. Gentle and distant, she lived alone in the last house, playing her piano for hours. Rhodri and I often sat under the hedge listening to the sweet, haunting music. About thirty years old, dark and elegant, she wore simple, expensive clothes, always dove-grey in colour. Every Friday, she left in a chauffeur-driven car for an unknown destination, returning on Monday morning. As she didn't attend Chapel or visit the shop, we knew nothing of her history. Finding that difficult to bear, the women talked about her continually. Where did she go, and where was her family? Why did she keep to herself so much? What was the big mystery then? I thought it was a sad mystery, like her music.

Mrs Morris came into the workshop saying she'd heard I was out of favour with Mrs Thomas. What if she asked Rhodri to join me for tea in her house, to make friends again? Nobody in his right mind refused one of Mrs Morris' teas. She made cakes like an angel, with dainties all laid out on lacy doilies in her cosy kitchen, clean as a new pin. Pride of place was taken by a modern, tiled fireplace, a large oven on one side and a hot water tank with a tap, on the other. The only one in the village and a sight to behold, it took two men from Aberteifi three days to set up.

Small and jolly with warm brown eyes and hair in earphone plaits, Tegwen Morris' favourite saying was "eat up". We did – creamy, jammy, delicious things – until we could barely move. We finished with a singsong led by Mr Thomas, a good baritone, prominent in the Chapel.

Rhodri and I were friends again but when I went to his house, there was no welcome there. I knew it would be a long time before his mother forgave me for hurting her little prince. His two brothers were grown, attending the County School in Aberteifi, where they stayed with Mrs Thomas' sister during the term. They were clever enough to go to college, if the money could be found, and be a credit to their family. Mrs Morris explained that Rhodri was all the more precious to his parents because he came to them late in life, to be a great comfort in their old age. I was to remember he was delicate, not robust like me, and I should treat him gently and kindly. I thought I did.

Pedro, my dog, was waiting down by the river with Dan, the old carthorse. I jumped from the big stone onto his back, so broad, it was like sitting in an armchair. Clinging to his long mane, the three of us took a slow walk along the riverbank. The sun was warm and I was full of delicious tea, but I knew a lecture awaited me at home regarding Rhodri's accident. Making sure we were alone, I stopped near my most secret place, a dry hole by the fallen tree. Dan and Pedro didn't make a sound, and no-one ever knew we were there, not even Col and Ita. I kept special treasures in the roots, odd shaped shells and stones from Llangrannog beach, two sticks of chalk pinched from school, one of Dad's cigarettes, a bag of yeast, and a broken watch found in a field. It was ages before supper, and nobody in the whole world knew where to find me.

Sunday

F'annywl Miriam,

Just a few lines before making tea to let you know the news. Haydn hasn't been too good lately, not ill, but a very tight chest in this hot weather. He's been a bit in the falen, he just can't get used to the farm work. It's too heavy for him, but he doesn't want to say.

To cap it all, on Friday, Mrs Davies wanted a chicken for today's minister. He was very good this morning, his sermon was not too long. Anyway, I told Haydn to kill the chicken, as I was busy making butter, which just wouldn't come, thunder about I think. If you can't wring its neck, I said, chop its head off. I knew he didn't want to do it, but he has to start somewhere. I could see him from the gegin fach window, looking all doleful. He hadn't even taken off his white coat. He took a chicken from the run, he'd never catch one in the yard, not enough breath. Well, he tried all shapes to wring that poor thing's neck. I don't know who was more upset, him or the bird. In the end, he put it between his legs, stretched its neck over the block, and chopped its head off. The blood was everywhere, all over him from head to foot, his coat was covered. He couldn't believe it, he went as white as a sheet, and made for the door. At this, the chicken got up and ran around the yard as they do sometimes. Haydn took one look and fell to the ground in a dead faint. Honestly, the sight of it turned him, he'd never seen anything like it in his life. Well, jawch erioed, I had to leave the butter in a hurry, to bring him round and help him in. Poor dab, he was in a terrible state, blood all over and feeling sick as a dog. Anyway, I cleaned him up, and after a bit he felt better, but he'll never eat chicken again, he says.

I had a surprise for him when he came home from the warehouse on Thursday. I think I've found a gwas to help us. He's a bit unusual but a marvellous worker, and so far we've hit it off very well. I'll tell you all about it on Thursday.

I hope your father's better by now. What will happen if he has to stop work? It's such a worry for you, Miriam fach, he's always been such a rock. We'll have a long talk when I come over ...

Love from,
Blodwen.

The dark was such a terror to me, Mam sat on my bed every night until I fell asleep. Sometimes, she was asleep first, but as long as she was there, I felt safe. Candles made it worse, shadows stretching and leaping, faces in the corners. I shrank from the shrieking of foxes in the wood, the call of owls, and the shufflings and moanings outside. I found the shrill, pain-filled screams from trapped rabbits so intolerable, my father stopped the laying of snares nearby. Although he hated the practice himself, trading in rabbits was an essential part of our income. That awful sound haunted my childhood, but the cry that came from inside the house never frightened me. I've heard it all my life. It was made by Col, our *gwas* and my best friend. He slept in the recess at the top of the stairs, a thick curtain drawn across for privacy. Every night and morning, the wooden rings clattered on the pole.

'Mam, tell me the story of Col looking over the gate.'

'*Cariad fach*, you should be asleep by now. All right then, but the words will be worn out soon, you've heard them so often. One day, when you were a little baby, I was teaching your Daddy how to milk the cows in the yard. He couldn't get the hang of it, see, so he left in a *pwdi*. I was singing to Bon, when I saw a man leaning over the gate. Strange he looked, his cap pulled low over his eyes, very serious and still. He was wearing working clothes, clean and tidy with a pack under his arm. He opened the gate, came across, picked up the stool and started milking. I could tell he was used to it, straight away. He didn't smile or say hello or anything. You're a funny looking cove, I said to myself, and nothing to say for yourself. I gave him a straight look and he didn't bat an eyelid. Well, you're not shifty anyway, I thought. There was something about him, you know, that made you feel he was as straight as die. When we finished milking, I said, "Thank you very much. Come in and have a cup of tea and some *bara brith*. You're very quiet, not much to say for yourself, is it? What's your name then?"

'He took a card from his pocket and on it was written, Collins. He pointed to his mouth shaking his head. I said, "Oh dear me, you can't speak, that's what's the matter. I'm very sorry, have another cup of tea." I felt he was sad and lonely without a friend in the world and somehow, I took to him then and there. "You can work for us, if you're looking." I said. "We need a *gwas* to help us badly, but there's not much money to spare. I'll look after you well, plenty of good food, a clean bed, clothes, money for tobacco and Sundays off. And when we've got money, there'll be some for you. What do you think?" He looked me in the eyes. His were very blue with those heavy lids of his down low. He nodded then, and took off his cap. Well, there's odd he looked! His hair and forehead were alabaster white, with the rest of his face as brown as a berry. All we had to do then was wait for Daddy to come home. He was surprised to see this strange man sitting at the table but when he heard the arrangement, he was so pleased to have help, he agreed at once. And he's never regretted it, has he? They've been good old pals from the start, yes indeed.

'We had a celebration supper that night, and we found out with nods and signs that Col knew a lot about farm work. We felt very lucky he'd come to our door. When it was time for bed, Col expected to sleep in the stable loft, but I wouldn't think of it. Much too damp for humans, enough to give you pneumonia. No, he had to sleep in the recess, no argument. He looked very unsettled by that, but I insisted, and up the stairs he went, bag and baggage.

'Well, as you know, in the middle of the night we heard the most awful noise! It was half screaming, half shouting, rising and falling, filling the whole house and out through the windows. Over and over, turning the blood to ice. I don't mind telling you, I was so frightened, I said a little prayer out loud! *Iesu Grist, aros gyda ni,* I said. When it died into a sort of moan, Daddy and I realized it was coming from the recess. We rushed to the landing and pulled back the curtain! Col was sitting up in bed, his eyes wide open and that terrifying sound pouring out of his mouth! I'll never forget that first time, we were scared rigid, too mesmerized to move. When I heard you crying, I had to do something to stop him, and quick! I touched his face gently and he went quiet, straight away. Closed his eyes he did, back to sleep without knowing we were there.

'Daddy and I were shocked to the bone. What had happened to this poor man, to make such a suffering cry in the middle of the night? And we weren't the only people awake, either. Mr Thomas and Mr Morris were banging on the door, expecting to find us dead in our beds. Mr Thomas was carrying a stick, and it took time to convince them we were all right. When they left, Mr Thomas said we should get rid of Col, and Daddy and Mr Morris agreed. But I wanted to think it over. Did this happen often? Was Col ill? He must have known about it, that's why he didn't want to sleep in the house. I expect other people had heard it before, giving him his marching orders, poor *dab*.

'By then, it was almost time to start the day's work. Daddy looked so pale and ill, I sent him back to bed and you were asleep on the *sgiw*. By five o'clock, first breakfast was ready to go on the table. I heard the rings go back on the pole and there was Col, standing at the bottom of the stairs, his pack under his arm. He was ready to leave, he didn't expect anything from anyone, no kindness, no understanding. "Sit down," I said. "*Bara llaeth* first, then you can prepare the cows. We'll do the milking and the work in dairy before you have a good wash and second breakfast. I'll show you the rest later."

'No bother at all after that. Every night, when Col had his nightmare, I touched his face and it stopped. He was part of the family in no time and your very special pal, wasn't he? Helped Daddy no end with the heavy work and always there when I wanted him, but never underfoot. And it's the same today, isn't it? We couldn't do without him now, it wouldn't be the same at all.

'That's the end, *cariad*, you know it by heart now. *Nos da*, Margaret *fach*, I'm almost asleep on my nose. *Nos da*, see you in the morning.'

Chapter Two

F'annwyl Miriam,

Just a few lines to let you know I can't come over this Thursday. Mamgu Poli came yesterday, caught me on the hop she did. She doesn't come in May as a rule, but Jono's been up to his old tricks again, I expect. Lucky it's warm for the time of year, isn't it?

I'm afraid there was no time to wash the sheets, so it was a flour job this time. Diolch i Dduw, the pillow slips were starched and aired. She's a case, too, phoned us on Friday night to say she'd be down yesterday. Col is sleeping on the sgiw, bendramwnwgl, and she's in Margaret's room. Everything with birds on it had to be removed in a hurry. Jawch erioed, it's a shambles here, I haven't finished my spring-cleaning yet. Haydn will be a handful, full of himself he'll be for days. It's always like that when Poli first comes, a proper babi losin he is. She's spoilt him rotten, so what can you expect? She brought him a new pair of shoes for best, and boots for the yard. She knows how he feels about clogs.

Now something very unusual happened this time. She always brings boys' toys for Margaret, as you know, that engineering Meccano, and a train set last Christmas. At last, she's acknowledged she has a grand-daughter, not a grandson. Calling the child John all the time, it was getting ridiculous. I tried talking to her about it, but not a bit of notice. Mind you, she loves our Margaret, can't do enough for her. Even though she's got funny ways on her, Poli and I are good pals. She makes me laugh, and she's got a heart of gold.

Anyway, to get back to it. She's brought Margaret a red velvet frock. Yes, indeed she has. Lovely it is, with smocking, and a very pretty cream lace collar. It suites her to a T, red shows off her dark hair. I trimmed her donkey crop, and she looks a proper little lady, for once.

They're in the gegin fawr at present talking history with Mr Llywelyn. Henry Tudor's getting it in the neck for the Act of Union almost killing the Welsh language, and thank God for Bishop Morgan translating the Bible. Poli is rampant for Welsh history, mind. All I remember is the Welsh Not. That placard was put on my neck more than once and the cane if it was still there at the end of the day. No wonder many of us can't write fluently in our own language! Poli's telling Mr Llywelyn that her family is belonging to some scholar from hundreds of years ago. Can't be through Jono anyway, he doesn't have a civilised bone in his body. He did have a first-class education, though, for all the good it did anyone. Me, I'd sooner have a good clonc any day, and value what you've got, I say ...

Love from,
Blodwen.

Pedro and I waited on the *twmp* at the top of school hill. The rain had stopped and the fields stretched glistening green towards the sea, steam rising in the sun. Behind us, the *cwm* was quiet, the river shining between alders and willows, houses tucked in, smoke climbing in straight lines, fires stoked up for tea. Skylarks sang high above and curlews far away. Wild flowers sprinkled pink and gold in the fields down by Cnwc, where hawthorn hedges, layered by Seth, were thick with blossom. Mamgu was late, I could hear Mrs Pryce, Brynfa, calling the cows for milking. It was so warm, I took off my pixie hood and scarf, placing them on the stone wall.

I looked forward to Mamgu's visits with such jumping up and down excitement, I didn't even mind her calling me John. She was different, unlike anyone else with her superstitious, funny ways, and in her company, anything could happen. Her antics made her the talk of the village, but they couldn't help being interested.

At last, I saw the big, black car approaching from the top road. It stopped at the bottom of the steep hill where Mamgu Poli and Mrs Mortymer stepped out. Climbing slowly, it stopped again on the brow directly below us, Trefor at the wheel. He was a tall, reserved man of about sixty-five with a calm, tolerant disposition, needing every scrap of it according to Dad. His dignified bearing made the brown, high-buttoned jacket and breeches look more like a uniform, accentuated by polished boots and leggings, cap, muffler and posh gloves, the gauntlets up to his elbows. Dad said Trefor was a decent, tidy man, honest and chapel going. Many wondered why he had never married. The new car, in Trefor's sole charge, received almost as much care as the horses. Horses were Poli's passion! She was a respected breeder and dealer, and in the old days, she owned a fleet of Hansom cabs. Trefor managed her stables, and woe-betide anyone mis-treating a horse in his sight! He politely insisted that passengers should alight at the foot of steep hills, unless ill or infirm. Now, he applied the same rules to the car. A journey could take twice as long as expected, hills being a prominent feature in Wales. Baskets of food and drink were always taken as a precaution. Poli indulged his eccentricities, having more than a fair-share herself. Feeling uneasy in the new car, she called upon her personal gods for protection, using three, a sacred number in Celtic culture to bring certain good luck. She insisted on travelling in threes or multiples of three, except for six, the Devil's number. Every sixth passenger had to be a child, making the group five and a half, Trefor counted in or out, as convenient. Dad said it was the antics of a deranged woman, how could she succumb to such irrational behaviour? Poli answered patiently, the Lord giveth and the Lord taketh away and in-between, it's wise to have all the insurance you can muster.

Mrs Mortymer's throaty laugh made me smile, even at a distance. The two women walked arm-in-arm, heads close together, talking nineteen to the dozen. What a strange pair they made! Mamgu looked slim and elegant in her dark-green, velvet costume, the skirt touching her buttoned ankle-boots. Her clothes were old fashioned but very stylish, with enormous hats to cover her unruly, red hair. Although the colour was fading, its curly mass refused to be tamed, popping strong, anchoring pins in all directions. In public, for the sake of decorum, she wore deep crowned, large brimmed hats specially made in Cardiff, decorated with silk flowers or large bunches of wax fruit. That day, it was a splendid creation in green and rust velvet, the brim undulating as she walked, a tall umbrella in her outstretched hand. *Diwedd annwyl*, there's grand she looked! If we went to Aberteifi or Castell Newydd Emlyn, she turned every head in the place, particularly when enveloped in her long, red-brown fur coat. It moved with a life of its own, Poli buried deep inside, two small feet at one end and a huge hat at the other. The coat was an object of derision in the family, but Mamgu was unmoved. It served its purpose and that was an end to the matter. Her impact on the village was considerable.

Martha Mortymer was shorter than Poli, heavily built, with a red face, bright, brown eyes and greying hair, severely drawn into a bun at the nape of her neck. Her clothes were dark, simple and untidy with the most nondescript of hats, showing a total lack of interest in her appearance. Nothing matched, and Martha didn't care a hoot! I was mesmerised by the strong hairs growing on her chin, and curling from a brown mole on her left cheek. She threw back her head when she laughed, deeply and often, opening her mouth so wide I could see into the depths of her throat. Mamgu and she were children together, and when Poli left for the South as a bride, Martha went too. Generous and good-hearted, she enjoyed being the third traveller, Trefor counted in, coming and going as required, visiting her many relatives in the district. She was married to a collier called Zac, and they had a family of six grown-up children.

It was time to tell Mam the visitors had arrived but we needn't have rushed, she already knew. Poker-faced, Col was parading daintily across the *gegin fawr*, one hand holding a stick, the other steadying the brim of an invisible hat. There was nothing of the clown about Col. A skilful, unnerving mimic, his fleeting gestures were uncannily accurate, ending with a "here they are" jerk of the thumb as the car appeared at the gate. Mamgu Poli swept up the front path.

'Have you taken down the curtains then?'

'Yes, yes, it's all plain cretonne everywhere, Mamgu Poli. Come in now, there's lovely to see you all. Hello, Mrs Mortymer. Hello, Trefor. Sit down by the fire. A nice cup of tea in the hand before we start. This child's been looking forward to seeing you all day, fit to burst with excitement. She's been up the *twmp* for hours. Where's your pixie hood and scarf then, Margaret? Don't tell me you've lost them!'

Big hugs from Mamgu, all scent, beads and lace.

'Well, you have grown, *cariad*, you're shooting up before our very eyes. Where are the presents, Trefor? That's it now, here we are. We'll go into the *gegin fach* and put on this new frock, shall we? Look everyone, isn't she beautiful? Red suits her, doesn't it, Mrs Mortymer? She looks lovely.'

Lovely, lovely, twirling about in my red, velvet frock. Mamgu was here at last and my pixie hood and scarf were on the desk! I blew a thank you kiss to Col.

My mother thought the world of Mamgu Poli, which was just as well, she could try the patience of a saint, according to Dad. Deeply and irrevocably superstitious, she brought drama and commotion into the lives of those around her. Special arrangements were essential before she could stay in any house, mainly concerning the image of birds. Indoors, it signified death, and many women of her generation felt the same. Some of my mother's curtains, cushions and best china were covered in birds. Two landscapes on the wall had minute ticks in the sky, never noticed until Mamgu's sharp eye sought them out. All were banished, and look out if she arrived without warning! Even Dad set to with a vengeance, pulling and pushing things around. Nobody seemed to mind, we'd do anything for Poli. She was funny, witty, and full of life, manna from heaven on a dreary day and we were happy to be swept along by her antics!

Bedclothes were a serious subject in our house, summer and winter. Efficient household management demanded at least five sheets to a bed; two on, two in the wash, one in the drawer for emergencies. There should also be a special set for guests, edged with lace. Our purse did not extend to such luxuries, making it top sheet to bottom and clean pillowslips once a week, weather permitting. Even so, things didn't always go to plan with three beds to keep and all that rain! Then there was the airing! Mam was mad on airing, damp being the mortal enemy of good health. Every single article of clothing and bed linen was baked to a crisp on racks in front of the fire, a faint layer of ash collecting on the surface. Never mind, better safe than sorry any day of the week, and what about Haydn's chest then? She had a habit of testing beds by placing a mirror in their depths. Any vestige of mist meant another session on the rack!

Excess rain, shortage of bedding, and zeal for airing sometimes resulted in the "flour job" conspiracy. Mam and I bustled up and down stairs, giggling like mad things, pummelling and stretching. The deception entailed stripping the bed to the bottom sheet, pulling it tightly over the feather mattress and sprinkling it with flour. After rubbing it well in, Mam stroked it carefully with a hot flat-iron, making it white and shiny. Surplus flour was brushed onto a tray, and the turnback on the top sheet given the same treatment. In candlelight, guests didn't notice a puff of white as they settle into feathered cosiness.

'*Shwsh* now, don't tell a soul what we've been up to. Keep it to ourselves, won't we? Our secret.'

'Oh yes, Mam, for ever and ever.'

Our daily routine was turned upside down when Poli arrived. Short shrift was made of the work with Mam and Mamgu pitching in, wearing large white aprons and cuffed caps, sleeves up to the

elbows. *Cinio*, the midday meal for the family and five school children, consisted of *cawl* and *tato bwts* – bacon or lamb broth with
vegetables, followed by potatoes and swede mashed up with lashings
of butter. We ate from our wooden bowls and oh! the glory of it, as
much as you could eat, couldn't move for a week!

The day's food was prepared after second breakfast, in case of
visitors, so after washing the dinner dishes, Mam and Mamgu had
five minutes in front of the fire. What a treat for Mam! Never idle,
for her it was like a holiday. I loved being with the two women in their
quiet moments. They were gentle and loving, sharing a sadness not
known to a child like me. We had a rare feeling for each other, like
being in the middle of a very special secret. Mam, Mamgu and me,
the lucky three. On rainy days, we talked, did the ironing, mending
and knitting, or lingered in the shop having a *clonc* with the wives.

'Who was that you were talking about again?'

'Well I never. Makes you think, doesn't it? I can't believe it.'

'It wasn't like that in our day!'

'Poor Mrs Jones. They say he was drunk again. Pity too. Doesn't
belong around here, does he? That's what comes of marrying an
outsider!'

'*Duw, Duw*, there's a bird pecking on the window, somebody's in
for it. Quick now, hold hands and say the Lord's Prayer three times,
we'll be safe then. No, no you've got to say it with feeling, as if you
really mean it. Start again.'

'You were saying about Mrs Jones. I never see her now.'

'She came down last night. That darling of hers has been borrowing again. He takes most of his pay as it is, not leaving her much. Poor
dab, she's so nice, all for her home and family. Never wastes a penny.
She and him had a terrible row. He swore at her and told her to go
home to her mother. If he did, *uffern dân*, she upped and threw a *sospan*
at him. Made his ear swell up like a pear. How she lives with him I
don't know, drinking and gambling all the time. We all have our cross
to bear, I suppose. I often thank God we had such good beginnings.'

'And what about Guto then? Dirty old *hwrgi*. Female flesh draws
him like a magnet, no matter how old they are. Hands in all directions, piggy eyes not knowing where to look first. Even Nain runs like

a rabbit when she sees him coming, and she's almost ninety! Thank God he's got a wooden leg, that's all I can say.'

'Talking about legs, I hear Ceri's shaving hers to stop any hair poking through those stockings. She'll be shaving her armpits next, then there'll be trouble. She wants her head read, if you ask me.'

'Mind you, she's a handsome girl. Bet you she'll find a stranger to marry.'

'More than likely, I'd say.'

'Have you seen that Miss Davies lately? Doesn't show herself much, does she?'

'*Duw Mawr*, can't believe it myself, it shouldn't be allowed.'

'*Shwsh*, there's Olwen coming. Mustn't show we're talking.'

I was invisible, sitting there hardly breathing, wanting to be in on everything. Half the time, grown-ups didn't notice I was there, just like Pedro. I probably knew more than was good for me, by a long chalk, but I learnt to keep what I heard to myself. Instinct told me there'd be ructions if I split, and I didn't want to be accused of sewing my ear to the keyhole. *Cau dy geg!*

Sunday

F'annwyl Miriam,

Tamping mad I am today. Haydn went to his father's three days ago, and came back with a cattle truck. They thought it would bring in ready money by carrying cattle from around here to Henllan, or to market. Well, this morning it wouldn't start, would it? Another white elephant, I can feel it in my water. I'm really grac, Miriam. The old man's up to his tricks again, especially now Poli's with Didi for a few days. I bet my boots it will never go again. Cheap it was, and no good with it. Haydn and Col are potching with it now, never mind the work. As soon as Jono pokes his nose in, we're in the domen. The money from the shop will not take the strain, see Miriam, if we go on like this. I thought we'd left his father and his rotten tricks behind us. It's upset me terrible, and I can see what's to come if we don't put a stop to it straight away. God forgive me for saying this, but I can't stand Jono these days.

We were supposed to go with Poli to the Horse Fair in Llanybydder on Thursday. She and Trefor still breed horses for pleasure. I wanted to take our Margaret to see Aunty Anne and Uncle Rufus while we were there, but I don't feel like it now with all this palaver going on.

It's too hot to move, isn't it? Haydn's sweating like a pig, not waiting any longer to take off his winter clothes. I caught our Margaret down by the river without her stockings, and I must say, I'm down to my jumper. The trouble is, if we change too soon, the old weather could turn in a whip, then where will we be? The children are sweltering, rushing about like they do. Have you taken off your woollens yet, Mir? Col's been down to his shirt for days, but that one's a law unto himself. Mamgu Poli says she's going home after my birthday, her clothes are too hot for comfort. I expect I'll find out eventually why she came down in such a hurry ...

Love from,
Blodwen.

There was thunder about, with dark clouds making a sultry lid over the *cwm*. Pedro flopped in the long grass by the river while I stroked Dan's soft mouth with water, leaning into his warm friendliness. I was missing Mamgu Poli, especially since Dad came home with the cattle truck. Mam was banging the china about, not a good sign. Col was watching points, but Dad didn't take a bit of notice, oblivious.

The rain came pelting down, enough to drench you in a minute. I was soaked through when I reached the *gegin fach*, but there was no Mam to be seen. Thunder crashed loud enough to frighten Pedro under the table, and me with him if I wasn't so wet.

I found Mam sitting in the wicker chair by the window in the *gegin fawr*, her hair dark against the pale cushions, her hands idle in her lap. She looked asleep. I drew closer but she made no sign. When I saw the tears on her face, I was so frightened I couldn't move. She cried without a sound, as if she was somewhere all alone. The rain ran down the window behind her like a waterfall, and in the gloom, I could barely see her.

'Mam, Mam!'

'Oh, *cariad*, I didn't see you there. *Duw, Duw*, you're dripping wet. Off with those clothes straight away, you'll catch pneumonia. Come by here now.'

Tender hands, sweet talk, Mam was mine again. I didn't ask why she was crying.

It was a day of strange happenings. I saw my mother lose her temper only three times in my life, and the first was on that day. Her anger was a sudden, searing thing, soon over but never forgotten. Thank the Lord, I was the object of it only once.

On Poli's return, she, Mam and I were in the *gegin fach* for coolness. I sat quietly, pretending to read, still unsettled by the morning's events. The two women spoke English for private conversation, but thinking I was immersed in my book, they continued in Welsh. Mam regretted the uselessness of the truck and Poli defended Dad, saying he needed to widen his financial horizons.

'Now don't talk to me about that sort of thing, Mamgu Poli, you know very well we've fallen flat on our faces already. Look at the geese we bought – Jono's idea again – thinking we could fatten them for Christmas. They all died, didn't they, of a disease unknown to man! Then buying the fruit on those plum trees, and not finding pickers in time. Ita and I worked our fingers to the bone, and lost money hand over fist. It's all right for you to talk see, Mamgu, you can make money out of a blade of grass, but not Haydn, he just doesn't have the knack. As for farming, he should listen to me a bit more, I know something about it. Please don't encourage him to dream up mad schemes, it's enough to deal with Jono in that department. I'm upset with it all, really I am.'

'Yes, yes, Blodwen, I know what you mean, and I'll speak to Jono. But I do wish Haydn could find an occupation befitting his education. I'm ready to help, as you know.'

'But we're here now, with a good chance of making a living, if we're left alone. You've spoken to Jono before, many times, but he doesn't take a blind bit of notice. It's almost as if he wants us to fail. You can look like that, Mamgu Poli, but that's what I honestly feel, and Haydn's not as ambitious as you think. All he wants is a bit of peace and quiet and no money worries. He's just starting to settle down here, things are getting easier and Col's marvellous, I don't know what we'd do without him. Haydn has more time for the shop, and his English is useful with all these new forms for the milk. The farmers are glad of his help, what with the telephone and the van. He's beginning to find his place.'

'I was hoping for more, Blodwen *fach*, my only son.'

Deep sighs.

When Col came in for dinner, he quickly caught the drift, rolling his eyes in my direction. Mamgu continued in the same vein, and Mam, serving up at the far end of the table, became seriously rattled. My father appeared on the steps of the *gegin fach*, immaculate in his long, white coat. He was sometimes quite lordly in Mamgu's presence, especially if she sang his praises. He said in a loud voice,

'Never mind the tittle-tattle, why isn't my food on the table?'

It happened in a flash! The plate flew over our heads, the whole length of the kitchen, hitting my father full in the face. It crashed to the floor, leaving a trail of gravy down his coat. *Duw Mawr*, nobody breathed! Mam, still as a nun, looking daggers! Dad opened his mouth to speak, thought better of it and left, Col following like a shadow.

For once in her life, Poli remained silent.

From the shade of the bridge, I watched swallows flying along the water, beautiful in colour and movement. Weasels played in the long grass in the corner of the field, two joyful acrobats. Before long, brilliant sunshine tempted me to remove my outer clothing. I was paddling in the river with Dan and Pedro when Mam appeared, saying a heavy cold would be the least of my worries, casting off my stockings before the last day of May. I was frog-marched home in double-quick time to find Mamgu Poli fanning herself by the door. She was about to remove half her clothes and if we had any sense, we'd do the same. It was ridiculous, roasting like this for the sake of a few days. We could get used to our summer clothes today and go to Llangrannog for Mam's birthday outing tomorrow. What a marvellous idea and wicked with it, casting clouts before May was out! Mam wasn't sure, but I was up the stairs like a *winci*, eager to shed layers of wool. First the cardigan, the pinafore skirt buttoned on the shoulders, my jumper and pretty, cotton petticoat, with lace, to hide the flannel one beneath. Over my head, throw them on the bed! Then the liberty bodice and pretty, cotton vest, with lace, to hide the knitted one, next to the skin. It was made from scratchy, Welsh wool and weighed a ton. All off, whirl them about, Mamgu and Mam laughing at my delight. Knickers to the knees and long, brown stockings, on the floor in a heap! Last of all, my band of silk with the golden pin. What a blessed relief! I'm free again to run and jump and climb trees! Back on with the cotton clothes but Mam insisted on the jumper and skirt. It mustn't be too great a shock to the system! Howls of protest! All right then, a blouse, skirt and cardigan and tomorrow, if it was still hot, I could wear a dress.

The women *shwshed* me out of the room while they did the same, rustling and laughing like a pair of girls getting ready for a party. But whatever they removed, including Chilpruf combinations and flannel petticoats, the corsets remained. Whalebone keeps you decent, whatever the weather.

'Margaret, back in here, I need nimble fingers for the buttons on this blouse.'

'You've got it on inside out, Mamgu.'

'*Drato*, quick now, a short walk up and down the yard, it's unlucky to turn it the right way round before going outside first. Where's my shawl? Won't be a minute, Blod.'

Parading around for luck, we didn't notice the chickens still in the yard. Too late! From the roof of the cowshed, Bomber descended like a howling banshee. He was Dad's huge, gleaming-white cockerel, not named in vain, who lurked in high places waiting to terrorize anything on his patch. Shrieks and screams brought Col at full stretch knowing Bomber always meant business. He could scratch your neck to ribbons from his favoured perch on the back of the head. Mamgu, whacking away to no avail, hair springing in all directions, and me running for cover under the doomed cattle truck. Pedro was there before me, knowing all about those mighty talons, thank you very much! Mam came out of the back door in her cotton petticoat, shouting like a sergeant-major, but Col was the expert and in a trice, Bomber was head down, flapping and squawking. Mamgu was beside herself, sweating and cursing flashes.

'*Uffern dân*, this *blutty* place, you can't do anything without the sky falling in. What's wrong with everything these last few days? All cross-grained! I'm on full stop until I've seen Besi to read the teacups. No good going on like this, no indeed, something's in the wind. Col, you tell Haydn when he comes back, this bird must meet his Maker. Today!'

Off she stamped, skirts flying, her hair in a huge, frizzy halo around her angry head. Col threw Bomber over the gate into the field, the chickens following with a deafening cackle. Brute that he was, no harm must come to the bird. Bomber was Dad's talisman, following him about like a tame pigeon, all *swci* and tender. A creature of strength and energy, he would remain cock-of-the-walk for many a long day!

Mamgu returned from Besi's, all smiles, with good omens for the foreseeable future. Besi was the old *ladi lwcus* of the valley, the herbalist and nurse who cared for my father during his severe bouts of asthma. The doctor, who lived miles away and needed payment, was only called when absolutely necessary. I was not afraid of Besi exactly, but when you looked into her extraordinary, silver-grey eyes, she held you and read your thoughts. I didn't want her to read mine. Did she know that since Rhodri's brother told us where babies came from, we were sneaking about, looking under all the gooseberry bushes? What if we found one? Could she tell I didn't like Chapel? Did she know about my hiding places, and my feelings about the little, china angel? One thing for sure, there was no secret safe from Besi.

The signs were right for our trip to the seaside, and Mam's birthday went well from the start. We emerged in summer dresses, slim and airy, like butterflies from a chrysalis of winter clothing. Our canvas shoes lay drying on the window-sill, cleaned with Blanco, the smell of holidays. Aunty Miriam and her children, Bryn and Eira, were to accompany us in the car, five and a half, Trefor counted out. Baskets of food and drink, rugs and shawls, rubber groundsheets, umbrellas for the rain and coats for the cold were packed away. No bathing costumes this time of year, it was far too chilly for swimming!

In the late nineteen twenties, Miriam went to the South to marry a young coal-miner. When he was killed in a pit accident four years later, she was evicted from her home. She returned with her children to live with her father, Datcu Jenkins, in a bright, polished, house three miles from our village. The rooms were filled with the scent of honey from apples stored in the loft. Datcu Jenkins was the best fruit grower and tree grafter in the district.

Good friends since they'd met in the South, my mother and Miriam were delighted to be together again. Bryn and I also enjoyed each other's company, being of a similar age and temperament. Eira, older and calmer, had grown into a tall, slender beauty with red, wavy hair, green eyes and a creamy skin. I longed to look like Eira. Both were waiting on the bridge, all smiles and a warm welcome. Plenty of time for a cup of tea and Welsh cakes before we went any further, the sun would last for ages! The table in the *gegin* was laid with the best china on a lacy cloth, glossily starched and ironed. Mam said Miriam was a marvel with the flat iron, never seen anything like it. After tea came the ritual. Each time I visited their house, Eira took me to see the mahogany box on the sideboard in the tiny parlour.

'There are loads of love letters in there from our Dad to our Mam. I know, because once I took the key from her dressing table and opened it, but she found out before I had a proper look. She cried, and said they were very private because they were all she had left of our Dad. I've never touched it since. Your Mam's letters are in there as well. Dozens of them! They tell each other all their secrets, things they wouldn't breathe to another soul. I heard our Mam say she might give them to you one day, when you're grown up. If you deserve them, that is. I bet you'd like to see one now, wouldn't you? Well you can't, because our Mam keeps the key somewhere else these days.'

We sat looking at the box, willing it to open and reveal all. Soon it was time to leave, and I took my turn to stroll down the rose path to the lavatory, built on a platform over the river. I enjoyed having a pee there. No chance of coming face to face with a rat in the eaves, its beady eyes enough to stop you mid flow. No, the only danger in Aunty Mir's *tŷ bach* was boys looking up from underneath, by far the lesser of two evils, in my experience.

I travelled in the front with Trefor, due to car sickness, and Eira and Bryn sat on the dicky seats behind. Bryn, always ready for a bit of mischief, flipped his up and down until frozen by a stern look from Trefor. To keep us in order, Mamgu told stories about the history of Sîr Aberteifi, its churches, chapels, standing stones and cromlechs.

'Once upon a time, well over a thousand years ago, a Celtic, holy man named Carantoc was sitting on the side of that hill down there, see? He was carving a new walking stick for himself when, suddenly, a fat pigeon flew down and took away some shavings in its beak. After several visits, Carantoc, being curious, followed the bird into the valley below, where he saw it place the pieces carefully on the ground. There was a feeling of great peace and blessing, and

Carantoc recognized it as a sign from God. On that very spot he built a church to the glory of His name.

'Look, it's still there, built in stone now. Inside, there's a very old font from Norman times for christening babies, and an ancient silver cup called a chalice. Shall we go and have a look? No, all right then, after you've had a paddle. In those days, villages and churches had to be hidden from any boats at sea, because more often than not, they were full of Vikings on the rampage. They were pagans, and never having heard of Jesus Christ, they didn't know any different. They were on the lookout for anything they could find, coming ashore here like savages to rob and burn and pillage. No mercy was shown. They took people, animals, goods...'

'*Diwedd annwyl*, Mamgu, it's a day out we want, not news of a massacre.'

'Children like drama, Blodwen, keeps them interested. Did you know that smugglers used the caves on Llangrannog beach? They left tea, tobacco, salt and drink inside, until it was safe to sell them cheaply in the villages, sometimes under the very noses of the authorities. They crept about in the dead of night, scaring people out of their wits, but even they gave Carreg Bica a wide berth, it being the tooth of the Devil himself. You can see it, look, all black and crooked like its owner. One day, the old Devil was marching up and down with a raging toothache. Unbearable it was, so he yanked it out himself and threw it down on the beach. Wallop! And there it stands to this day, to remind us to keep on the alert, in case he chooses us for his wicked ways! Well, here we are then. Watch out, I don't want to be trampled in the rush!'

After a long, lazy day on the beach, our journey home was hard work, in and out of the car every five minutes, the incline from Llangrannog enough to take your breath away. Bryn and I raced about while Eira preferred to be very sedate, walking quietly with the women. Sometimes, we stopped at the Stone of Dyffryn Bern where, under Mamgu's instructions, we clustered around, eyes as big as saucers. She threw her hat on the ground.

'Put your ears to the Stone, children, and be very, very quiet. Can you feel the vibrations from ancient times? Close your eyes and concentrate. Yes, I knew you would. A deep and powerful hum it is, once heard, never forgotten. Look at these letters carved here in the olden days. Latin they are, the language of the Romans, who came to our country not long after the death of Christ. They didn't conquer us, mind, just came for a look! Hold hands and circle around and thank God we live in such a rich and beautiful country. Who would ever want to live anywhere else?'

My favourite beach was Penbryn where we swam and played in the deserted sand-dunes all day long, free as air. I loved the steep walk through the green, ferny woods to St. Michael's Church at the top of the cliffs. From the graveyard, we looked down on a huge, grand sweep of sea, blue, gold and silver to the far, far horizon.

The church is one of the oldest in Wales, built within a circular wall, to prevent the Devil hiding in corners. We crept into the dim stillness, nervously passing the coffin bier and leper squint to press ourselves against the very cold walls, near the altar. It was as holy as Heaven! Overwhelmed by silence, we were glad to find the women in the sunlight, reading gravestones through clouds of butterflies.

One summer night, I woke to find the candle out, and Mam no longer lying on my bed. I had a great fear, not only of noises, shadows and phantoms, but of the darkness itself. It was alive, pressing against my body, my face, my eyes, waiting to inhabit me, to be inside my head, enveloping my senses. Moonlight dispelled my terrors, especially the brilliant, shimmering silver of that night, shining directly on my face, burnishing the walls and mirrors. I wasn't afraid, I liked lying there quietly in my bed, savouring the magic. In the stillness, I heard voices from the *gegin fawr*, Mam and Mamgu Poli.

'Stay for the picnic, Mamgu, it won't be long now, the weather being so hot.'

'No, I must go back, Blodwen, to keep an eye on things. I can't impose on Dai any longer, he's so willing. The travellers and the warehouse must be paid at the end of the month and I can't leave that to Jono, just in case.'

'I don't know how you put up with him, honestly I don't. He doesn't know he's born the way you look after him.'

'He can't help himself, I'm afraid. He's let his past defeat us both. The bitterness of his father's death has never left him, Blodwen *fach*. Terrible thing, mind you, finding your own father hanging in the barn like that! Enough to turn you for life. A privileged family, rich merchants with a high position in the town, and then – nothing! Gone, gone to the bottom of the sea, ships, men and every penny he had. He'd mortgaged all his assets to buy that huge cargo of grain and he lost everything. Awful thing to happen and it finished him off. *Ach a fi*!

'It was the end of the boys' expectations too. Jono was the youngest, spoilt rotten by his mother, always giving him his own way. He didn't get over it as well as Dai, no indeed. Now there's a fine man for you, upright and decent as the day is long, and a good friend to me. I could never leave the business for five minutes, if he didn't take over while I was away. Such a contrast between two brothers, completely different characters, you wouldn't believe. Yes, I'm sorry to say, Jono has been irresponsible and deceitful once or twice in his life.'

'Once or twice! Give it a rest, Mamgu *fach*. Look what he did when he ran off to the army, leaving you with all those debts. Not a single word for years! Then he turns up on your doorstep, saying he was injured in the trenches and lost his memory, when all the time he was in the Catering Corps in Aldershot. You shouldn't have taken him back then.'

'Yes, yes, you're quite right, I know what he's like, but he is my husband after all. He did do a low thing this time, though, yes indeed he did. I didn't want to tell you before. He stole my mother's silver tea service, and I didn't see the going of it either. He's given it to that fancy woman of his, I expect, she still has a hold over him, after all these years. He denied it, of course, but I know when he's lying, I can see it a mile off. It cut me to the quick to see him stoop to that, when he can help himself to the till anytime he likes.

'I know I'm much older, but when I married him, I was daft enough to think I could help him, give him a safe place to get over his grief. He seemed so lost somehow, he touched my heart. But he doesn't understand love, he doesn't see the gift of it, only the gain. My brother said often enough, he only wanted me for my money. I made my choice, I had to stand by it and I still have feeling for him,

God only knows! What worries me, he's starting to upset Haydn again. Look at that cattle truck, he won't pay his half, of course, but I'll see to that. He's jealous of Haydn, always has been, never behaved like a proper father. You'd think after losing one child, he'd cherish the other, but no, he wasn't interested. All self with him, gallivanting about like the big "I am," no thought for his family. He set a very bad example for Haydn and that's why I sent him to private school, thinking he'd be much better off, away from all the talk. Who knows if I did the right thing? At least, it saved him from the worst, except for that last time. It had to be in front of the boy, didn't it? It's left its mark on Haydn to this day, but he still wants to give his father a chance, doesn't he? We only need half a kind word, even now.'

'Don't cry, Mamgu *fach*, he's not worth it, he doesn't deserve a woman like you, still defending him when you can.'

'I'll be all right now just. Comes over me in waves sometimes, behaving like a daft old girl crying behind her apron. That was a long time ago and I told him then, if he ever threatened me again, I'd tell his brother. It did the trick! Dai is the only person he's afraid of, this side of hell. It kept him in line, but afterwards he never even pretended to be a decent husband and father. Shamed us openly he did, shamed us with that woman, and his shady dealings up and down the valley. That's what your people have against us, not Haydn or my doing. Once your good name is dragged through the mud, people have long memories. I'm sorry, Blodwen, here I am grumbling like this when there are thousands worse off than me.'

'Why don't you come and live with us, sell up the old business and enjoy yourself for a change? Haydn and I would love to have you, and Margaret would be in her element. Think about it, I can't bear to see you being treated so shoddily.'

'I know, *bach*, I know you mean it, but I must see to the business, or there'll be nothing for Haydn. I want him to have it when I'm gone, set you both up. Don't you worry, I know what I'm doing and I don't get down in the mouth often – no time! I don't know what I'd do without you both, honest-to-God. Blodwen, *fach*, you're a true-blue friend to me as well as a daughter-in-law. A rock in time of trouble. Nice cup of tea now, is it?'

Chapter Three

Sunday

F'annwyl Miriam,

... The hay is almost ready. Seth is passing regularly after dark to see if Ita's there. Margaret is waiting too, up the twmp half a dozen times a day, can't be long now. Ita's special, she is, but I can't see what will become of her and Seth, they've waited long enough, yes indeed.

Haydn was in the top field yesterday, testing the hay, when he heard music coming from the Rhys' garden. It comes right down to the corner there into the trees. Haydn looked over the hedge, but all he could see was Mr Rhys' brand-new gramophone on the grass, belting out, 'Come into the garden, Maud.' The old man would have a fit if he knew! They went to Aberporth for the day, leaving Dilys on her own. Not often that happens! She doesn't get much freedom, poor girl, proper slave she is in that house. Old Rhys is such a misery and so sanctimonious with it. If you ask me he should have his own pulpit on wheels. Do you know what he said to me the other day? He said, 'If you work night and day to get the Lord on your side, when the Great Day of Judgement comes, he won't charge you so much interest.' Before I could stop myself, I said, 'How do you know, Mr Rhys, you haven't had the bill yet!' There's flat he went ...

Love from,
Blodwen.

I liked lying snug in bed in the morning, listening to Mam's footsteps on the flags, in and out of the *gegin fach*, poking the fire, kettle on the chain; the clatter of dishes on the table and the smell of bacon frying for second breakfast. Safe and sound, I didn't want to be anywhere else. The men were out, and Mam and I had our special time together, sitting on the *sgiw*, making toast on the long fork. I didn't like *bara llaeth*, the bread soaked in milk stuck in my throat like a slug.

'Will Ita come today, Mam?'

'I don't know, *bach*, but she's bound to come soon.'

'Will she ever come again, Mam?'

'Yes, of course she will. They've always come for haymaking, long before we came here to live. Col will know, he'll tell you straight away.'

'Sometimes I think she's in my imagination and she belongs to the *Tylwyth Teg*.'

Mam laughed and gave me a hug.

'Don't you worry, *bach*, she'll come soon enough, as real as you or me, and you'll play on the rock on the top.'

'Why can't Ita go to Seth's house?'

'Seth's mother is not well and it's best not to upset her, see.'

'But why should she be upset?'

'You want to know a lot this morning! How shall I put this now? Seth is her only child, and she doesn't want him to go away. It's unusual for a village man to be courting a gypsy girl, and his mam doesn't want them to get married. That's why we don't talk about it, not to put her into a fit, her with a bad heart. It's a sort of secret, not to upset her, so we can't go chiming in and spouting things about. *Cau dy geg*, if you see what I mean, *cariad*. Seth has to stay with his mam.'

'Why can't Ita stay with her too? If she knew Ita, she couldn't help liking her, could she?'

'Quite right, but I expect Ita would hate living in a village. The gypsies like to be free to go where they want, not stuck in one place like us all the time. The top and bottom of it is, Seth can't expect his mam to understand.'

'I don't understand either.'

'You don't have to, plenty of time for understanding.'

I was sure Seth's mam did understand. She was always asking me strange questions about Ita. On warm days like today, she spent much of the time sitting just inside her front door in her frilly white cap, black bonnet and shawl. Her bird-bright eyes watched for movement. When she wasn't asking about Ita, she questioned me on my verses. She knew her Bible backwards, quoting long passages by heart, peppering her conversations with the Scriptures.

'*Merch y siop*! Do you know your verses?'

'Yes, Mrs Morgan.'

'Please recite one for me.'

'*Eiddo yr Arglywydd y ddaear, a' i chyflawnder, y byd, ac a breswylia ynddo.*'

'Where is that written?'

'Psalm twenty four, first verse, Mrs Morgan.'

'Very good. Do you know how many books in the Old Testament?'

'Thirty-nine, Mrs Morgan'

'And the New Testament?'

'Twenty-seven, Mrs Morgan.'

'Excellent. How many words in the Bible?'

'I don't know, Mrs Morgan.'

'You don't know how many words in the Bible? Whatever do they teach you in Sunday School?'

'God is love, Mrs Morgan.'

Before she drew breath, I fled to the Misses Bowen to thread needles and eat sweet things. While they treadled their sewing machine, I was allowed to search the patch basket for scraps for dolls' clothes.

'I hope you haven't been bothering Mrs Morgan, she's upset enough as it is,' said Miss Siân. 'Ianto's been plaguing her this morning saying we're definitely descended from apes!'

Several times a day, Pedro and I walked up the school hill to see if Ita had arrived. Every summer, two caravans, painted red, yellow and black, camped on the *rhos* near the river. The men worked on the top farms throughout the season, leaving after the harvest. The Romanies came and went, unbeknown to the village, on the old, back road. In the past, there were many *vardos*, children, horses and dogs, but only one family came to their *aichin-tan* during my childhood. I thought if I sat on the *twmp* long enough, the whole, wide world would come to me. My dearest Mamgu Poli, Ita and her magic, Ceri, all modern from Swansea, big Zac and Martha, the mysterious *Ladi Llwyd*, and Col, with the cobwebby shadows of his past.

Haleliwia! Ita was there! I ran down the slope into her arms.

'Ita, Ita, you're here at last, I thought you'd never come. I thought I'd lost you, Ita!

'Never, never, my little *rakli*. You'll never lose me, I'll always find you. I've made more dressing up clothes and we'll play every day!'

'Hurray! Hurray! You're here! You're here!'

Shouting, wild with joy, I leapt and danced up and down the *twmp*. Pedro and Mara, Ita's greyhound, circled and barked, adding to the excitement. Summer had really begun.

I can't remember when I first saw Ita, following her around the village, watching her every move. Young and lovely with a fine, fierce face, dark eyes and curly, black hair, she was my stranger from another world, spun from light, vivid and dazzling. I wanted to wear gold-hooped earrings, long, full skirts and bright shawls. I wanted to live in a *vardo*, sleep in a *bender* and wash in the river.

Although the Romany family were well known in the district, they kept to themselves, hard-working and independent. Dad said Ita's father couldn't be matched with a scythe in the hayfield, or for putting a good edge on a bacon boning knife! Only Ita came to the village, selling pegs and collecting pots, pans and chairs for mending. She sat on our wall, telling me stories, laughing and calling me her little *rakli*. If my Dado didn't mind, she'd teach me how to dance and play her tambourine. She'd show me where the otters and badgers lived, where the birds had their nests and where the *hotchiwitchi* slept. My friendship with Ita delighted and enchanted my childhood in the village.

Sunday meant Chapel three times and very quiet with it, but between Sunday School and teatime, Col and I played our game. He strolled up to the *twmp* and I followed, pretending to be invisible. Ita's family sat around the fire, cooking, whittling pegs or polishing harness. Col had kept company with the Romanies for many years, silently sharing a smoke and a cup of tea, but I never followed him down the slope, a rule obeyed from the past. I waited for Ita and we wandered about, often riding Asia and Dan, with the dogs nearby. As the years passed, she taught me where to find wild strawberries, damsons and blackberries, herbs and hazel nuts. We said thank you for the fruit of the elderberry, and sorry if we damaged the tree, making sure not to offend the witches and their magic. We watched the kingfisher, perched motionless before his brilliant dive, the birds feeding their young and scores of magpies flashing black and white in the fields. Near the top road, noisy rooks gathered on the big trees, dark against the rose-red and purple sunset. Together, in secret places, we discovered the first snowdrops, primroses and bluebells. Too beautiful to pick, we never told a soul where they grew, except Col.

Our favourite place was the rock at the end of the valley, a big, stone shelf jutting from the hill, facing the sea, out of sight and out of earshot. There, Ita and I day-dreamed, pretending to be grand ladies from the *Mabinogion* stories told to me by Mamgu Poli. Leaving out the sad bits, we threw ourselves wholeheartedly into the characters of Olwen, Branwen and Elen. My imagination blazed and soared, relishing the flamboyant gestures, the lavish curtsies, our wild singing and dancing to Ita's tambourine. I was in seventh heaven up there on the rock in my swishy skirt, bangles, scarves and feathers. Col played a reluctant King Arthur to my Queen Gwenhwyfar. For some reason, it was not a favoured role and he refused to wear a crown. His cap low over his eyes, a cigarette clamped in his mouth, he strutted about only to please me.

Sometimes, Seth came to meet Ita by the iron gate. They glowed, all melting and smiling, no eyes for anyone else, their sweet tenderness bringing a catch to the throat. Seth was quiet and serious, with hardly a word to say for himself, but when Ita came he was a changed man, chatting and smiling as if he'd won the *Eisteddfod*. It would break their hearts not to be together and he'd better hurry up, some said, or he'd lose her one of these fine days. I knew when Ita sang her gypsy love-song, deep in her throat, she would wait for Seth until the sea ran dry. Her family didn't want her courting a *gawje*, an outsider, and as a girl of sixteen, they'd often left her with relatives when they came to the village, hoping she'd forget him. She didn't change her mind and five years before, at eighteen, she'd given Seth her pledge. They'd wait until Seth told his mother and then they'd be together.

'One day, you'll come to my wedding, the day of all days,' she said whirling me about in my bright, gypsy skirt. I was her very special little *rakli.*

The Women's Picnic took place on the riverbank on the first hot Saturday in June. It was a time to share family news, have a good *clonc*, and show off delicious cooking on brilliant, white tablecloths. Most importantly, the women discussed their arrangements for hay-making, when they went from farm to farm, cooking, serving food in the fields, raking, turning and gathering. Although the work was hard, they enjoyed the companionship of shared labour, rushing between sunshine and showers, praying haymaking would end before the wheat ripened. If the rain persisted, hay turning could last into August, threatening the harvest. Buying in winter feed could ruin a small farmer.

What a crowd! Aunty Mir, Eira and Bryn came in Dad's van and Ceri made sure she was home from Swansea, in a blue dress smart enough to put Dilys' teeth on edge. Mrs Morgan was wheeled down in her chair by Mrs Rhys, both stern in summer black, followed by Mrs Davies with a card from her daughter in London, wishing she could be there for the picnic. The white and downy Misses Bowen, in lacey, high-necked blouses, giving their pearls an outing, and Besi in her best, black hat ready for a busy day ahead, reading the teacups. Nothing serious, mind you! Mrs Morris brought a basket of her best dainties, while Rhodri's mam looked rosey posey in a new, pink dress.

'There's lovely you look in pink, Mrs Thomas, suits you down to the ground.'

'Made it myself, thank you very much.'

'A credit to you, yes indeed, a credit.'

Olwen and Miss Davis, standing together, a united front.

'How's Guto then?'

Miss Davies, 'Very well indeed, thank you for asking.'

Olwen, 'Yes, very well indeed.'

'Glad to hear it, ladies, there you are then.'

Mam and I, summery in our green florals.

'There's pretty you both look. Got to be careful this time of year. Can't throw off too many clothes, too soon for safety.'

'You and Rhodri have grown since we last saw you, Margaret. Nice to have each other to play with. You'll both be going to school with ours before long, pity we don't live nearer.'

Mrs Emrys made sure Mrs Jones and her children were there to enjoy the afternoon.

'Haven't seen you for ages, Mrs Jones. You look as thin as a rake, my girl. Over by here now, cup of tea and some *bara brith*, made fresh this morning. That's a nasty cut on your hand. Has Besi looked at it? How's Mr Jones? Still working away?'

The women made a fuss of Nain Pritchard, almost ninety-years-old, still sprightly and dressed in the old way like Besi, Mrs Morgan and some of the farm wives. She knew everyone, had a brain like a clock and a tongue like a razor if needed, according to Dad. Miss Eirlys, her daughter, was pleasant and sociable but looked as if her mind was on other things. The *Ladi Lwyd* was away in her big, black car, and Ita never came to the picnic. After a huge tea, the children played hide-and-seek, ring-a-roses, statues, or paddling and skimming stones on the pool. Dan made sure he was elsewhere, wise to the demands for rides, up and down, around and around. When we were too tired to move, we sat near the women and listened to the *clonc*.

'It was a posh wedding by all accounts. Fully choral, but half the family didn't go, unseemly haste they thought. The bride bought her rigout in a big shop in Caerfyrddin and just as she got into the car, the dress split down the back from top to bottom! The cotton must have been rotten. Her father rushed her to the drapers, there's presence of mind, isn't it, and they sewed her up, no charge. She was late for the service but lucky to get there at all. Hope it wasn't a bad sign, things coming undone at the very start like. But she's a very sensible girl, I've been told.'

'My Modryb Ann died last month, eighty-nine she was, house-proud to the end. It was a cold day, but she insisted on washing the steps as usual. She was carrying a bucket of hot water and she fell in her length. Got up like a *wiwer* and said she was fine, but she never recovered from the shock. Caught pneumonia and died she did, died in her sleep. Good way to go, mind you. She never did like fuss and bother, very tidy minded, my Modryb Ann. It was a big funeral, she was well known. I bought a new, black hat in Aberteifi as a mark of respect. She would have liked that.'

'Twm had a very nasty accident a couple of weeks ago. Did you hear? He was drilling some iron bar when the drill broke and hit him, a huge cut over his left eye. It knocked him right out. It looked so bad, they had to get the doctor. He put in seven stitches and said he was a very lucky man to have saved his eye. His face is still black and blue and he's gone very, very quiet.'

Nain enjoyed talking about the old days. She'd lived in the village all her life and nobody knew the valley better. The picnic wasn't just a social occasion when she was a girl.

'Do you remember, Besi? On the first, hot Saturday in June, just like today, the men came down to the river, early in the morning and made three or four fires on the bank by the bridge. They put on big cauldrons and filled them with water to boil. The women came carrying baskets of food and washing, babies in shawls, children and dogs all over the place. There's excitement for you, the old winter over. We didn't have the conveniences women have today, it was easier to wash all the heavy winter blankets, curtains and clothes down here by the river. In those days we used soft soap for washing wool, to keep its warmth and lustre. Beautiful thing Welsh wool, nothing like it. Scrubbing and wringing for hours we were, while the young ones swilled off the soap in the river. Falling over and getting soaking wet, we were in our oils, shouting and laughing like ruffians, no thought for tomorrow. Running up and down, with washing streaming out behind us, like the sails of a ship. What a grand time we had, mothers saying we would have pneumonia as sure as eggs, with us so soon out of winter clothes. Catching us, rubbing us dry until we were red and glowing, hair standing on end! The washing was spread out on the grass and bushes to dry in the sun. Nothing to match that sweet smell! After a big dinner, we had the rest of the day to play, just like you children today. Brings back pictures, I can tell you.'

Towards evening, the men joined us for supper and the conversation turned to the prowess of past and present reapers in the hayfield with Ita's father high on the list. Ianto's views were much in evidence when debating the type and quality of each scythe and the time taken to cut every field. An elderly bachelor, living on a small farm, he preceded most of his sentences with "Samson says". Samson, his old dog, sat impassively on his lap, the fount of all wisdom. Col stayed close to Dad, ready to leave if the wind changed. Mic and Huw Pryce, Brynfa, and the other farm boys strolled by, giving the girls the eye. Presently much giggling could be heard in the shadows.

If the weather held, we sat around the fire singing hymns, reciting poems and telling stories. The day ended when Mr Wil Morris, in his special waistcoat, sang *Dafydd y Garreg Wen* so tenderly, it melted the heart. Mr Emrys asked for a blessing through the night with the children's prayer,

'*Diolch iti, Arglwydd,*
Am Dy ofal cu,
Drwy yr hirnos dywyll,
Gwylia drosom ni.'

It was a drowsy, humming day, perfect for haymaking. There were no clouds in the west and if it stayed dry, our small crop would be down before evening. Col, Seth and Ita's brothers moved like stately dancers, their scythes swishing in perfect time, their hypnotic movements making me forget my task.

'Margaret, dreaming again! Off you go, quick march!' Down the side of the field pell-mell, Pedro at my heels, to spread tablecloths in the corner under the trees. Mam, Aunty Mir, Mrs Morris, Mrs Thomas and Mrs Olwen Guto carried large baskets of food, billowing and chattering in their starched, white aprons and caps. Dad, Ita, Eira, Bryn and Rhodri followed, balancing jugs of lemon barley-water and cold tea. We sat in the shade, relishing thick slices of ham and chicken, leek and potato pies, bread, cheese, and fruit tarts. Before stretching out for a rest and a smoke, the men untied the string circling their trousers below the knee, and we children waited for awful creepies, or worse, to slither down over their clogs. Seth, pretending he'd trapped a snake, chased us screaming and shouting, until we realised it was only his tightly-rolled, green handkerchief.

The women returned to spread the hay after washing-up in the house, and the children romped about making dusty clouds of golden speckles in the sunlight. Suddenly, my father fell to his knees and Mam and Col were running across the field. They bent over him, loosening his clothes, trying to ease his distress. I watched fearfully as he fought for breath, his face turning a mottled purple. Gently, the men carried his shuddering body into the house. Mam nodded as she passed and I knew what to do. I ran to find Besi who came at once to prepare steaming, herbal vapours, which Dad inhaled from a bowl, his head draped over with a towel. The heaving and gasping slowly subsided and he sat, pale and spent in his wicker chair in the *gegin fawr*. The heart was taken out of the day. Col remained by my father's chair, never taking his eyes from the bowed head. Driven by the fine weather, the reapers continued and with the help of friends and neighbours, all the hay was down and turned by late afternoon.

Dad stayed in his chair for three days and nights. The house was quiet and still, nothing could be touched, not the ashes in the grate or even the cloth on the table. We lived in the *gegin fach* to give him peace to recover and I only saw him at bedtime, blowing him a kiss as I walked softly through the room. He nodded and winked, his face haggard and unshaved, his eyes very dark and burning. I longed for my cowboy-playing Dad, when we punished the poor old sofa, riding hard, six guns blazing.

Col sat with Dad every night, easing Mam, and Aunty Mir came to help in the shop. Besi brought her herbal medicines and Mrs Morris tempted Dad's appetite with delicate broths and junkets. Neighbours continued working in our hayfields until Saturday when Ianto rolled the stalks between his palms and, after consulting Samson, pronounced it fit for gathering. But not on Sunday, the seventh day, no work was ever done on Sunday. It was God's day, to be spent in Chapel. On this Sunday, it rained, pelting down the entire afternoon and evening. No rest for the wicked, Mam sighed, the turning would have to start again when the weather improved. It did, but not the baking-hot dryness of the previous few days, and although some of the larger farms with horse-drawn machinery were ahead, it was touch-and-go for them too.

Shoulders to the wheel! Aunty Mir cycled over in the mornings, and Ita, Col, Mrs Thomas, and Mr and Mrs Morris raked away like mad things. Customers for the shop either came looking for Mam in the field, or helped themselves, paying later. Clouds gathered in the west and although there was still a little moisture left in the hay, it was now or never. Even Dilys was allowed to lend a hand, and Mr James, Brynmawr, kindly sent his *gwas*, a good-looking stranger, hardly ever seen in the village. He entered the field with quite a swagger, smiling all round. The women gave him a keen look, some tightening their lips as he cracked a loud joke with the men. I was standing close to the hedge with Dan and the cart when he passed by, touching his cap to Dilys. She went bright red to the roots of her hair, dropping her rake, she was so flustered. He pitched hay into the cart, and after watching him for a moment, she picked up her rake and hurried off to the far side of the field. The sky grew dark and hope was fading fast when Ita's father and brothers came striding into the top field. Then things went with a swing, the tension easing as they silently pitched and loaded. Several children came after school, hoping for tea and some fun before the long trek home. It was the best time, a chance to laugh and chase about, covered in hay, looking like scarecrows. Struggling to climb onto the cart, begging for a lift on that last ride to the Dutch barn, we were kings of the castle, singing our heads off.

'*Oes gafr eto? Oes heb ei godro*
Ar y creigiau geirwon,
Mae'r hen afr yn crwydro.
Gafr goch, goch, goch,
Ie, fingoch, fingoch, fingoch,
Foel gynffongoch, foel gynffongoch,
Ystlys goch a chynffon
Goch, goch, goch.'

It looked so heavy with rain, the women laid out tea in the barn. The heavens opened just as the children arrived carrying bundles of hay to sit on. Men, horses and dogs clattered through the big doors, spraying raindrops like diamonds in the gloom. Watch what you're doing, boyos, shouted the women, rescuing food and tablecloths in the commotion. At last we sat down to tea, the lanterns lit against the shadows. Dilys had left earlier, and there was no sign of the *gwas* from Brynmawr.

'Isn't that Maldwyn coming in for food then?'

'We haven't seen him since it started raining.'

'He isn't from around these parts, is he?'

'No, he came from away somewhere to help when Mr James was taken ill, back last summer. Friendly enough chap, and a very good worker. But between you and me, I've heard on good authority that he's a Roman Catholic, through and through!'

'A Roman Catholic! What on earth is he doing here?'

'I don't know, but it's the honest truth I'm telling you, drop dead.'

'He must be Irish.'

'He doesn't sound Irish, and Maldwyn's a proper Welsh name, isn't it?'

'Well, that's something, anyway.'

'Roman Catholic or not, he's a good-looking chap. Wonder if he's courting?'

'He's not likely to find anyone around here, him being a stranger as well.'

'Talking of courting strangers, I hear someone's got his eye on your Ceri. Works in a bank in Swansea, with prospects, is that right?'

'I don't know who told you that, I'm sure. Nothing serious, you can put your mind at rest. Our Ceri wants to concentrate on her training.'

'She'd make a good matron, if you ask me. Plenty of spark, she knows how many peas make five. She's a credit to you, Mrs Morris, no doubt about it, she's got style, your Ceri has.'

'Thank you, Blodwen. She works hard and keeps herself decent, and that's what counts, isn't it? By the way, have you heard, Dilys is going on holiday soon?'

'Is she? Who's paying, not her father, I'm sure.'

'She's saved enough egg money to stay in Ceri's lodgings in Swansea for a week.'

'Swansea? Far enough away, isn't it? Why's she going to Swansea?'

'Swansea isn't that far, is it? And our Ceri will be there for company, won't she? She wants to see a bit of life, I expect, and who can blame her? She's been kept close for too long. She's a good girl is Dilys, doesn't get much of a chance really. Deserves a home of her own at her age.'

'Nice for her to have a change, she'll never manage another, old Rhys will see to that.'

'He's not that bad with his family, except for paying for vegetables. Mind you, they always keep a very good table.'

'To give him his due, he's generous to the Chapel and very free to the missionary fund. Top of the list every year. Well you can't have everything, can you? Good luck to Dilys, I say, I hope she has a good time.'

'I expect you're right, but I can't see any good coming of it myself, gallivanting about like a gypsy. Sorry, Ita, no offence, I didn't mean you.'

'None taken, Mrs Guto.'

'By the way, Olwen, how is Guto?'

'Very well, thank you for asking.'

'And Miss Davies?'

'Very well, thank you.'

'There you are then.'

The morning Dilys went to Swansea with Ceri, the water came off the roof through the broken shooting like a waterfall. Pedro and I sat by the window, cheated by the weather, knowing Mam wouldn't let us out to say goodbye and wave them off. I expect Dilys was wearing her best, blue, two-piece suit with her cream, straw hat and crochet gloves. She said she'd make me a pair for the *Cymanfa Ganu*, with embroidered daisies on the backs.

On his return, Dad said Mr and Mrs Rhys looked a bit glum when he and Ceri called in the van, and Dilys cried as if she was going to Australia.

'You look like a ghost, girl, what's the matter with you?' Ceri said. 'We'll put on a bit of box when we get to the station, some rouge and lipstick will put you right.'

'I've never seen you wearing box before, Ceri.'

'Oh yes you have, but I'm cute about it see, not to scandalize Dat. Just a little makes all the difference, I'll show you. You should buy a pair of joking pearl earrings when we get to Swansea, gives you a glow. Not as good as the real thing, but good enough. Cheer up now. You look as if you're going to a funeral.'

'Bit nervous, I expect. Never slept away from home before, except at Aunty's in Aberporth.'

'*Duw, Duw*, nothing to cry about, Dilys *fach*, going on holiday you are, and we'll be together so you won't get lost. Look, your handbag's undone. Why on earth are you taking your Bible? Your Dat afraid of sin around every corner, is it? Crying again? We better get there quick, Mr Sharrol, or Dilys will be *siwps* before we reach Swansea.'

Ceri always rang with a message to reassure her parents of her safe arrival, but that evening, she wanted to speak to her mother urgently. Mam rushed out of the house, telling Dad not to ask questions, she'd explain later. She and Mrs Morris were back in a flash, shutting the door to the telephone room firmly behind them. Something was in the wind! Normally, Mrs Morris wouldn't go near the telephone in a month of Sundays, like most of the people in the village.

Early next morning, after mysterious comings and goings, Dad took Mam and Mrs Morris to Henllan station. It seemed Ceri wasn't well, and Mam was taking Mrs Morris as far as Caerfyrddin because she was nervous of travelling.

'Won't be long, *cariad*. Look after Daddy and Col until I come back.'

'What's happening, Mam? If Ceri's so ill, why was she talking on the phone?'

'You don't miss much, do you?'

'Why can't I come with you? I like the train. I've only been on it once, when we went to Mamgu Davies'. Can't I come too?'

'Not this time, *bach*, Ceri needs her mam and we've got to go quick, see. I'll be back before you know it and I'll tell you about it later.'

'Why can't Mr Morris go instead?'

'He's got a gravestone to finish, and you can't put that off, can you? Don't fret, I'll be home in time to put you to bed.'

Dinner was late, and the school children were already seated in their usual places when Dad laid the table. Goggle-eyed, they watched Col serving the *cawl*, wearing a white apron, his movements identical to those of my mother. Dad and I were in stitches, but after eating in complete silence, the others left in haste.

A dry afternoon meant we could continue my bicycle-riding lessons in the yard. Dad and Col had spent hours repairing a two-wheeler to replace the pushchair on my outings with Mam. I was making slow progress, unable to ride unless Dad held the saddle. When he ran out of breath, Col took over. No matter how much we practised, every time he released the bike, I fell off. Pedro and Bomber watched with a superior air. It was hopeless! Much to everyone's relief, I admitted defeat, and we decided to play cowboys and Indians instead.

Our games began when Mamgu Poli suggested I should learn to speak English. Dad started by reading the usual fairy stories, including *Snow White*. I thought they were really terrifying, preferring Col's favourite passages from *The Mammoth Book of Thrillers, Ghosts and Mysteries!* Finding these difficult to translate, Dad resorted to play-acting, his dramatic gestures and various voices much appreciated by Col and me. Best of all, we enjoyed Zane Grey's books about the Wild West, which arrived by post every month. Dad had always wanted to be a cowboy, riding the range on his bucking bronco, driving cattle across the wide prairie. It would make up for being such an old crock, he said.

Bedecked with headdresses and tomahawks made by Col, the action began. Our roles rarely differed, with Col playing Hiawatha to my Minnehaha, and Dad as the sheriff wearing a metal star and a

battered hat. We whooped, war-cried, fought and died, Dad frequently sitting on the gate for a quiet smoke, Bomber perched
peacefully by his side. We shouted, "put 'em up, pard", "drop that six
gun" and "move them critters, you old cowpoke". The phrases did
little for my English vocabulary, but I had a wonderful time. Col's
death scenes were spectacular! One moment he was spread-eagled
against the hedge with lengthy twitchings, the next flat on his back,
madly shaking each limb in turn. The longest act entailed being shot
in the head. Throwing off his cap, he reeled about, clutching his
white head, crashing into the gate before finally falling to the ground
with his tongue hanging out. Slowly and painfully, he froze into a
grotesque pose. Pedro kindly licked his face to bring him back to life.

'Ten out of ten for that Col, my old pal. Marvellous, much better
than last time. I think we've polished off them there varmints for
today.'

For the grand finale, Dad sang his favourite cowboy song, about
Wildcat Kelly, accompanied by Col, blowing on his comb through a
cigarette paper.

'Give me land, lots of land, under starry skies above,
Don't fence me in.
Let me ride through the wide open country that I love,
Don't fence me in.
Let me be by myself in the evening breeze,
Listen to the murmur of the cottonwood trees,
Send me off for ever, but I ask you please,
Don't fence me in.'

Years later, I learnt that Mrs Morris and my mother were having a
drama of their own. Ceri's phone call revealed that Dilys was in serious trouble and needed help urgently. They were travelling from
Swansea to Caerfyrddin the following morning, and could Mrs
Morris meet them at the railway station, without fail? She would
explain then, and not a single word to anyone in the village, except
Mr Morris and my parents. It was alarming news! Mrs Morris, read-

ing between the lines and fearing the worst, asked my mother to ring a trusted friend in Llandysul, a district nurse with a car, and a very handy person to know in a crisis. Besides that, she was Mrs Morris' middle brother's wife's sister, one of the family! Knowing Dilys, she was only too pleased to help, promising to meet them at the station, and take them back to her house, if necessary.

Mrs Morris and Mam arrived in Caerfyrddin to find the two girls sitting on the platform, looking as if they'd been pulled through a hedge backwards. Even Ceri, who was usually so particular about her appearance. She was overjoyed to see them, but Dilys paid no attention, staring into space as if in a trance.

'Thank God you're here,' said Ceri, 'I've been frantic wondering what to do. We've been up all night, and I haven't had a *gec* out of Dilys since yesterday afternoon. Nothing has passed her lips, she just sits there as if she's off with the *Tylwyth Teg*. I can hardly believe what's happened. I'm going to cry now, I'm shaking like a leaf. I'll have to go back soon, I'm on duty to-night.'

'Look, the buffet's empty,' said Mrs Morris. 'We need a cup of tea to calm us down, and you can tell us all about it, Ceri *fach*.'

My mother took Dilys' arm and she went like a lamb, but she didn't touch her tea.

'Everything was fine to start off with,' said Ceri. 'Dilys was full fuss on the train, excited about seeing Swansea for the first time. But when we reached my lodgings, there was a big surprise in store for me, I can tell you! Dilys wasn't on holiday at all. She was marrying that chap Maldwyn in the registry office, at half past three! I almost fainted, especially when she asked me to be a witness cum bridesmaid. How on earth could she be getting married when she's only known Maldwyn five minutes? But no indeed, it turns out they've been seeing each other for almost a year. She met him at the Eisteddfod in Aberteifi last August. They were there to hear Mrs Rhys' cousin singing in the choir, Handel it was.'

'Well, that's an end to Handel in that house,' said Mrs Morris.

'Maldwyn was standing in the same *gwt* as Dilys, waiting for a cup of tea. They got talking, and when he said he was looking for work, she told him Brynmawr wanted a *gwas*, and it went on from there. Where did they meet then, I asked her, considering her father kept her so close? When her mam and dat went out, she put *Come into the garden, Maud* on the gramophone, and if Maldwyn was in the fields, he came to the house.'

My mother and Mrs Morris exchanged meaningful glances. One mystery solved anyway!

'I said she couldn't do this to her family,' continued Ceri, 'it would kill them for sure. She gave me one of her looks, and I could see her mind was made up. Nothing to stop Dilys when she looks like that. Her father would never let her marry a Roman Catholic, so there was no point in talking. It was now or never, she said, while she had the courage. She'd written to her mam and dat, explaining everything, asking for forgiveness in time. We talked things over, and in the end I said I'd go with her to the registry office, but not to take part.'

'Very wise, Ceri *fach*.'

'I couldn't very well be her bridesmaid, could I? It didn't seem right, and if Mr Rhys ever found out, he'd put a curse on me, silly old devil.'

'Now then, keep a civil tongue, our Ceri.'

'Well, Mam, it's so ridiculous. Look at the state she's in, all because she's been cooped up for a lifetime. Dilys is thirty-two years old, not a child! Anyway, there was no turning back. I gave her my pearl earrings for a wedding present, and I did her hair and put on a bit of box. There's lovely she looked, like a young girl really. I'd never seen her look like that before, as if she was looking forward to something special in her life for once.'

Ceri dabbed her eyes and blew her nose. 'We were early at the registry and while we were waiting for Maldwyn, it came into my head that Roman Catholics could only get married in their own church. I'd heard it somewhere, but I didn't think it was the best time to say anything. Well, half past three came and went, and Dilys was as pale as a lily, shrinking in her skin, looking like a little, old woman. It was awful to watch! When the office closed, I expected to go back to the lodgings to talk things over for the best, but Dilys had other ideas. She had Maldwyn's address in Swansea, and she was going to see what was wrong. She said he must have had an accident and if I didn't go with her, she was off on her own. We tramped across the town and when the landlady opened the door, Dilys asked if she could please speak to Maldwyn. The woman said he'd only stayed a few days, his wife and children had come to fetch him the day before and they'd gone back to Monmouth.'

Mrs Morris and my mother were thunderstruck. A Roman Catholic and a married man! That was bad enough, but all three shared the same thought. Was Dilys in such a terrible state because she had a secret? God forbid, could she be in the family way? They didn't say a word, just looked at each other.

Ceri returned to work shortly before Miss Evans arrived. Dilys was looking very poorly by the time they reached her house in Llandysul. After settling her on the sofa, Miss Evans said she was in a state of acute shock and she would call the doctor. Did they know why Dilys was in such a bad way? Mrs Morris said they didn't, but feared the worst from the very beginning. Very protective of Dilys, Tegwen Morris decided to stay with Miss Evans until the poor child regained her senses. They would keep in touch with Mam and let her know the consequences, whatever they turned out to be. Dilys was no better when Dad collected my mother, but she was in good hands.

Mam looked very tired when she arrived home in the van. She said she was whacked, as if she'd been up Snowdon half a dozen times. No story that night, she was asleep before I'd finished my prayers. *Nos da*, Mam, it's lovely to have you back.

Next morning, the phone rang during second breakfast.

'Blodwen, Miss Evans from Llandysul wants a word with you.'

'Iesu Grist aros yda ni.'

My mother's prayer showed her agitation. A few minutes later she was talking to my father in the shop.

'In all the commotion, we completely forgot Dilys' letter to her mam and dat. I don't care what you say, Haydn, and I know it's against the law, but no post for the Rhys house today until I've seen it. We could be holding Dilys' future in our hands.'

'I'm afraid you're too late, Blodwen, Mrs Rhys came while I was doing the sorting. She asked if there was a letter, and I gave it to her.'

'Was it Dilys' handwriting?'

'I'm afraid I couldn't say.'

'*O diawl*,' my mother swore, 'the fat's in the fire now. She's guessed something's up with all the comings and goings. She'll be back after reading the letter to see what I've got to say for myself. There'll be hell to pay, you just wait and see. What can I tell her? I must play for time until Miss Evans rings me again. The doctor is seeing Dilys this morning. She's no better, still hasn't said one single word or eaten a morsel. I'm afraid there's something drastically wrong there.'

'I must say, I'm surprised at Dilys,' said Dad, 'I didn't think she'd say boo to a goose. But I remember now, she did come to collect several letters last summer, with a Swansea postmark. It seemed a little odd at the time, they had *The Garden Club* printed on the envelope.'

'*The Garden Club! Duw Mawr!* Didn't you think that was strange? Nobody ever has a letter from a garden club in this village. Didn't you put two and two together?'

'Keep your hair on, Blodwen, I don't have a crystal ball. Why should I know about Dilys' private life?'

'If only you'd mentioned it, we might have saved the day!'

'I can't see how. What could you have done?'

'You never know. You should have said.'

'Now the whole affair is my fault! In heaven's name, I'll never understand the workings of a woman's mind!'

'Lucky for you then,' my mother replied.

When we sat down to *tê deg*, Mam drank three cups of tea and started biting her nails. Dad soon went to busy himself in the shop, and Col began rolling his eyes.

'Have you heard anything about that Maldwyn, Col? You often know more than the rest of us, and that's a fact.'

Col shook his head and left.

A knock on the front door startled us both.

'It's you, Mrs Rhys, please come in.'

'No, thank you just the same. I think you know why I'm here.'

'I expect it's about Dilys, but I ...'

'I knew by the state of my daughter when she left that she wasn't going on any holiday. I felt sure there'd be a letter this morning and

I was right. I know the facts, but something even worse has happened, hasn't it? You and Teg Morris didn't go off yesterday because Ceri was ill. I want to make things quite clear. Dilys is my daughter and my only child, and whatever trouble she's in, I intend to help her. I'm not angry, Blodwen, so please tell me what's happened.'

'You've taken the wind right out of my sails, Mrs Rhys. Teg Morris and I thought there'd be a real rumpus, and we were playing for time until we knew what to do for the best.'

'I appreciate that, but Dilys and I will decide what to do for the best. I'm not completely daft, you know. I've guessed for some time that Maldwyn was lurking about. Whatever you tell me will be between us women. Mr Rhys doesn't need to know until the time is right.'

'You must come in, Mrs Rhys, I can't tell you everything out here on the doorstep.'

Mrs Rhys was not a favourite of mine. Her stern face and black, pebble eyes indicated she was not fond of children. I went to the *gegin fach*, leaving the door open behind me. My mother closed it firmly. It seemed like hours before she called to my father.

'Haydn, could you please take Mrs Rhys to Llandysul as soon as possible?'

Shortly afterwards, Dad left with Mrs Rhys sitting stiffly in the car wearing her best black. He returned with a very excited Mrs Morris.

'I had the shock of my life when I saw Mrs Rhys standing on the doorstep. Dilys was still bad, the doctor'd been, but no change. She was sitting in the chair when Mrs Rhys went in and put her arms right round her. Dilys seemed to come to herself, looked at her mam and burst out crying like a little girl. Miss Evans and I went into the garden to give them a bit of room. When Mrs Rhys called us in, she thanked us very much for our kindness and trouble. She was taking Dilys to her sister in Aberporth for a change of air, and please could I take a note to Mr Rhys? Then she said, very confidential, she felt we ought to know that Dilys was definitely in the clear.'

'Oh, Mrs Morris *fach*, I can't tell you how relieved I am. It feels as if a ton weight has been lifted. The thought of her being cast out of

Chapel's been haunting me. Terrible thing that, never held with it myself. I saw it happen once, I couldn't witness it again, too heart-breaking for words. The shame for the family, with most of the women in the congregation thanking God it wasn't them or theirs. Those poor culprits standing in the big seat. But worse for a girl on her own, of course, not much mercy for her. If her family turns their back on her as well, there's nothing but the workhouse. Cruel I call it, what a way to treat your own. Well, Dilys won't have to go through that, anyway.'

'We ought to say a little prayer of thanks that she's been spared, Blodwen.'

As they bowed their heads, my mother crossed her fingers.

Chapter Four

Sunday

F'annwyl ffrind,

Poli is coming down for Dydd Iau Mawr, next week. She's bringing Martha and Zac, three, Trefor counted out. She's not quite so fussy about the numbers these days, getting used to the car now. I hope so, makes things very awkward on times, mind. Still makes Haydn caclwm mad, but she doesn't take a blind bit of notice.

    I'll be glad to see Zac, he and Haydn being such good friends. He misses him, wishes he could see him more often. He needs a bit of cheering up, he's got a boil coming up on his left side, very painful it is, all swollen and reddish-blue like. Zac will give us a good laugh, full of politics as usual, I expect. Even Col cracks his face behind his hand when Zac's spouting about the old days. They're staying with Jess for a week. She's been bad too, have you heard? Something wrong down below, the doctor wants to do an op for repairs. Sounds nasty to me, doesn't it? I expect Martha will stay on if she's needed. You can always rely on Martha for help.

    Nain is hiring the bus to take us to Tresaith this year, leaving at ten o'clock. Are you coming? Nain told me to be sure to tell you to come, she's expecting you and the children. The bus will pick you up on the way, he's going to Penrhiwpal as it is. Write and tell me and I'll phone the garage. We'll meet you there, Trefor's taking us in the car, as Margaret is very bad on the bus, as you know...

Love from,
Blodwen.

Mamgu Poli was at Besi's, Dad was in bed, and everyone was doing something important, no children underfoot, thank you very much! Fortunately, Nain Pritchard always had time to talk. I loved sitting at the long table in her *gegin fawr*, listening to stories from the past. The whole room glowed, from the polished red and black floor tiles, to the copper lustre in the corner cupboard. Two panelled settles flanked the huge, open fireplace, its mantel lined with pewter plates and candlesticks. Nain had the best dresser I'd ever seen. Colourful jugs and dishes crowded the shelves, and six, matching, china dogs sat on the board.

Sometimes, as a special treat, I was taken to see the brass-bound Bible in the parlour. The flyleaf held the dates of all births, marriages and deaths in the family. Pictures of God and the Prophets, Jesus Christ and the Apostles, divided the books of the Old and New Testaments. Next to the grandfather clock, a glass-fronted cupboard displayed the best china dishes and ornaments. It was kept locked, and no fingering the glass, if you please. Above it hung a portrait of Nain's prized Friesian bull, painted by a journeyman painter, all the way from Holland! That was a long time ago, when Nain and her husband were still young.

'Have you always lived here, Nain?'

'Yes, *cariad*, born and bred in this house I was and I shall die here too. I've never wanted to be anywhere else. My Hen-Datcu and Mamgu worked hard for years to build up this farm. They lived in the *bwthyn* out there, look, the washhouse it is these days. When there was enough money, my Datcu built this house, and a Dwgan has lived in it ever since. My father brought my mother here as a bride, and when I got married, my husband came here too. Now there's a fine man for you. Dafydd Pritchard. See his picture by the glass? Our Evan and Twm are like their father and Eirlys has his eyes. Young Dafydd and Islwyn were more like me, gone now, God rest their souls.

'Yes indeed, we've been here a long time. The farm prospered and when the Chapel was built, the village grew around it, with the school, the shop and the Post Office. We had everything we needed, a blacksmith, cobbler, carpenter and harness maker. We looked after ourselves and kept the old ways. Things have changed a lot, but I can see much bigger changes coming, selling milk every day for one, and there's talk of a bus coming through on Fridays. It'll be all different before long. I'm glad I won't be alive to see it. When you grow up, nobody will want to remember the old days. This bus to Tresaith on *Dydd Iau Mawr* now, not so long ago the whole village went by *gambo*. Grand it was! Everyone had the day off, and the farmer, my father it was then, treated us all to a trip to the sea. The women helped my mother prepare food and the men cleaned the carts, putting bales of straw to sit on. The journey was as much fun as the beach! You should have seen the horses! Like silk their coats looked, their manes and tails brushed and combed and plaited with ribbons. Your Mamgu Poli will remember that, the brasses like gold in the sun. One cart was full of food and drink with no shortage of anything, big hams, chickens, pies and faggots. As for the cakes and puddings, you've never seen anything like it! You could eat non-stop for a week! Cold tea, lemon barley-water and home-made beer to drink. My mother kept a strict eye on the beer, mind you.

'Off we went in a procession, proud as *Pwnch* we were. Girls together, Besi Puw, Siân and Anni Bowen, Dai's mother, Neli's and Wil's. In our best, starched, summer dresses and bonnets, pretty as a picture, making eyes at the boys on the sly. They looked very hot in their chapel black, but down to their shirts in no time. There were some good-looking men in the village, old Madoc Hopcyn for one. He never got married though, looked after his dat he did, to the end. I was a bit sweet on him but not a word to a soul, mind you, or I'll never hear the end of it! Then I met Dafydd, didn't look twice at any man after that. The Bowen girls had a good-looking father too. He married a nice little girl from Sarnau, delicate she was, died on confinement with Anni. The girls never married either, very spic and span. Elias Rhys' father was as serious as a judge and passed it on to his son. Never known anyone for carrying his spirits in his boots like him, always looking for wrongdoings. He wouldn't have put up with Guto's antics, I can tell you. Out in the open for everybody to see, it's beyond belief. Olwen's people must be turning in the grave. They never thought much of him in the first place and he had both legs then! Olwen was afraid to be left on the shelf and Guto was the only bachelor around. No other woman would have him, that's why. Full of himself that one, always was. We used to run like rabbits when he was about, not safe for five minutes.'

'Not safe from what, Nain?'

'Never you mind, just talking I am, remembering the old times. No indeed, he would have got the *ceffyl pren* in my day, not just the straw plait.'

'What does it mean, Nain, hanging a straw plait on someone's gate?'

'Not for children to know! But whoever puts it there must surely see it takes more than that to show what we think of Guto. Disgusting! Olwen's daft to put up with it, always backward in standing up for herself, that one.'

'Put up with what?'

'Never you mind. What was I saying before you interrupted? Oh yes! Going to the seaside was the best of the summer for all of us. Now we go by bus, but still nice when we get there, if the weather stays dry. Right, now let's have some of this *bara ceirch* with fresh butter. I still think oats are better for you than wheat. You can take one to your Mam, I know she's partial to *bara ceirch*.'

After dinner, Ita and I were sitting by the railings in front of the house.

'Come to Tresaith with us, Ita, come on. You can come in Mamgu Poli's car with me. You'll like it, Col's coming this year.'

'No, I don't like the bus or the car. Shut up you are, like a cat in a cage. It's not for me, bach, you can't see anything, going so fast. I'll take you on Asia's back one day, just the two of us. Look, here come Mr and Mrs Mortymer to see your Dado. *Dydd da*, Mrs Mortymer, *dydd da* Mr Mortymer.'

'Hello, Ita *fach*, there's lovely you look. And here's Dewdrop. How's my girl, then?'

Uncle Zac swung me over his head, tickling me with his long, spiky eyebrows, making me laugh.

'Where's your Dad then, not very well, is it?'

'He's bad in bed with a carbuncle, Uncle Zac'

'I'll give him carbuncle, poor old bugger.'

Martha's voice was very sharp.

'Mind your language, if you please, Mr Mortymer. None of that in front of the child.'

'Sorry, Dewdrop, forgot myself, penny in the swear box. Can't get away with anything, your Aunty Martha's got ears like a bat.'

Uncle Zac spoke halting Welsh like Dad, laced with the everyday language of the pit. He wasn't very tall, but well built with legs like pit props, according to my father. He had a vivid, humorous face, thick, black eyebrows, dark, brown eyes and a thatch of white, wavy hair. Small, blue scars on his forehead and chin indicated a life spent working underground. In his best, dark suit and white, silk muffler, he was an arresting figure, still turning women's heads, Mamgu Poli said. There was a sense of strength and energy in his movements, belying his sixty-odd years. He filled our *gegin fawr*, sweeping Mam into a bear hug, and slapping Col on the back.

'Upstairs to Haydn then, see what we can do for the poor old b—— Yes, Martha I know. Not in front of the kids, eh, Dewdrop?'

The house shook as he clumped back down the stairs.

'Blod *fach*, that poor *boyo* needs seeing to, on his knees he is, the pain something awful. Looks very nasty to me. He says to ask Besi to bring the bottle to get it over with.'

'Besi said she'll come anytime, but I don't know, it could be agony if it's not ready to burst. I've been pondering since yesterday. He's going down hill fast, can't sleep at all for the pain. What do you think, Mrs Mortymer? Come and have a look.'

Dad was lying on his stomach, covered only by a sheet. When Mam lifted the poultice, I saw the large swelling above his waist, an angry, dark red boil in the centre, surrounded by several smaller ones. My poor Dad was in the wars again, his breathing shallow and painful.

'We'll bathe it once more and if nothing happens, I'll send for Besi, at least he'll have a proper night's sleep. What do you say, Mrs Mortymer?'

I was at Besi's with a note before tea. She packed her basket with a wide-necked glass bottle, a long silver spoon, a jar of ointment, a

small hammer and some spotless, white strips of cloth. I knew what
it meant, I'd seen the treatment before. Why was my Dad always ill?

Col and Zac were with my father, and the kettle was boiling on
the chain. Besi asked Mam to take it upstairs, no children allowed!
Sitting on the *sgiw*, Aunty Martha and I heard every sound; Besi's
quiet words, the rattle of the spoon, the gurgle of hot water being
poured in and out of the bottle, the creaking bed as Col and Zac held
my father down.

'Hold on, *bach*,' from Besi as she placed the steaming mouth of
the bottle over the carbuncle. A howl from my father to bring down
the plaster.

'Don't move, Haydn *bach*, it's drawing out now, you're almost free
of the *blutty* thing at last.'

Besi then, 'Mr Mortymer, hold him still, the bottle won't come
off. Where's the hammer, Blodwen? Wrap the towel round the bottle,
quick now, sharp tap, there you are, all over.'

I was having a good cry on Aunty Martha's lap, my hands over
my ears.

We were already on the beach when the children scrambled from the
bus in Tresaith. Plunging into the sea, we remained there until din-
ner-time. My father, still unwell, had travelled in the van with Col,
intending to leave early. The men carried baskets of food into the
shadow of the cliff before settling down to a quiet smoke. They cer-
emoniously removed their shoes and socks, rolled up their trouser
legs and placed knotted handkerchiefs on their heads. All except Col.
He hung onto his cap as if his life depended on it. Mamgu Poli
brought everyone to a halt, in a pale-lilac outfit with purple trimmings, and a hat large enough to cast a shadow over Llandaff
Cathedral!

During the noisy picnic, Col began to look ill at ease. As I led him
to the deserted bay beyond the waterfall, I saw a tall, slim girl on the
beach road, with a black dog on a lead. I liked the way she walked,
light and graceful, her dark, curly hair shining in the sunlight. A soft,
cream dress fell almost to her feet, the deep hem richly embroidered

with leaves and flowers. She was a stranger, and beautiful enough to be one of the seven princesses in the legend of Tresaith! Suddenly, the dog pulled free and raced along the sand, scattering picnic baskets and licking empty plates. Women shouted and flapped, making him more excited than ever, until Mr Thomas finally chased him away. Although the girl called and called, the dog went in the opposite direction. Some way off, he joined a group of children and a scrawny terrier, who were jumping in and out of the waves. When the growling began, the black dog was taken by surprise and the children ran away. The girl screamed as she ran towards us, but Col stood in her path, indicating she should stay with me. His stillness held her. Together, we watched him walk steadily to the water's edge, where he crouched beside the fighting dogs, legs apart, hands on his knees. A swift lunge caught the black dog's collar, pulling him aside. Col stared intently at the other, his face inches away from the bared teeth. The trio was absolutely motionless, breath suspended, until both dogs sat meekly on the sand. A few moments later, the terrier joined the watching children and Col returned, the black dog at his heels. Smiling happily, the beautiful girl thanked him over and over, shaking his hand.

'Thank you very much for all you've done. My name's Deborah. I hope we meet again, I think you're a wizard.'

How did *she* know Col was a wizard?

'It's like the Houses of Parliament in there, Col, Mr Mortymer going on about politics, full force. Mamgu Poli's putting in her pennyworth, and Haydn's lifting his sleeve as fast as he can go. It's a mad house, *caton pawb*. Listen to it!'

'A scandal to shake the nation, that's what it is. Those *blutty* coal owners still making money on our backs, and we haven't got two ha' pennies to rub together, *mun*. Half the kids on our street with no shoes to their feet. Call it justice, aye, by God, justice for the *crachach*, starvation for the workers. Always been the same, of course, my father before me. Hell's fire, we work our fingers to the bone, what for? Dust on the lung and nothing in the belly. Politicians? What do they know? Bugger all, that's what, and what do they care? Even less! Rabble we are to them, *mun*, not fit to live decent. Digging our lives out down there, we were better off fighting the Romans! My father died young in the Rhondda. Big, strong as a bull he was, a fighting man. Like a pimple on a haystack I am next to him. Many a time I saw him fight for money on the mountain, to put food in his children's mouths. Quick on his feet for a big man, and very particular about the nose. It was a fine nose, see, didn't want it squashed over his face, no indeed. Taught me from a kid how to look after myself. Mind you, he had strict rules about fighting. Keep a cool head and never go for the privates. Marvellous man, ready for burying by the time he was fifty. Dust. Born in 1845, he was, fourteen years after Dic Penderyn was hanged for the Merthyr Riots.

'And that's another thing. Did we get justice then? Did we, hell and damnation! Where were the politicians, the church and chapels, when they starved the poor into their coffins? In the pockets of the coal and iron masters, that's where! I could tell you a thing or two, and so could you Col, old *butty*, if you had the words. Listen now, remember Crawshay, the ironmaster? After all the terrible things he did, he had the blasphemy to put 'God forgive me' on his gravestone. Too late, *boyo*, too late. We won't forgive what you did to us in a hurry. Mind you, ten tons of concrete they put on his grave to keep him safe. Aye, I'd give him forgiveness, me and hundreds like me. And what have we got now? The Depression, if you please. Are the *blutty* coal owners depressed, I ask you? Oh, aye, of course they are. We feel for you workers, is it? I'd like to feel their puny chins under my fist. Kids starving in Merthyr, *mun*, dropping like ninepins! And what about the unions? Where are they in our hour of need? One in four unemployed! Aye, aye, Haydn, my son, you did the right thing coming down here. When the worst comes to the worst, at least you'll starve in peace and quiet!'

Zac cut off a length of twist with his pearl-handled penknife, and lodged it between gum and cheek. As he drew breath for another onslaught, Martha was on her feet.

'For goodness sake Zac, put a sock in it. Ranting and raving as if the end of the world is coming. Half that's in the past, anyway. Come on girls, let's go for a walk. Enough is enough! Right then, you men have a good jaw while we're out and when we come back, some quiet from politics for a bit, is it? Where are my shoes, Blodwen, by there look, under that chair. Puts years on me he does. And the language! Not fit for decent people. God help us, we've got enough to do to keep body and soul together for the here and now. But he'll never change, too long in the tooth for that!'

I loved watching Uncle Zac in the *hywl*, standing there waving his arms, looking like one of Mamgu Poli's Celtic warriors, jabbing the air with his finger, his eyes on fire, shouting for justice. But I had to leave with the women, to walk in the quiet of the early evening along the riverbank. Elderberries ripened, deep and dark, and crabapples on the old tree in the hedgerow were turning a brilliant red. Leaning against the bridge, the women were at ease, relaxed and happy in each other's company. I could tell a long *clonc* was about to begin.

'You'll be coming with us as far as Lampeter then, Blodwen? Your mam and dat spending a few days with the old people at Haulfre, are they?'

'Yes, Mrs Mortymer, I'm looking forward to it, I feel as if I haven't seen them for ages.'

'Still miss your people, do you? I saw them in *Cyrddau Mawr* in Bethania Chapel a few weeks back. Smart women in your family, Blodwen, always turned out to a T. I think your Teify is the image of your dat, although Glyn's the one with his grey eyes. I hear your Ifor's thinking of going to London.'

'He's studying by correspondence for the Tradesman's Guild certificate. I think he'll go if he passes.'

'Won't make your mam very happy, I'm sure.'

'No, I don't expect it will, being her eldest son. But he wants to spread his wings, I suppose.'

'Aye, aye, you bring them into this old world, and keep your fingers crossed they'll mostly land on their feet. I pray hard every night for my lot, I do. Our John's out of work now. Not many prospects, he might have to go back down the pit. Four mouths to feed see, but he hates underground. Poor *dab*, no choice really, no indeed. I must say, Blodwen, Col looks a picture of health. A credit to you, wouldn't believe he was the same man. A bag of bones he was, poor old devil, he's seen some hard times, I know. Zac says he's sure he's worked down the pit, something about him, you can always tell.'

'Did you see him with those dogs on the beach?' Mamgu Poli asked. 'He's got the power with animals, I've seen it before. Trefor's marvellous with horses, but Col's got something else. Remember the time when that horse went mad in the hayfield, Blod? Col had him eating out of his hand in a flash, without a word passing his lips. It's a gift from the gods, that's what it is.'

I fell into a daydream when they started talking about someone I didn't know, someone by the name of Annie Jones.

Love from Blodwen

F'annwyl Miriam,

I hope your father's better now, we were sorry to hear he wasn't himself. He's getting on and he mustn't work so hard in the garden. But he couldn't have a better nurse than you, that's for sure. I'll be over to see him when we come back from Haulfre.

You would have enjoyed yourself in Tresaith. We had a champion day, the weather was warm, and all went A1. There was a bit of bother with a young girl and her dog, but Col saw to it. Yes, he came with us this year, but sat on his own mostly and he left early with Haydn and Zac. Haydn didn't want to be too wanged out. He's much better, but still very dark around the eyes.

We went to the café for a lovely cup of tea and then back on the beach. Wil Morris started singing hymns, and we all joined in, quiet like. Then the other trippers joined in as well. It was a proper Cymanfa Ganu in the end with plenty of hwyl, I can tell you. They sang all the way home in the bus, by all accounts.

We were having five minutes on the bridge last night. Poli was telling us about Annie Jones from Brynglas Street. Do you remember her? She was in your class at school, or was that her cousin? She's a teacher, remember, been living in her mother's front room for years. Calls it her sitting room, plenty of swank in her, always has been according to Poli, and she's got a fur coat as well. She doesn't pay her mother much rent, I expect. She's been a spinster for years now.

Anyway, last year, along came some chap to lodge with Mrs Lewis, next door. You know her, don't you? She's got a stiff leg and her husband works for Thomas the mason, a big noise in Clafaria Chapel like his father before him. She's always taken in lodgers as long as I can remember. This chap is an official in the pit, a widower, very clean and tidy, quite la-di-da, by all accounts. After a bit, he starts giving Annie Jones the eye, and to everyone's surprise she started walking out with him. Very superior they looked, her in her fur coat and him in his Homburg hat. Lots of twitching curtains up and down the street that day, I know. Well, the other day they got engaged and when she was in Poli's shop on Friday, she said her marriage was going to be different. She said, "We have each other's confidence entirely," whatever that means. She said, "I'll always be completely open with my husband, as equals should be."

Then Poli made me laugh. "Don't you worry, Blodwen fach," she said, "she'll soon learn. She doesn't know yet, you only tell men what they need to know, and you keep as much money as possible in your knicker pocket!"

She's a case, Miriam, always makes me laugh she does...

Love from,
Blodwen.

'What if Mamgu Haulfre says I must go to bed on my own, Mam? She did last time we were there. I was frightened to death until you came. She said I was a proper *babi losin*. I'm not going if I have to go to bed on my own.'

'*Cariad fach*, it'll be all right, I promise, criss cross my heart. I'll take you upstairs myself and I won't leave until you're asleep. Mamgu Haulfre wouldn't want you to be frightened, I know that for sure. I'll explain things to her. She isn't well, that's why she's sharp now and again. She suffers from pernicious anaemia, see, which means she has to eat raw liver every day. That's enough to make any-one irritable, isn't it? Come on, no black looks for our holiday. Sit on this case, quick now, I can't shut it properly. Trefor's waiting, it's time to go.'

We were about to spend the first days of our holiday with my maternal great-grandparents and great-aunt at Haulfre, Llanfair Clydogau. The family used the name of their house to distinguish them from the other grandparents. My mother's parents from the South were also visiting, and during the course of the week we would stay with several relatives in the district. A grand meeting of the family was planned to take place at Soar-y-Mynydd on the last Sunday of our holiday.

Mamgu Haulfre sat on the *sgiw* in her shawl and cuffed cap. In spite of her age and poor health, she was a sharp-tongued, formida-ble figure, much respected in the family. The mother of six daughters and three sons, she had little time for my bedtime antics. I kissed her nervously and her eyes warmed momentarily before the inevitable question,

'Still making a fuss about going to bed on your own, are you?'

Denial was useless. I couldn't risk having to prove it later. My Great-Aunty Ceri gave me an understanding smile, a toffee and a means of escape.

'Go and tell the men, tea will be on the table in twenty minutes. They're in the shed, Margaret *fach*. Your Mamgu Davies isn't here at present. She's spending a few days in Llain-Goch, but you'll see her on Sunday.'

I was gone like a shot! Both grandfathers were favourites of mine and I loved spending time in their affectionate, uncritical company. Datcu Haulfre, my great-grandfather, was a joiner and carpenter, and his cosy shed held a special fascination for me. On the rafters above the workbench were two handsome coffins, one for each of my great-grandparents. Unwilling to trust the task to anyone else, Datcu Haulfre had made them himself, using the best oak and brass. The exceptional craftsmanship brought many customers to order coffins of the same calibre.

Datcu Haulfre, an impressive figure in his late seventies, had a full head of white hair, a moustache and beard. He and his son shared the same kindly, grey eyes and calm, tolerant disposition. Beneath their mildness, lay a strength of character and purpose rarely imposed on others. Both men were Nonconformists, each faithful members of an Independent chapel. Datcu Haulfre was a deacon and conductor of singing in Capel Mair, Llanfair Clydogau. My grandfathers were well liked in their own communities, respected for their honesty and fair dealings.

Dadcu Davies, my grandfather, learnt his trade from his father, working locally until he and Mamgu Davies became engaged. He left Sîr Aberteifi, like many others, to seek a better living in the industrial valleys of the South. A particularly severe winter hastened his departure when, in the spring, he and his father buried several old people who had died of starvation, sitting before an empty hearth. He found it hard to forget the rasp of saw on bone. Never again, he said. For a time, he lived with relatives in Nelson, often cycling over the Brecon Beacons to see his sweetheart in Lampeter, a journey of about seventy miles each way!

After years of hard work, he and Mamgu were married and she came over the mountains in a wagon, bringing her dowry to a house in Mount Pleasant Terrace, Miskin. They had seven children, all surviving except Dilys, who died of meningitis in her youth. Although I saw little of my mother's immediate family as a young child, we were later to become very close.

In the evening while the women talked in the *gegin fawr*, my grandfathers and I looked at the brown, leather, photograph album kept in Datcu Haulfre's inlaid cupboard in the parlour. I enjoyed his family stories, especially the ones about his mother-in-law, Mamgu Sarah, Tŷ Capel. Knowing her Bible off by heart, she corrected any preacher misquoting his text in the pulpit. I liked the look of her strong, humorous face, dressed in her be-ribboned bonnet and shawl. Datcu Haulfre, the son of Sarah and Daniel Davies, was one of ten children. His mother belonged to an even larger family with two of her brothers becoming famous men in America!

'This is one of them,' said Datcu Haulfre pointing to a very stern young man in the album. 'See his gown and mortarboard? That means he's high-up in the world of learning. One of my mother's younger brothers he is, by the name of William Walter Davies, born in 1848, only eleven years older than me. He left his home, Tŷ Gwyn, in Llangybi, when he was eighteen years old with no language but the Welsh, to go over the Atlantic Ocean to a foreign land. Took some courage that did, a young lad leaving his family, his home and his country, perhaps never to see them again. Mind you, he wasn't on his own. Hundreds of people went from these parts because of the hardship and poverty. A man called True John used to travel with them on the ships to see them settled on the other side. Two hundred and fifty people went from the Blaenpennal district alone! They called it the Ohio Fever around here.

'Most of them went to Cincinnati. Yes, that's right, Cincinnati, and that's where your great-great-great Uncle William Walter went too. There was a minister there called Michael Jones, who wanted to start a Welsh colony in Patagonia. His dream came true, but he was never to see it, that was left to others. No, William Walter didn't go to Patagonia either. He stayed in Ohio to work hard and learn English. When he was twenty-four, he got his B.A. in the Ohio Wesleyan University of Delaware. Clever chap, don't you think? My mother was very proud of him and she kept this article about him in the back of the album, in English, of course. Tell the child about it, Tom.'

'Look, Margaret, they've spelt Cardiganshire with a K! It says here he was a very learned man with at least ten books to his name. He became a Doctor of Divinity and after being a minister for while, he went to Europe to study languages, earning his Ph.D. in Halle University, Germany. Then he returned to his University in Ohio to teach and become Professor of Hebrew and modern languages. According to this, he was a stickler for hard work, truth, honesty and accuracy and he practised what he preached. There you are then, can't have better than that! His wife was an educated woman, by the name of Mary Elizabeth Chase and she taught at the same University. Doesn't say if she was Welsh or not. Look, their house is very grand, more like a mansion, really!'

'Where is he now?'

'Well he must be ninety, if he's still alive. We never heard much about him or his brother, John Walter, after my grandmother died. Just think of it, between the two of them, we might have a big family over there in America!'

'Did you ever want to go to America?'

'No, Margaret, I saw plenty of foreign places in the war and that cured me forever. There's no place like Wales, that's what I say.'

'Me too, I'm not going to leave either. I'm going to help Dad in the shop.'

'Quite right, *merch fach*, quite right.'

'What's this place here?'

It was a photograph of a *plasdy*, a mansion where Datcu Haulfre once worked. The lady owner was a staunch Tory supporter and even though the ballot was secret by then, she discovered that Datcu Haulfre had voted Liberal in the General Election of 1885. She told him if he wished to continue working on the estate, he would need to change his politics. He packed up his tools and quietly informed her ladyship that only his labour was for sale.

'Look here', said Datcu Haulfre, 'this photo shows Fachddu in Cellan, our first home after we were married. That new thatch was finished the day before this was taken. My brother-in-law said it looked so handsome he wanted to take photos. He was a dab hand with a camera. Ceri and the boys were little then, they're standing in the doorway with your Mamgu. The landlord had just called for the rent, and while he was inside, his horse ate a big chunk of the thatch. Mamgu was furious! Spoilt the look of it entirely she said. Good thing the horse belonged to the landlord.'

Fachddu was once a *tŷ unnos*, a dwelling built on unenclosed, common land. Any such building, erected overnight, with smoke coming from the chimney in the morning, was the legal property of the builder, together with any land that lay within the throw of an axe, in each direction. The original cottage was usually constructed in the summer, with the help of all one's friends and neighbours, to be replaced by a more permanent home before autumn.

'The land belonging to these places was later taken away from the people and given to the gentry by Act of Parliament,' said Datcu Haulfre. 'Only someone who'd lived there for over twenty years was allowed to stay. Very generous, these politicians, always looking after the interests of the poor. That's why so much of Wales fell into private hands around that time. Things are not easy now, but, *caton pawb*, nothing like it was in those days.'

Dadcu Davies pulled a bag of sweets from his pocket.

'You've got him in the *hwyl*, Margaret *fach*. We'll need some refreshments until supper's ready.'

'The child's interested, Tom, and we should all know our history and what we stand for. I remember my Datcu telling me how the people were kept down in the old days. No education for the poor, no indeed. If it hadn't been for the Methodist Revival with its chapels and ministers, they wouldn't have had a chance. It was only a couple of hundred years ago that Griffith Jones, Llanddowror, started his Circulating Schools in the winter months. Thousands learned how to read then, and of course, there were the Sunday Schools and the Band of Hope to teach the Bible. When the Charity Schools came, very few families could spare a penny a week for each child. Mind you, we had the best preachers in the world, and the old ones could hold you spellbound. Think of them, Daniel Rowland, Llangeitho, for one. People used to come from all over to listen to him, even by sea from the north. He came through a door at the back of the pulpit, all of a sudden, like God's avenging angel! Then there was Christmas Evans, Llandysul, with one eye, which made people tremble in their boots. My Datcu said Howell Harris' sermons could turn you to stone, out there in his open-air meetings on the mountain. He was a Breconshire man, but none the worse for that. We went to a few outdoor meetings when I was young. Hundreds upon hundreds came, depending on the preacher. If he had the *hwyl*, we were in the palm of his hand, dozens crying and shouting *Haleliwia* over and over. Very stirring it was, but some went too far. Religion was everything then with only hunger and the workhouse for so many. No wonder the Rebeccas tried to do something about it. My father, Daniel, was a boy of eight when they destroyed the tollgates in Whitland, and attacked the workhouse in Caerfyrddin. That must have been a sight, mind you, all those men disguised in women's clothes, riding around the countryside intent on justice for the ordinary people! The authorities brought the regiment from Shrewsbury, but the Rebeccas were never caught. They made their mark, and most of the tollgates were taken down. But there was still plenty of poverty, and that's why the Welsh left in droves for London, America and the Valleys, like your Dadcu and your Uncle William Walter.'

Photographs of babies sitting on fur rugs filled the back pages of the album. You couldn't tell the boys from the girls, dressed as they were in velvet frocks and lacy smocks. None of them were smiling, but one had a particularly solemn expression.

'You know who this is, don't you?' asked Datcu Haulfre. 'She's your mother, such a pretty little girl.'

'She's very serious for a baby,' I answered.

'Yes, as if she knows the sadness to come. A Thursday's child, our Blodwen. A Thursday's child has far to go.'

'What does that mean? I'm a Thursday's child too.'

'It means,' said Dadcu Davies firmly, 'you have a long and healthy life ahead, starting with supper on the table now!'

I began to fidget as my bedtime grew closer. An owl cried out in the wood behind the house. It's great, yellow eyes were waiting for me in the back bedroom. When Mamgu Haulfre said it was time for bed, I wasn't brave enough to go to the *gegin fach* to find my mother. The owl hooted again, and as the tears came, my Dadcu Davies winked, took me upstairs, and stayed until I fell asleep.

It was all fuss and flurry on Sunday morning with dinner on the table early enough to be in Soar-y-Mynydd Chapel by half past two. A close friend of the family was preaching in Cyrddau Mawr, Big Meetings, and the Davieses would be there in full force, except for my great-grandparents who now rarely left their village.

Soar-y-Mynydd Chapel was situated in the heart of the wild, lonely mountains, the remotest place of worship in the country, accessible only on foot or by horse. You were nearer to heaven in Soar-y-Mynydd than anywhere else on earth, according to Mamgu Haulfre. Services were held every Sunday during the summer, attended by families living in the scattered sheep farms. When the snow fell in November, they were isolated until the spring.

We set off in a neighbour's hay-lined cart, with Dadcu Davies and I on the tailgate. Mam and Aunty Ceri were very sedate in summer dresses and hats, coats over the arm, just in case, best shoes for Chapel in the bag. Mam was only two years younger than her aunt, and having much in common, they'd remained friends since childhood. Ceri was bright-eyed and lively, always well-dressed, being a tailoress by trade. The talk flowed to start with, but as we journeyed softly into the high, enclosing mountains, silence fell. On the rim, all around, the blue-pink sky became a shimmering band of bronze. Dadcu called it the hem of God. Steep slopes grew greener as they swept to the valley floor with water glinting, sheep grazing and dark trees lying in giant shadows in the distance.

Dadcu left the cart to walk awhile, frequently wiping the inside of his hat. Before long, he removed his heavy jacket, placing it beside me, the hat on top. Taking a silk handkerchief from the breast pocket, he knotted the corners and put it on his head. In the middle of nowhere, tall and straight, he sauntered along in his waistcoat, swinging his malacca cane with the silver top, whistling through his teeth. I stretched out and closed my eyes. I could smell the sweet hay, the sweat from the horse, Mam's Evening in Paris scent and the wool of Dadcu's jacket. When I woke, I found myself sheltered from the sun by Aunty Ceri's big, black umbrella.

The simple, whitewashed building stood in a grove of beautiful beech trees, the river running below. There were two tall, arched windows in the chapel end, and under the same roof, lodgings for a preacher and his horse. Crowds of people sat quietly in the graveyard, sharing the grass with four, grey gravestones, the seats inside taken by the mountain people and our elders. I stood under the trees in the vast, silent mountains, empty of people except here in this place. This dreaming, drifting, other place. Sweet singing floated through the open doors, but I was caught in a different spell.

After the service, the family came together for tinned salmon sandwiches, Welsh cakes and lemonade, down by the water. I was delighted to receive special hugs and kisses from my beautiful Mamgu Margaret, all cool and smart in her navy blue and white. I'd never seen so many of my relations in one place before. There were dozens of them! My great aunts and uncles on both sides – Aunty Hannah and Uncle John, Llangybi, Aunty Bess from London, Aunty Lisa and Uncle Eben, Llanbedr, Uncle John and Aunty Mari, Llain-Goch, Aunty Ellen, Aunty Dora and Uncle John, Aunty Peggy and Uncle Dan from Farmers, Aunty Anne and Uncle Rufus, Llanybydder and Aunty Sarah, all the way from Aberystwyth. Pity David Rhys and Connie couldn't be here from London! Dinah, Dai, Edrud and Elwyn, May and David Dan, John, Haydn, Bethan, Trefina and hordes of other first and second cousins of all ages flocked around to welcome Mam and me. I sat close to Mamgu for the picnic, savouring the pleasure of belonging to such a large, affectionate family. She held my hand and stroked my hair. Oh how I'd grown! *Fy merch fach smala*, my funny little girl.

The Davies tribe was the last to leave and the journey home was slow, amiable and noisy. Women swapped places in the carts, catching up on the *clonc*, young people walked in animated groups and the children ran around until they were fit to drop. By the time we came to the parting of the ways, I was tired out and content to sit quietly between Mam and Mamgu. Tonight, she would lie on my bed and tell me the story of Llain-Goch, her childhood home. The story of how she and her large family lived in the barn while her father and brothers built their house.

Summer was over when Ita and the caravans left the village. Swiftly moving clouds made shadows on the *twmp* where two magpies strutted, urging us to leave their territory. Pedro chased them half-heartedly, sensing the sadness of our parting. Whenever we said goodbye, I felt I would never see Ita again. She gave me special tokens of remembrance – the breastbone of a kingfisher for protection, a stone with a hole in the middle to keep away the evil eye and some coral beads for luck. Before telling stories to keep while we were apart, she promised to return, hand on heart.

'Rhodri's brother told him a story about a girl called Blodeuwedd. Do you know it, Ita? It's sad, but I like it. We can play it on the rock if you come back. Long ago, a man called Llew Llaw Gyffes had a curse on him, which meant he could never have a wife made of flesh and bones. His friend, Gwydion, the great wizard, saw he was very lonely and used magic powers to make him a wife from wild flowers. She was beautiful, with long, fair hair and a gentle face and Llew fell in love at first sight. They lived in a grand castle with many servants, and everyone thought they would be happy ever after. One day, Llew went to see the King and while he was away, a handsome knight called Gronw Pebr came to stay in the castle. Before long, Blodeuwedd preferred him to her husband. When Gronw said he wanted to stay, they had wicked thoughts and they decided to kill Llew. Blodeuwedd knew he could only be killed in a very special way, so when he came home, she tricked him into telling her. She passed the secret to Gronw and, on the river bank, he threw a special spear through a hole in a great stone, right into Llew's chest. He gave a terrible scream, changed into an eagle, and flew away. Blodeuwedd and Gronw were frightened, but glad to be together. I don't suppose she felt very sad, because if she was made of flowers, she didn't have a heart, did she?

'Gwydion soon heard what had happened to his friend and he rode pell-mell to the castle. When Blodeuwedd saw him she ran towards the lake, followed by her ladies. They were so busy looking over their shoulders, they fell into the water and were all drowned. All except Blodeuwedd! Gwydion found her, proud and beautiful, standing alone on the bank, trying to hide her fear. The wizard took no mercy on her. He said her wickedness was so great, he was ashamed he'd ever created her. Blodeuwedd must face her punishment, and before she could say one single word, he turned her into an owl! She was doomed to live by night, never to share the company of other birds. The cry of the owl is Blodeuwedd breaking her heart through loneliness. That's why it sounds so sad and screechy. I know where she lives too.'

'Where's that then?'

'In the wood behind Mamgu Haulfre's house in Llanfair Clydogau. She cried every night I was there, but I'm glad I didn't know who it was at the time. Do you like that story, Ita?'

'Yes, it's good but not very cheerful, I must say.'

'What I want to know is why did they have to kill Llew? Couldn't they have lived together like Mr and Mrs Guto and Miss Davies? When I asked Mam, she said, *twt, twt* that was the end of that topic. But I've heard the women say Mrs Guto shouldn't put up with it, she should throw Miss Davies out. Does Guto prefer Miss Davies to Mrs Guto? Pity she doesn't have Gwydion for a friend, he could change Guto into something small and dainty with two legs!'

'I don't know about that, I'm sure. But I know a magic story about a bird too. Come on, I'll tell you as I walk you home, it's getting cold out here.

'Long ago, in a land where my people travelled, far across the sea, there lived a beautiful bird. Like gold its wings were when it flew over the mountains. One day, a great Prince was out hunting and he saw the shining bird. He'd never seen anything like it in his life, lovely beyond words. He followed it for miles and miles as fast as his horse could carry him. Suddenly, an old man jumped out from behind a rock.

'"Stop," he said, "If I were you, I wouldn't follow that bird. A bad-tempered, nasty, old witch lives on that hill over there and the bird belongs to her. Its beauty is a trick to make young men follow it to her cave where she casts a spell, changing them into white marble statues. Look, you can see dozens of them standing on the mountain yonder."

'"But I must see the bird again," said the Prince, "Please tell me, is there a way, old man?"

'"You're just like all the rest of them, young and foolish, they didn't listen to me either. There is a way, but it's very dangerous, and nobody's been able to do it yet. If you can creep up behind the witch without her seeing you and grab her tightly by the hair, she can't harm you."

'Quietly, the Prince moved up the mountain. He didn't make a single sound and when he got to the cave, the old witch was fast asleep outside. The Prince pounced on her, holding her scraggy hair tight in his two hands. She struggled and screamed her head off but he hung on for grim death.'

'"What can I do to make you let go?" she shouted.

'"First of all, I want you to turn those statues back into people, and then I want you to give me the golden bird," said the Prince.

'Puffing herself up like a huge frog, the witch blew an enormous blue breath toward the statues. Straight away they turned into handsome young men. When she called the bird, the Prince let go of her hair and *pwff* she disappeared into thin air! The golden bird sat quietly in his hands, looking so gentle and lovely, he kissed its head. I bet you know what happened next?'

'Yes, it turned into a beautiful girl, the other way round from Blodeuwedd. What happened then?'

'They all went down the mountain and the Prince and the girl had a big wedding and lived happily ever after.'

'Like you and Seth, one day.'

'Yes, just like Seth and me, one day.'

Chapter Five

Cadw dechreunos began on the evening of the twenty-sixth of September. Every house in the valley lit a candle to challenge the darkness of the coming winter. The working day shortened to six o'clock when family life once more centred around the hearth. Chilly days and river mists brought out our heavy clothing which made my skin itch furiously. Rebellion was unthinkable. A good Welsh wool vest was a lifesaver, no argument!

I helped my mother with ritual household tasks. Newspaper soaked in flour and water filled gaps in window frames and floorboards. Heavy curtains replaced summer cretonne, and tubes of flannel stuffed with old stockings stopped howling draughts under doors. Dampness descended on the parlour until mid-summer. We shrouded the furniture with sheets, packing away velveteen cushions, curtains and carpet mats. Two oval watercolours of desert scenes were removed before cleaning the wallpaper with balls of bread. Mould gathered, masking the smell of brown paper cigarettes smoked by Rhodri and me on wet Saturday afternoons. Once, after using the pages of a mildewed Bible found in the cupboard, we spent days expecting to be struck by lightning.

Severe weather, especially snow, meant isolation. Pantries were crammed with jars of jam, honey, pickles, salted green vegetables and crocks of preserved eggs. Shiny onions hung in ropes and root vegetables were bagged or clamped against the frost. No medicine cupboard was without goose grease or Besi's elderberry cordial. Buildings and gates were repaired, sheds stocked with coal and wood, hedging and ditching completed. Sheep were brought to home pastures to mate for spring lambing and dung was carted out ready for spreading.

In the old Celtic calendar, winter began after *Nos Galan Gaeaf* on October 31st. It was unwise to be far from home on All Hallows Eve, when ghosts and spirits of the dead were known to roam abroad at midnight. The sighting of the *Cannwyll Gorff*, the *Ladi Wen* or the *Ceffyl Gwyn*, (the corpse candle, the headless white lady, or the white horse) was a warning of imminent death.

Nain gave a *Noson Lawen* party, everyone home by midnight, thank you very much! The men built a bonfire in the yard using nine different kinds of wood, as they did for *Nos Galan Mai*. Children danced around at dusk, eagerly awaiting potatoes and apples baking in its embers. After ducking for apples from a huge copper bowl on the *gegin fawr* table, most of the games involved predictions for the coming year. A marriage lay ahead if nuts or ivy leaves burned brightly when thrown into the fire. Girls peeled apples in unbroken strips, throwing them over their shoulders to seek a sweetheart's initials in the way they fell. Young men, persuaded to walk around the dung heap nine times in the dark, called, *'Dyma'r esgid, ble mae'r droed?'* (Here's the shoe, where's the foot?) In answer to the question, the face of a future bride would surely appear. Besi was kept busy all evening, reading palms and teacups. Nothing serious, mind you. Before leaving, children threw stones into the fire, promising to retrieve them the following morning, bringing good luck for the future. The party ended with ghost stories, leaving plenty of time to reach home before the dreaded midnight hour.

One *Nos Galan Gaeaf*, Mam and I spent the day at Aunty Miriam's, expecting Dad to collect us in time for the *Noson Lawen*. About four o'clock, he phoned the shop across the road to tell us the van had a flat tyre and changing the wheel had brought on his asthma. Best to set off and Col would meet us as soon as he could. The light was fading and Mam looked nervous. We left Aunty Mir's at a brisk pace with me in the pushchair, no nonsense if you please. After hurrying up the steep hill through a tunnel of hedges, Mam started singing *Pen Calfaria*, a sure sign of unease. It grew dark and I joined in. Where was Col for goodness sake?

Close to home we began to relax, but at the crossroads, Mam stopped dead. In the gloom, in the middle of the road, the *Ceffyl*

Gwyn was standing on his hind legs, pawing the air! It floated slowly towards us, hesitated and receded. The harbinger of death on *Nos Galan Gaeaf!* We were transfixed, mesmerised by its awful, dragging movements. On its second advance, Mam took to her heels. Plunging through the gate on her right, she ran like a hare along the stubbled field with me bouncing wildly in the pushchair. I hung on like a limpet knowing it was a matter of life or death. Clamping my mouth shut, I touched the silk strip on my neck, praying it would stop the *pwcibo* going down my throat.

Mam was out of breath when we rejoined the road, her stockings torn, her legs scratched and bleeding. On the verge of tears, I knew it was no time to add to her troubles. With any luck, the apparition would stay at the crossroads, its preferred haunt. As we approached the *Ladi Llwyd*'s house, we saw a light in the parlour window.

'I'm shaking like a jelly, *bach*, I can't go another step. Private or not, I'm knocking on this door.'

The *Ladi Llwyd* appeared, as elegant as ever in her pale, grey clothes.

'Whatever's the matter? Please come in at once and tell me what's happened.'

She ushered us into her parlour, seating us near the fire. Hesitantly, Mam described her plight.

'Honestly, I feel a fool now but out there in the dark it was enough to make your hair stand on end, what with all the old stories about ghosts and spirits about tonight. But it was there for sure, we saw it with our own eyes. Not something I want to go through again, I can tell you, especially with my own child. Sorry to be a bother like this but my legs gave way when I saw your light.'

'What a dreadful experience for you both. I know the stories, of course, but I can't say I've ever believed them. Are you sure it wasn't a trick of the light?'

'No indeed, it was plain to see, floating, coming and going. My feet are firmly on the ground usually but, *ach a fi*, it was enough to give you a fit.'

'Sit there quietly for a while. I'll make you a cup of tea and then I'll walk you home.'

Her comforting words calmed Mam and soon they were chatting like old friends. She wanted to attend to Mam's scratched legs but the cup of tea was just the thing, thank you very much.

I'd never seen such a room. It was posh in a different way from Nain's, softer, more luxurious. You could see it was used for every day, not kept for Sundays and visitors. Thick, plush carpet stretched from wall to wall, two of which were covered in books from floor to ceiling. There were rich paintings without glass, photographs in silver frames, and rose velvet armchairs with long curtains to match. The best side of the material could be seen from inside the room! A small desk stood under the window, and opposite, the piano, in pride of place. Through the open door, the carpet stretched across the passage into the *gegin fawr* with its polished table, sideboard and big looking glass. A stove covered in blue and white tiles showed flames flickering behind glass. Wait until Rhodri knew I'd been in the *Ladi Llwyd's* house! Nobody in the village had ever set foot beyond the front door. I wanted to see more, my fright forgotten, but it was time to leave.

'Thank you very much for everything, you've been kindness itself. Your light was manna from heaven. There's a warm welcome in our house any time you like. Oh look, Col's here, you don't need to come out. Good night now then.'

Col was waiting by the gate, surprised to see my pushchair outside the *Ladi Llwyd's* house. Taking a deep breath, Mam described our eventful journey.

'Col *bach*, I do wish you'd come sooner, saved me from a near heart attack it would. Mind you, on second thoughts I'm glad you didn't see it. We won't spread it around, we don't want to make people jittery tonight of all nights. Don't really feel like going to the party now but I expect it will cheer us up, won't it, Margaret *fach*? We'll go home before the ghost stories, I've had enough for one day! Daft how it can upset you like that, but you won't find me scoffing anymore, I can tell you. No indeed. Can't help wondering about the consequences, however down to earth you are.'

Dad's disbelief was overcome by concern as he tried to distract us with comic explanations and recollections.

'I know you're trying to make everything normal, Haydn, but I know what I saw. It was the *Ceffyl Gwyn*. Guto said he saw it once on the top road and his brother-in-law died within the month.'

'Come on, Blodwen, you're not quoting Guto surely, he'll say or do anything to be in the limelight. Good heavens, he's even displaying his wooden leg now at every opportunity. Although I must say, it's a remarkable object he's made there. The mechanism is first class and those carvings of flowers and birds are very artistic. But you can't believe half he says, he tells lies as long as his arm!'

Col appeared making signs for Dad to follow, it was important. Dad was smiling broadly on their return and Col's cap was pulled low over his eyes. Information advertising a sale on a nearby farm had been printed on a large, white flour sack and nailed to the sign-post at the crossroads. Dislodged from the bottom, it was still floating on the breeze.

'Oh yes, put your arm around me and say you're sorry, but laughing your heads off you are. Yes and you Col, I can tell. It's all very well for you two, but it wasn't funny at the time. I'm glad Poli isn't here, she'd have us locked in Chapel for a month! Anyway, I might have lost my head, but I think I've gained a friend.'

Love from Blodwen

F'annwyl Miriam,

...We're killing pigs tomorrow. Margaret hates it, she says she can hear them screaming all over the cwm. I worry sometimes, she gets so upset if anything happens to the animals, she has nightmares about it. Anyway, Mamgu Poli has taken her to stay with Didi Fawr for a few days. They'll call in Nevern on the way, Poli goes there whenever she can. She believes the story of the Cross, like the old people used to. You'd think they'd have a look by now, wouldn't you? Perhaps it's best not to know one way or the other, keep the mystery of it. Margaret couldn't wait to go. That child has Poli's mark on her for sure. She'll have a good time with Didi, she's not frightened of the dark there. All cosy in one room, she says. Poor Didi, she'll never get over her loss. Moses is still on guard, by all accounts...

Love from,
Blodwen.

We kept four pigs, placid, comical things, who spent most of their time having a mud bath by the river. They ate whey and swill, a pungent mixture of bran, leftovers and vegetables, boiled on the brick hearth in the outhouse. Dad said pigs were economical to keep and profitable to sell as bacon in the shop. In late October, early November, the slaughterer travelled from farm to farm and his appearance in our yard gave me the horrors. The sights and sounds were so unbearable, Mamgu Poli made sure she took me away until the pig man left the valley. It was her last visit of the year. During the winter, she considered the veil between this life and the next to be at its most frail. No need to meet trouble head on by gallivanting around the countryside. The best place was home and chapel. Our autumn journey took us to Didi Fawr's cottage in the Preseli Mountains. She was Mamgu Poli's cousin and a great friend of mine. During our stay, we sometimes visited Poli's sister-in-law, Modryb, and her daughter Ceinwen.

We left the village in time for dinner at the Black Lion Hotel in Aberteifi. Many of the tables were occupied by smartly dressed people in shoes, and a few sedate children with no elbows on the table. The room fell silent as Mamgu Poli swept in wearing her long mulberry wool two-piece and matching hat of corded rep, decorated with pale pink flowers, the colour of her tucked silk blouse. Several rows of beads and the gold locket and chain made her glorious to behold! I felt very smart in my new green coat and pleated dress, a present from Mamgu for the occasion. A pair of black, patent leather shoes completed the picture. I wriggled with joy, storing every detail to relate at home. It was no ordinary day for me, seeing the big, outside world in Mamgu's company. She poured tea, holding her little finger high in the air! I tried not to laugh and a wink from Trefor made him an accomplice. Mamgu was enjoying herself. Thank goodness there were no birds on the china!

The town was full of people as we paraded around the shops drawing glances from right and left. Quite unaware, Mamgu Poli concentrated on her purchases. One of my presents was a picture-book of a very pretty little girl with ringlets, called Shirley Temple. Crisp tissue paper was wrapped around a plaid shawl and leather gloves for Didi, sparkling beads and handkerchiefs in an embroidered sachet for Ceinwen, and several pairs of stockings and scented soap for Modryb.

The heavens opened just as the car drew up outside the shop. Mamgu's hat, always a hazard in times of stress, was handed to Trefor before we dashed for cover. Wet or fine, Mamgu would not miss her pilgrimage to Nevern. She described it as an ancient, most holy place, full of comfort and blessing.

'When I was young, my father brought my four brothers and me to Nevern every Eastertide, as his father did before him, to pray at the Pilgrims' Cross in the rock. I brought your daddy here too, many times, and I told him the story my father told me. And now I shall tell you.

'Nevern was a sacred place even in ancient Celtic times, long before the Romans came to Wales. Now, they liked it here so much they stayed for about four hundred years. Before they left, the story of Jesus and the Crucifixion had already reached these shores, through the ministry of Joseph of Arimathea. As it happened at the time, the Emperor of Rome's mother was a British queen called Elen. When she heard of Jesus and his works, she became a Christian and persuaded her son, Constantine the Great to do the same. No more throwing the Christians to the lions after that, I'm sure! One day, it looked as if the Cross was in danger of being destroyed by the barbarians, so Elen decided to put it in a safe place. Knowing the country, it was natural to choose Wales, wasn't it? We were already Christian and as far west from Jerusalem as she could travel. The story says she brought the Cross along Sarnau Elen, showing it to the faithful followers of Jesus on the way. Many of the villages were named after those in the Bible. Finally, it was placed in the holy cave at Nevern.'

'Has anyone you know ever seen the Cross?'

'No, *bach*, nobody, but the old people believed it was there and who are we to say it's not?'

'But why don't they take a look?'

'That I don't know. As far as I'm concerned I believe what I believe and always stop to say a prayer when I'm passing.'

'Can we see the yew tree first, Mamgu?'

We crossed the stone bridge, halting outside the Church of Saint Brynach. It was very still with the pungent smell of damp earth after rain. Walking down a towering avenue of yews, we came to the tree with the severed branch which dripped sap upon the ground. Red sap, the colour of blood. Long ago, a man hanged himself from that branch. The villagers removed it, regarding the suicide as blasphemous. The cut never healed and the sap still flowed after a hundred years. I lingered, tempted to place my hand beneath, knowing from experience that the stain was difficult to remove. Mamgu, sensing my fascination, called me to look at the Great Cross, a tall stone covered in Celtic carvings.

'Come on, trace them with your fingers. Feel the vibrations. Stretch your arms around the stone. And you, Trefor, we'll do it together. The energy stays in your bones, sets you up it does. This other one by the door has Latin written on it, the language of the Romans. Your father learnt it at school in Llandovery, Margaret. I hope you'll do the same one day. Nothing like Latin to improve the mind.'

'Miss Poli, if you want to see the Pilgrims' Cross, the time's getting on and it's going to rain again,' interrupted Trefor.

Crossing the road to a path at the foot of the cliff, we passed beneath quiet green-gold trees to stand before the Pilgrims' Cross cut into the rock. Mamgu held my hand before kneeling to pray on the hewn ledge beneath. Trefor removed his cap and closed his eyes. For a long time, we were lost in the faraway silence of rocks and trees.

It was gone teatime when we reached the narrow track leading to Didi's cottage at the end of a small valley. Behind black clouds above the mountain rim, wide shafts of light fell to earth, the brightest silver.

'Oh *pechod*, I expect Didi's gone already. Put on your clogs, *cariad*. Where are my galoshes, Trefor? We'll walk up anyway. Moses might be elsewhere.'

But Moses was never elsewhere. Another Bomber, he stood on guard in the doorway daring anyone to enter while Didi was away. Mamgu swiped her umbrella at the black cockerel but he stood firm turning a baleful, red eye in her direction. Trefor had tried many tricks over the years to outwit Moses, always in vain. He was the boss. There was nothing for it but to sit by the well, huddled under Mamgu's big fur coat and glad of it.

Didi appeared on the mountain, her tall figure black against the silver light. She walked steadily towards us, occasionally lifting her hand in greeting, the skirt of her long coat flapping in the wind, her shawl streaming behind her. Every day, Didi Fawr went over the mountain to meet her son from school. Every day, she returned alone because Gwyn was lost. He'd been lost for years, but Didi behaved as if he'd soon return to join her at the table where she laid his place every mealtime. No questions were asked on her arrival and, as always, she was delighted to see us. Moses stepped politely aside, perching on the chair by the door and a hot cup of tea appeared like magic.

Although Mamgu and Didi were cousins, they bore no physical resemblance. Tall and spare in a plain, black frock, Didi's dark eyes were deep set in an austere face, her straight, white hair covering each ear in a plait. She was older and quieter, giving a feeling of tested strength and patience. When she laughed, which was often in Poli's company, she threw her hands over her head, rocking in her chair. Didi and I liked each other and she tenderly understood my fear of the dark. She never mentioned Gwyn or the pain and sorrow of losing him, but I knew she wouldn't be happy until he came home. I wanted to please her, and I convinced myself that I would be the one to find him. Whenever we walked on the vast, empty mountain with the wind clean from the sea, my thoughts were always of Gwyn. Trefor and I watched black ravens on black rocks and high-flying buzzards in a cloudless sky. Reluctant to leave, I climbed higher and higher, but there was never a sign of Gwyn. One day, Trefor spoke of an Iron Age fort at the top of the mountain where people once lived in olden times.

'Perhaps that's where Gwyn's been all this time, Trefor. We must go up and look straight away.'

'What do you mean, *bach*, why should Gwyn be up there?'

'He's been lost for such a long time, he must have found somewhere to live.'

'Who told you Gwyn was lost, Margaret?'

'Everyone talks about poor Didi losing Gwyn on the mountain and how she'll never get over it.'

'I think there's a bit of explaining to do here, and I don't know if I'm the one to do it. I'll talk to your Mamgu when we go back.'

'What is there to explain, Trefor, please tell me.'

'Well it's like this. When something terribly sad happens, people often don't use the exact words to describe it. They skirt around it, like, trying to make it sound not so bad. Are you following me here?'

'Yes.'

'Say now that one of your Mamgu's horses was hurt and we couldn't help him, do you know what would happen?'

'Yes. Mamgu would give him the tablet from her gold locket to put him to sleep and then he wouldn't feel any more pain. That's why she doesn't take it off and I must never touch it.'

'Quite right, you've hit the nail on the head there. Do you know what putting the horse to sleep really means?'

'Yes, he'll die and go to heaven and never come back.'

'Yes, that's it. Well, how can I put this? In Gwyn's case, lost is another word for dead. Margaret *fach*, Gwyn is dead, dead and gone to heaven, poor little lad.'

'But everyone kept on saying that Didi lost Gwyn on the mountain. What happened then?'

'Well, Didi went to meet him from the school bus, as usual. He ran around the back, something you should never do, you know that, don't you? The brake wasn't on properly, the bus rolled back and he went under the wheel. He was killed outright on the mountain road. Come on now, *cariad*, don't cry, it was a long time ago.'

'But if he's dead, why does Didi go to meet him every day and lay his place at the table?'

'You know what I said about using softer words for death, to ease the pain?'

'Yes'

'Well, Didi has not been able to ease her pain, see. She can't accept Gwyn's death because she can't bear it. Meeting him from school and laying his place makes it easier for her. Keeps the past alive, a special place to go for her memories. It's like a story, a favourite story you listen to over and over again, to give you comfort. We all do that from time to time but Didi takes it a little bit further, that's all. Am I making sense here, *bach*?'

'Yes, I think so. Didi knows Gwyn won't come back, but doing those things keeps him in her mind. But I don't understand...'

'Time for tea, race you to the house. The last one there's a donkey!'

After tea, Trefor brought in the coal and went to his friends nearby. There was no room for a man to sleep at Didi's, the space in the roof hadn't been used for years. The lamp was lit, the fire banked up and we sat around the table in the cheerful room, talking, knitting and sewing. Didi taught me chain stitch and daisy faces, but I could not master French knots.

'Now then, a song before bedtime. How about *Nant y Mynydd*, we all like that. Altogether, a one, a two, a three...'

'We sang that loud enough to lift the mountain. I know there are no nightingales west of the Severn, but we've made up for it tonight.'

The doors of the box bed at the end of the room were opened and after prayers, I snuggled into the warm feather mattress. No need to worry about Gwyn tonight. I decided it was better to be in heaven than all alone on the mountain in the dark. I watched the two women sitting in the firelight until I fell asleep.

When Mamgu Poli visited her sister-in-law, I usually preferred to stay with Didi, but sometimes my curiosity overcame my apprehension. My mother put it less delicately, calling me a nosy little monkey, wanting to know the ins and outs of everything. Nosy or not, it took all my courage to meet Modryb, who was frightening enough to be a witch. I made sure I wasn't alone with her for a second, staying close to Mamgu Poli, not uttering a single word.

The grey, stone house stood at the bottom of a steep valley beside a fast flowing stream, mostly in shadow even on the sunniest day. Whitewashed stones edged a path to the door where a motionless black dog watched our descent. As we reached the bottom step in the bank, he pelted across the yard, his chain jerking him to a halt just below us. He was not a pet, he had no name. To name a dog was not Modryb's way. Ceinwen opened the door, her bright red hair startling against the greyness, the only colour in sight. Gentle and hesitant, she had the face of a saint from our Sunday school book. Modryb appeared, to call off the dog, but she gave no greeting.

We entered the bare, scrupulously clean *gegin fawr* with its scrubbed deal table, chairs and large cupboard. No dresser with bright dishes, no mats, curtains or cushions to soften the starkness. The shutters were half closed and a small fire barely took the chill from the air. Trefor left immediately after delivering the parcels and baskets, his presence unacknowledged by Modryb, who placed her unopened gift on the table, clicking her tongue disapprovingly. Ceinwen's face lit up at the sight of the glittering beads, but Modryb's glance stilled her thanks, making her look more like a young girl than a woman of my mother's age. With permission, she took me to the parlour to see her books of pressed flowers. We sat in the grey-green room, silently turning the pages, like two children in a cave under the sea.

At tea-time, Mamgu Poli folded back the shutters and she and Ceinwen laid the table with food from the baskets. I sat close to Mamgu, watching Modryb consuming large pieces of cake in a very lady-like fashion, her little finger in the air. It wasn't funny at all and I began to feel nervous, regretting my visit. I fiddled with my hair. Modryb stretched out a bony hand, clutching mine! I tried to follow Ceinwen into the *gegin fach*, but an outraged look pinned me to the chair. Modryb spoke sharply,

'It's the afternoon for Ceinwen to wash my hair and you coming will not be an impediment.'

'Not at all, we'll go for a walk. Trefor won't be long,' said Mamgu.

I dragged my hand away from Modryb's and leapt to the door to find it was raining heavily. We were prisoners! Where was Trefor? Mamgu winked, taking me on her lap to hide my face in her fox furs! But when the ritual began, I could not tear my eyes away after all. Ceinwen removed Modryb's cap, shawl and woollen shirt, placing a towel around the gaunt shoulders. After pouring warm water into a bowl on the table, she unpinned the long, grey hair and began washing it carefully, her face impassive, almost blank. The soap slipped to the floor. When I picked it up to place it on the dish, my eyes were level with the back of Modryb's head. To my astonishment, a V of thick dirt stretched from her hairline to the nape of her neck! It was as black as ink! Ceinwen's dark eyes looked into mine and I saw something there that froze the words in my throat. Calmly taking the soap from my hand, she continued washing her mother's hair.

Sunday

F'annwyl Miriam,

Thank you very much for coming over while we were away. Col was glad of the Welshcakes and the pie. Diolch o galon.

I'm sure the day of the funeral was the wettest in living memory. It tipped down the whole time. Our Margaret stayed with Didi while I went with Trefor on my own. The garden was so overgrown you could hardly see the house, brambles everywhere. Trefor had to clear a path to the door for the coffin. But the inside was as spotless as ever. Ceinwen managed on her own even when her mother was very ill. Modryb wouldn't let a soul near the place until they were forced to send for Poli and Haydn.

There was a fire roaring half way up the chimney when I got there, but it was still quite chilly. I've been worrying about Haydn down there in the damp. It's like living under a waterfall. There's something about that place that gives me the creeps. I was glad there weren't enough beds for me to stay the night. Trefor and Haydn are sleeping on camp beds in the gegin fawr as it is. Poli's got some guts sleeping in Modryb's bed. You wouldn't catch me doing that, I can tell you. The house is as bare as a nunnery, and the parlour cold enough for a morgue. Modryb's body could have lasted for months in there.

Don't let this go any further, Miriam, but Poli had an awful job scrubbing a thick croften of dirt from the back of Modryb's neck! I could hardly believe it when she told me. Then it came to me. Modryb couldn't stand having her neck touched since that goitre operation years ago. When she washed, the rheumatism stopped her poor fingers reaching right around. But Ceinwen must have known it was there. Of course she did. Just think of it, that might have been her one little bit of freedom, leaving that dirt there, out of her mother's sight. Ach a fi gives you the shivers mind.

Ceinwen surprised me, I must say, very calm she was. Mamgu Poli found her next to the coffin that first night, holding her mother's hand, but she was all right after that. She's still such a beautiful girl with those great big eyes looking somewhere we can't see.

And the funeral! Uncle Henry came, but there were only six of us, not counting the bearers. The minister's wife was there to swell the numbers, but it was really heart breaking. Poor old Modryb, frugal to the end. I only found out in the service that her Christian name was Gwladus ...

Love from,
Blodwen.

Ceinwen was moving to a pretty house of her own in a nearby village. A week or so after the funeral we were present at the last family gathering in her old home. My father and Trefor had repaired the steps, weeded the path and swept the yard. The garden was clear of undergrowth and any sign of spring flowers. Its bare-boned austerity would have appealed to Modryb.

The first thing I noticed was the absence of the dog without a name. Dad explained that a strange thing happened when Modryb fell ill. The day she took to her bed, she unchained the dog. He stayed in his kennel, Ceinwen feeding him as usual. When my father arrived, he sat quietly by the door showing no sign of his old ferocity. However, he was completely unresponsive and disliked being touched. Shortly after Modryb's death, the dog disappeared. Trefor looked everywhere, but he could not be found. Pity our Col wasn't there. He would have found him, for sure.

Mamgu Poli and Mam were preparing dinner when Ceinwen invited me to look at her pressed flowers. Her red hair glowed against the black frock, her face gentle and withdrawn. The parlour was warm with bright rugs draping the armchairs! A vase of daffodils stood on the window-sill and beyond, far down the valley, the sun shone. We sat close together by the fire, Ceinwen describing each flower in a soft, low voice. I was almost asleep when she bit me hard on the arm! I saw the look in her eyes, that chilling look I'd seen once before. She leant towards me. I ran from the room into my mother's arms.

In spite of much sobbing and a little blood, I felt more frightened than hurt. Trefor finally made me laugh by wrapping my arm in a huge bandage from wrist to shoulder. Mamgu stayed in the parlour with Ceinwen and dinner was laid aside. My mother wanted to leave, but Dad decided a walk by the river would calm the nerves. There he told me Ceinwen's story.

Edward, the eldest of Mamgu Poli's four brothers was a successful businessman in his middle fifties when he married Gwladus. A jolly, practical woman ten years his junior, she became known in the family as Modryb, or aunt. They were overjoyed when Ceinwen was born, but sadly, as she grew older, her behaviour became unstable.

Her parents devoted their lives to the comfort and protection of their beloved daughter. Edward retired to educate her at home, controlling her aggression. She adored him and they became completely inseparable. Few people outside the family ever knew the extent of her condition.

A month after Ceinwen's twelfth birthday, Edward died suddenly of a heart attack. Utterly distraught, she became increasingly violent. She began attacking her mother, often biting her ferociously. Frightened that Ceinwen could be removed from her care, Modryb became more reclusive. She'd promised Edward on his deathbed that their daughter would never be placed in an institution. She sold their comfortable home, dismissed the servants and moved to this remote place. There was ample money to provide professional nursing at home, but refusing to be influenced, Modryb chose to carry the burden herself. Convinced that Ceinwen would then be safe, she severed all connections with family and friends, until gradually, they were forgotten by everyone except Mamgu Poli. Modryb thought simplicity and unrelenting hard work would resolve most of their difficulties. In time, Ceinwen became quieter, the fits less frequent.

'Modryb had a dream that Ceinwen would improve sufficiently to return to their old life,' my father continued. 'But she knew in her heart it would never come true. Your Mamgu Poli and I used to visit often when I was young. Mamgu has a certain influence over Ceinwen. I think it's partly her resemblance to Uncle Edward. All that red hair! Modryb was a very different person then, but as the years passed, she changed considerably. Hardly surprising, living here on their own in this depressing place, not seeing a soul from one month's end to the next. Even their provisions were left at the top of the bank. Finally, to anyone who didn't know their story, Modryb was the strange one. She never complained though. She kept her promise to Uncle Edward, and she loved her daughter to her dying day.

'Ceinwen's been quiet for many years now, but that's no excuse for what happened today. I should have expected something after the shock of her mother's death. I'm so very sorry you were the one to be hurt, my little Snwny.'

Determined to banish the gloom, Mamgu had arranged a surprise on our return to the house. It was the first thing we saw from the top of the bank. Mam laughed so much she almost fell down the steps. Long sticks were dotted all over the garden, each displaying one of Mamgu's flamboyant possessions. Hats, shoes, feathers, beads, scarves, her fox furs and goodness knows what! Where on earth did she find those red balloons? I flew down the steps to join Mamgu, whirling around the sticks while she draped her finery around my neck. Unable to peer over the furs, I fell to the ground in a laughing heap. To my amazement, Ceinwen picked me up and gently placed Mamgu's biggest hat on my head! She smiled and clapped her hands. Swinging a pretty shawl over her shoulders, she held Mamgu's hand to waltz sedately along the path. Two red-headed women in funeral black dancing in a make-believe garden! My mother cried.

I never saw Ceinwen again. Mamgu visited frequently making sure she liked her new home and the trusted couple who took care of her. She preferred to be alone, listening to something inaudible to the rest of us. Not many years later, she died peacefully in her chair by the window, her books of pressed flowers in her lap.

Y Gwyliau Mawr, the long Christmas holiday, lasted three weeks, spanning the quietest time of the year on the farm. When Nain was young, the celebrations continued until the beginning of February, with wassailing, the *Mari Lwyd*, the Wren's House and *Calennig*. In 1752, eleven days were lost when a new calendar became law in the United Kingdom. It was ignored in many remote, rural areas like ours. Almost two hundred years later, village elders kept Christmas Day and New Year's Day on the sixth and twelfth of January respectively. With the rest of us as guests, a long holiday encompassed the jollifications, which included both my father's birthday and mine.

Christmas was close when Dad bought several geese from Mr Pryce to sell in the shop, together with capons from our yard. Mam, Miriam, Mrs Morris, Mrs Thomas and Olwen did the plucking and dressing in the barn, keeping the feathers for mattresses, pillows and cushions. Under the light of a hurricane lamp, milking stools were placed in a circle and soon laughter and feathers filled the place. Dad, unable to tolerate the dust, prepared tea and lemon barley water served by Rhodri, Eira, Bryn and me. We jumped in the feathers, bringing screams of protest from the sneezing women. The *clonc* flowed.

'Miss Eirlys has gone to Llangrannog to see to her house. Her husband will be home soon. Good looking man, the Captain, I've always thought so. Lovely beard.'

'How's Guto then, Olwen?'

'Very well, thank you for asking.'

'And Miss Davies?'

'Very well, thank you.'

'There you are then.'

'I hear you had a bit of bother on Friday afternoon, Blodwen.'

'Who told you that, Mrs Morris?'

'Oh, a little bird.'

'That little bird had eyes to see through doors then'

'You could say that. Come on, girl, tell us and give us a good laugh. Most of us know already.'

'*Uffern dân*, you can't keep anything secret around here. Well, you know that Idwals, the traveller? He calls every now and then hoping for an order. Haydn's told him we get everything we need from the warehouse in Castell Newydd Emlyn, but he keeps on coming and I notice it's mostly when our van's not outside. On Friday, I was halfway down the steps from the loft when the shop bell went. I shouted I was coming but before I could turn round, there he was at the bottom of the steps. He'd walked straight through, quiet as a cat. Then, if you please, the dirty old devil put his hand on my ankle. Yes he did, honestly. "What the hell do you think you're doing?" I said. "It's irresistible", he said, "You've got such dainty ankles." I'm going to have trouble here, I thought, if I'm not careful. I couldn't come down the steps any further, I'd be right in his arms, see. So I bent down and gave him a smack in the chops. I didn't want to hurt him, just a warning to say no nonsense, if you please. I must have hit him harder than I thought. Out shot his teeth and smashed to *jibereens* on the floor! Couldn't believe my eyes. He let go my ankle, picked up the pieces and marched off without a word. Won't be seeing him again in a hurry!'

'Good riddance to bad rubbish! Irresistible ankles indeed, what-ever next? I've heard plenty about him before.'

'Got what he deserved then.'

'Wonder what excuse he gave to his wife, she's a proper Tartar by all accounts.'

'Better keep those ankles under cover, Blodwen, or we'll have a riot on our hands!'

Amid shouts of laughter, the feathers flew up to the roof.

Chapel was the centre of our social life, more so in the winter. Sunday dinner became a lively occasion if bad weather kept outlying families in the village for the day's services. The big oil lamps, the smell of paraffin and beeswax, the *hwyl* of the singing and the ser-mon brought a warmth of their own. A soft light from high windows fell on honey coloured wood, white walls and delicate plasterwork making a serene, peaceful interior. And always the wind, the lulling sound of the wind.

Seated before a huge fire in the vestry, the long evenings were filled with Bible readings, prayer meetings, Band of Hope and Tonic Sol-Fah classes. I loved drama practice best, especially rehearsals for the Nativity Play, when our minister, Mr Emrys, spent patient hours encouraging our talents. Early Christmas week, Mrs Emrys checked on any family in the district in need of help. Food was collected or purchased from the fund and brought to the shop for packing and distribution.

'Anyone new on the list this year, ladies?'

'Rhian will need help with the cooking. She's much better, but no grain on her yet, still in bed.'

'They've had the influenza something awful in Pen-y-Pant, taking turns in and out of bed. Mair found Illtyd behind the door in the *tŷ bach*, collapsed in a heap. Very nasty it is, they say they're dropping like flies in the South.'

'Don't forget Ianto and Samson. They're not going to his sister this year, she's off to see her new grandson. How many more children is that girl going to have? She's got a house-full already. Nice girl mind you, cheerful as the day is long.'

'Needs to be with that brood around her feet.'

'Our Emyr saw Eirwen in Aberteifi. You remember her, don't you? She and her mother sing duets. You've never heard a better contralto than her mother. They're a singing family and everyone wants them for the *Cymanfa*. Well, her mother-in-law, Eirwen's that is, died sudden a week ago, dropsy they said. I didn't know her myself, she came from Pembroke somewhere. Eirwen was buying a new hat for the funeral, the second one this year. Can't see why the first one doesn't do twice, can you?'

'Bit of swank, I expect.'

'We'll have to help Mrs Jones, she's very upset. She was going to her family in Beulah for Christmas, a treat for the children. But that rotten husband of hers has done the dirty on her again. He phoned to say he couldn't come home he was too far away. Too far away for Christmas, if you please. When I told her she cried awful, poor *dab*. He hasn't sent her a penny piece, so she's rock bottom, nothing in the house.'

'Come, *cyfeillion*,' said Mrs Emrys, 'She'll be top of the list this year. We'd better get on, plenty to do before dark.'

Dad and I distributed the Christmas boxes in the van and after the warmest hospitality, we took away as much as we delivered. During the afternoon, Seth provided each house with a yule log, placed at the back of the hearth to smoulder throughout the twelve days of Christmas. All lamps and candles were lit by a flame from the log to bring good luck. On Old Twelfth Night, Besi collected a handful of ash from each fire, mixing it with seed corn in a pot. Come springtime, Rhodri and I watched her scattering it on the ploughed fields ensuring a bountiful harvest.

Love from Blodwen

F'annwyl Miriam,

This weather is beyond, it's like the North Pole upstairs, ice on the inside of the windows all day long. My hands are chapped and bleeding today, I expect yours are too. That Snowfire's no good and Besi's run out of her salve already, we're clamouring for it.

I had a letter from our Dinah to say she'd tramped up to see if Elwyn was all right. A couple of years ago he burnt half the furniture. The two big sgiws, two ffwrwms and those lovely old chairs. God help the grandfather clock, my Mamgu and Datcu would turn in their graves. Why doesn't he stack up in the summer like everyone else, I ask you? I've sat on those ffwrwms hundreds of times. They used to celebrate Hen Ddydd Nadolig, remember you came with me one year? They brought the plough in under the table, all polished for Gwyliau Mawr. We had to touch it for luck before we sat down. Anti Mari piled our plates with food, and before we'd finished, she'd plonk the pudding in the gravy! I can see her now, shawl tight around her, that flat cap on her head, and men's clogs up to her knees. She was a case too, worked like a man, strong as a horse, but she was a hopeless cook. Uncle John never complained, a real gentleman he was.

Then the boys dressed up for Mari Lwyd, remember? You could always tell it was Dai Banc in the horse's head because of his huge feet. Our Dat wore that comical hat, and that little chap who played the sergeant was as bandy as a coot. They thought they were the bee's knees chasing us about. We had a rattling good time, didn't we? Then out came the old photos with stories to match. I've got some of them somewhere, I'll have to find them, we'll have a good laugh. Nain's the same, loves to keep the old ways she does. Are you coming for her tea on Hen Ddydd Nadolig this year? Haydn will come and fetch you, if it doesn't snow...

Love from,
Blodwen.

The shop and *gegin fawr* were crowded with people on Christmas Eve afternoon, many of them expecting a phone call from relatives in London. Unable to take a holiday from their dairies and milk rounds, they rang to exchange seasonal greetings, confident my father would answer the telephone. Older people in the valley refused to enter the store room, let alone hold the receiver. The caller spoke to Dad in English, he shouted to Mam who translated to the listener, and then the procedure was reversed. A lengthy business! Mr Davies' role as barber was much in evidence, the men smoking and talking politics as they waited.

The performance of the Nativity Play in the evening was the main attraction, creating much excitement amongst the children. We couldn't wait to show off our dazzling talent, all dressed up with rouge and powder. My dream came true the year I was chosen to play Mary when even Dad, who never attended chapel, came to hear me singing a lullaby to the Baby Jesus.

> 'Suai'r gwynt, suai'r gwynt,
> Wrth fyned heibio'r drws,
> A Mair ar ei gwely gwair,
> Wyliai ei Baban tlws.
> Syllai yn ddwys yn ei wyneb llon,
> Gwasgai Waredwr y byd at ei bron,
> Canai ddiddanol gan,
> Cwsg, cwsg, f'anwylyd bach,
> Cwsg nes daw'r bore iach,
> Cwsg, cwsg, cwsg.'

Christmas morning was magic! First of all, I emptied the stocking hanging on the bed frame, full of sweets, nuts, apples and a shiny half crown in the toe. Sometimes it contained an orange wrapped in pink tissue paper with blue and gold lettering.

'*Nadolig llawen*, Mam and Dad, all downstairs for presents.'

'It's too cold, *cariad*, I'll see to the fire first.'

'Col's doing that, Mam. Come on, I can't wait.'

Coloured paper chains had appeared overnight to festoon the

gegin fawr. My big presents were hidden under a sheet, and a pillow-case hanging on the brass rod under the mantelpiece contained books, pencils, paints, chocolate and a tray of hard toffee with a small hammer! I hopped about like a mad thing, loving the mounting antic-ipation, the thrill of different presents from the family every year. A doll's cradle, or pram, with satin covers from Mamgu and Dadcu Davies and either a three wheeler bike, a blackboard and easel, or a desk and chair from Mam and Dad. Once, Dadcu Davies made me a grand doll's house with furniture in every room. Playing with it helped me through many miserable days to come. I cherished Col's presents which he always made himself – a beaded collar, a feathered head-dress for Minnehaha, or a box covered in pretty shells. Unsuitable gifts from Mamgu Poli stopped when I was about five. I regretted the passing of the Meccano, train set, bagatelle, clockwork tip-up lorry and bright-red wheelbarrow. My mother, however, was relieved when I received a china doll with a wardrobe of exquisite clothes. She was very special, her butter-blonde hair, delicately painted face and lace dress making her the prettiest of my family of ten. Although a label around her neck named her Gillian, I called her Blanco. Running home after showing her off in Rhodri's house, I fell heavily, smashing her head in several pieces. I was heartbroken when Col carried me gently into the house. A few days later, he presented me with a box covered in coloured paper. Inside, on a bed of moss, lay Blanco, every fragment painstakingly pieced together. Her eyes opened and closed and her hair was carefully brushed. My lovely old Col had made her beautiful once more. I threw my arms around him, my lovely, lovely old Col. Battered Blanco was my favourite evermore.

Rhodri and I wished every household *Nadolig Llawen* before attending chapel for carols at half past ten, dressed in our Sunday best. Under the warm light of the big lamps, we sang *'O deuwch Ffyddloniaid'* loud enough to raise the roof. Wil Morris' solo, rich in the lower register was a great favourite. Best of all, we enjoyed a haunting duet sung by Susan and Dwynwen from Tegfan Farm. As we left the service we saw the *Ladi Llwyd* driving away in a black car.

A day of pure pleasure followed our huge dinner of roast goose. Mam made sure she stored the fat for medicinal purposes! Every other housewife performed the same ritual. At the merest hint of a cold, the victim's chest and neck were massaged with grease and wrapped in flannel or a sweaty sock. You could smell us a mile off!

Old customs also prevailed on New Year's Day, setting high standards of courtesy and consideration for the coming year. Borrowing was forbidden, debts settled, quarrels made up and adults were more likely to exchange gifts than on Christmas Day. Children rose early to collect *calennig*, a small gift from each household in return for a song or recitation. The tradition ended promptly at midday, for fear of bad luck. If the weather stayed reasonable, Rhodri and I joined older children from the farms, venturing further afield in our quest for silver. Dressed for Iceland, we sang greetings at each door.

> 'Mi godais yn fore,
> Mi gerddais yn ffyrnig,
> At dy Mrs Morris i'nofyn am g'lennig,
> Os clywch ar ei'ch calon,
> Rhowch swllt neu chwecheiniog,
> Blwyddyn newydd dda,
> Am ddimai neu cheiniog.'

The *Noson Lawen* on New Year's Eve, was always well attended. Hosted by a different village each year, the entertainment included music, vocal and instrumental, poetry recitals and *cynghanedd* competitions. This entailed a group of people, usually men, composing two lines of verse with alliteration and rhyme within each line. Failure to speak in turn, in a given time, meant dismissal from the contest. The winner was a man of distinction.

On one of these occasion, my father became the hero of the hour for a very different reason. Due to bitterly cold weather, he was relaying the village elders to a neighbouring *Noson Lawen*. Our van's unreliable engine needed Col's presence on every trip. The successful concert, the feast and the folk-dancing afterwards put everyone in a festive mood. Outside, a heavy frost had fallen, transforming the countryside. We admired its shimmering beauty, seeing it as a good omen for the coming year.

The van engine, covered with sacks, sprang to life after a few cranks of the starting handle. The Misses Bowen, Mam and I were the first passengers, Col in the back. About a mile down the road, we passed a group of men cycling furiously back towards the vestry, calling as they went. What did they say? Why were they going so fast on this icy road? We soon found out! Around the corner near the wood, a man was standing in the middle of the road, shouting at the top of his voice. He held an axe, swinging it wildly from side to side. Silver pale in the moonlight, he was completely naked. Around him danced a red radiance.

'Iesu Grist, aros gyda ni.' My mother breathed as he plunged towards us, the axe raised above his head.

'Get down,' my father shouted, 'I'm going to pass him. Keep calm. I'm putting my foot down. Hold on, here we go.'

Lurching towards the raging figure, the van swerved abruptly. The man hurled himself on the bonnet, the axe crashing on the roof. His face, hideously pressed against the windscreen, made the women scream loudly. Dad veered from side to side and after a lifetime, the man disappeared. A roaring shout, a heavy jolt and the van stalled. Silence.

Col was first out. Dad sat, drawn and haggard, his face bathed in sweat.

'I ran over him, Blodwen. I think I've killed him! Stay here, I'll see what's happened.'

He returned within minutes. 'He's still breathing, thank God, and his pulse is strong but I don't want to move him. Col's gone for help. Are you all right?'

'Yes, Haydn, don't worry about us, take these rugs to cover him up. Margaret *fach*, it's all right, Dad and Col will see to everything and the man will be as right as rain, you'll see.'

She held me tight, turning to comfort the trembling Misses Bowen, their faces hidden in their scarves. Peering through the window, I saw Dad standing with his hands on his hips, expanding his chest to ease his gasping breath. It must have looked a triumphant posture to the gathering crowd.

'Good old Sharrol the Shop, you polished him off good and proper.'

'Didn't know you could pack such a punch, *boyo.*'

Appalled, Dad tried to explain, but the congratulations continued.

'Scared the living daylights out of us, he did.'

'He's as drunk as a lord, you can smell him a mile off.'

'Who is he, then?'

'Stranger around here, they only came just before Christmas. Up to their eyes in debt, I heard. Bailiffs on the warpath.'

'Looks a lot smaller now. *Duw Mawr*, he was ten feet tall back there!'

A sturdy woman came down the road towards us wearing a flat cap, a long thick coat, and clogs.

'You've found him then?'

'Well, he found us actually,' replied my father, 'I'm afraid he's hurt.'

'He'll be all right. He's *meddw talpe*. Hope he didn't do any damage. He went mad when they took his harp, see. The bailiffs didn't seem to know it was against the law to take a man's harp. Got raving drunk he did and ran off. I followed his clothes down the road. No, don't touch him, he's mine, I'll take care of him. Up you come, you poor old sod, home to no supper and a thumping headache in the morning. *Nos da* to you all.'

She picked him up, held his arm around her neck and carried him off like a child, stark naked.

'Margaret, you come back in the van this instant, if you please.'

The crowd gradually dispersed, still praising my extremely embarrassed father.

'I tried to explain I was no hero, my knees are still knocking. I feel such a fraud. They must know in my condition I can't knock the skin off a rice pudding.'

'Never mind, Haydn *bach.* We're all safe, that's what matters. You kept a cool head back there. God knows what might have happened!'

'Yes indeed, Mr Sharrol, you showed real presence of mind, yes indeed you did.'

'I'm so sorry you had such a shock, ladies. I hope you're all right.'

'It was a shock I must admit,' said Miss Siân. 'It's not every day you see a naked man on the road, is it? In front of respectable women and children, *ach a fi!*'

'Yes indeed,' agreed Miss Anni, 'If he had to go around waving an axe, he could have left his clothes on, I'm sure. He ought to be ashamed, frightening decent people out of their wits. Naked as the day he was born, disgusting, he ought to be reported.'

I'd never seen a naked man before and neither had the Misses Bowen by the sound of it.

'As long as you're not hurt, ladies. Are you still frightened, Snwny?'

'No, Dad. Did you see the red ring?'

'Red ring, what red ring? I didn't see any red ring.'

'Did you see the red ring, Mam?'

'No, what do you mean, *bach*?'

'There was a ring of red light all around that man.'

'It must have been a trick of the headlamps. Come on, you're very tired. Let's go home.'

In the *gegin fawr*, I asked Col, 'Did you see the red ring?'

Nod.

'All around him?'

Nod.

'Were we the only ones to see it?'

Nod.

'Why?' He made his sign,

'Magic.'

It was still bitterly cold at the end of *Gwyliau Mawr*. I tried to keep my toothache a secret, knowing the inevitable, but when my face started swelling, Mam rubbed my gums with oil of cloves and sent for Besi. It had to be taken out, no doubt about it. Dentistry was performed by Mr Davies, the blacksmith, a man of many skills. He treated his patients gently, extracting teeth with a small pair of pinchers made for the purpose. He'd made an even smaller pair for children, but nothing diminished the anguish of that slow, sombre walk. Grown men were known to cry on that stretch of road to the forge, only pain preventing a quick retreat. The breath of bellows, the glowing pinchers, the acrid smell of hissing water. A prelude to misery! Blood flowed. After the torture, Mr Davies produced a bag of toffee to soften the blow. I vowed to scrub my teeth every day with salt and flannel, as instructed.

Besi said teeth were always a nuisance. She and her brothers had theirs removed by the blacksmith as a twenty-first birthday present from their parents and false ones fitted in Castell Newydd Emlyn. It was common practice in her day, she said, no more trouble with old teeth after that! There was one small drawback though. With only one dentist in the district, every set of false teeth looked exactly the same!

A thin covering of snow fell during the afternoon making the valley silent and remote. I was still nursing a sore mouth in front of the fire when Besi sent word to phone for the doctor. Seth's cold had turned into a high fever, causing concern. Dr. Tuffin arrived before dark, in his big car, to diagnose the influenza. He left strict nursing instructions with Besi, in case bad weather prevented his return the following morning. Overnight, the village was cut off by a heavy snowfall.

A few days later, Mam was serving Mrs Morris when Ita appeared in the shop! Looking pale and anxious, she said she knew Seth was very ill and she wanted to see him at once.

'Ita *fach*, come in, you're frozen through, girl. In by the fire now, no argument.'

I was surprised and delighted to see her but she wasn't my summer Ita. Bundled up in dark clothes, she looked small and fragile, her eyes shadowed. Taking my hand she sat by the fire, tired to the bone.

'Eat this *cawl*, now, it will warm you up in a jiffy. How did you know about Seth then? Did anyone fetch you?'

'No, I just knew. I must see him, Mrs Blodwen.'

'Haydn will go up straight away. I'm sure Mrs Morgan will let you see him, things being as they are. You're right Ita, Seth is very ill, we're all worried about him. You must stay with us, can't have you wandering about in this weather. How on earth did you get here through all this snow?'

'My brother's digging out the wagon on the top road. He'll stay with me until I see Seth.'

'Haydn will send help to bring him down to the yard. Don't worry now, *cariad*, we'll see this through, Seth will be better soon, I'm sure.'

Dad returned with a harsh answer from Mrs Morgan. She insisted they knew nobody by the name of Ita in her house. Ita stared into the fire, saying nothing. She was very still for a long time, so far beyond reach, I felt frightened. I said a prayer over and over in my head asking for Seth to be well again. When her brother arrived, she thanked Mam and Dad and left for the wagon, her shawl pulled tightly around her.

The next day, all the talk in the shop was about Ita and Seth.

'Poor girl, she looks terrible, I hardly recognised her.'

'Funny how she knew about Seth, nobody told her, did they? Didn't know where she was anyway.'

'If she can read the hand, she can tell other things as well, I expect.'

'Surely, Mrs Morgan will let her see Seth. What if he gets worse?'

'Yes, but who's to say the first words? Who'll risk letting the cat out of the bag, it could make her ill as well.'

'She must know by now they want to get married. She must have a hint after all this time.'

'Perhaps Mr Emrys could have a word. Something will have to be done.'

'But Mrs Morgan does know! She's always asking me funny questions about Ita and Seth.'

'What do you know about it, Margaret? What sort of questions, my girl?'

'*Shwsh, cariad*, off you go and find Col, he was looking for you just now.'

'But I know...'

'Do as I tell you, go and find Col, he's in the barn.'

'Col, why can't Ita see Seth? She's so upset, she's not talking to anyone. If Seth dies, Ita'll die too, I know she will. Mrs Morgan knows they want to get married, I can tell by the questions she asks me. You must do something, Col, please do something.'

Col held me in his arms and dried my tears. He shook his head and gave the thumbs up sign.

'Seth's going to get better?'

Nod.

'Does Ita know that?'

Nod.

'Why is she so upset, is it because she can't see him?'

Nod.

'Will she see him soon?'

Nod.

Mam rushed into the barn, all smiles. 'Don't worry you two, we've just heard this minute that Seth's over the worst. Besi's worked like a Trojan and the fever's broken. He'll be as good as nine pence in no time at all. Ita's in the *gegin fawr*, her old self again, thank goodness. Come on now, no more tears, everything's going to be A1. We'll have a bit of a do when Seth is well, a posh tea, is it?'

They met in our house, Seth all pale and spindly. We went next door to give them five minutes, before a special tea of ham sandwiches, *bara brith*, Welsh cakes and one of Mrs Morris' creamy trifles with sugar violets on top. Ita was her laughing self, hanging on to Seth's arm like a limpet and the sweetness between them was there for all to see. The colour returned to Seth's face as he announced they were engaged to be married, the week after harvest. They planned to live in Cnwc, seeing poor Mrs Jones had already left the village. He would tell his mother that very afternoon.

Mrs Morgan was never to hear the news. The fever developed quickly and her condition deteriorated rapidly. Doctor Tuffin called daily, allowing only Seth and Besi in the house, the influenza being very contagious. Brown paper and herbs were burnt in the sick room, and sheets soaked in disinfectant hung on every door, to prevent the illness spreading. Mrs Morgan was delirious for over a week, then she felt a little better and asked for her Bible. As Seth placed it in her hands, she closed her eyes and slipped away.

Chapter Six

F'annwyl Miriam,

I'm sorry I haven't written lately, what with the weather and Haydn's chest, I've been up to my eyes. Thank you for your letter with all the news. I'm glad your Gwen is coming to stay for a bit, do you good, you've had a hard time of it. You need to get your strength back after nursing your Dat. A blessing he went so peaceful in the end. We'll miss him terrible, a lovely man he was, a proper gent. The house is empty without him, Miriam fach, always there when needed. Such a bad old winter with your Dat gone and Mrs Morgan too. I'm glad your Eira's better, she did have a packet, didn't she? Our Margaret had it for a week, but nothing like your Eira, poor thing.

It's good to see the spring's coming at long last. Ita and Seth won't be married this year again, pity too, but you can't have a funeral and a wedding in the same year, of course. Yes, they've finished the threshing at long last. We were the bottom of the list with the machine this year.

We are all looking forward to the Eisteddfod. The children always do well, marvellous really, all credit to Mr Llywelyn and Miss Jones. Our Margaret will be with them next year, starting school in September. I can't believe where the time's gone. I don't know how she'll take to it, not very keen at present. It would have been better if she'd started last year, the same with your Bryn, but rules are rules I suppose. Mr and Mrs Morris want us to go to the Eisteddfod in Pontrhydfendigaid with them this year. It would be lovely, but I'll have to see how things go. Teg's cousin is competing in the solo, she's a beautiful soprano.

I've been to Aberteifi for new glasses. Went on the bus on Friday, very comfortable it was, surprising how many we picked up! The man said I must have a special lens for my left eye. Remember I splashed it with ammonia when I was in service with Rachel? Scarred it, he said. More expense, but I can't do without glasses. Lovely shops, Miriam.

I saw a gorgeous hat for the Cymanfa but too much, so I bought new trimmings for my navy instead, pretty shell-pink flowers to match my dress. The Misses Bowen are making a powder-blue costume for our Margaret with a blouse to match. Mamgu Poli bought her a Deanna Durbin halo hat, cream it is. Are you coming this year? We've got a good baswr, my favourite. I love a good baswr. I hope we'll have fine weather. We're expecting a good crowd with a special dinner and tea in the vestry. I'm really looking forward to it. We'll be cleaning up the cemetery soon for Sul y Blodau...

Love from,
Blodwen.

On the day before *Sul y Blodau*, Flowering Sunday, the men scythed the grass in the cemetery and the women cleaned and weeded in preparation for Easter. Glass domes, about eighteen inches high, stood on many of the old graves, covering exquisite, white porcelain flowers decorated with birds, bees and butterflies. My favourite contained a tiny, seated angel with outstretched wings, holding a book. I longed to touch its fragile beauty, but the dome always held fast. Watching from our haystack near the cemetery wall, I saw my opportunity when the domes were removed for washing. Climbing down, I took the angel, intending to replace it after a moment. The temptation was too great. Back over the wall like a *winci*, I ran pell-mell to my river hideout. I knew it was wicked. I knew the intense glow of pleasure as I gazed at the stolen angel was wrong. But now it was mine. I hid it in the roots, a secret never to be shared.

My over-casual air when I rejoined the group didn't fool my mother and one of her straight looks made me feel uneasy. I knew I was in serious trouble when Mr Emrys accompanied us to the house. What did I have to say for myself? I'd been seen removing the angel from the grave, so there was no doubt of my guilt. Mr Emrys was as gentle as ever but this was not a trifling matter. I turned to my protector and a cold realisation crept through me. For the first time I could remember, my mother was immune to my pleading look. I'd shamed her. I was a thief. When Mr Emrys asked me to return the angel, I felt such panic, I denied having it.

'Well, Margaret *fach*, you say you haven't taken anything from the grave and others say you have. We must prove it once and for all. Here I have a magic piece of straw which grows in the hand of anyone telling a lie. I'll measure it with this inch tape and then ask you to hold it. If you are guilty, it will grow a whole inch. Your mother and I will close our eyes and see what happens.'

I knew at once what was happening! I could see the straw growing in my hand! Unable to face the look in Mam's eyes when she found out I was a liar as well as a thief, I tore an inch off the end! Measured again, both my guilt and deviousness were revealed. I must return the angel and take my punishment. I ran like the wind but although I searched everywhere, I could not find the angel. *'Iesu*

Grist aros gyda ni.' Ashamed and miserable, I returned empty-hand-ed, full of remorse. My apologies were accepted but I was not allowed to attend the Cymanfa Ganu Children's Service. What about my powder-blue costume and halo hat? Misery enough, but the quiet chastisement I received from my mother was unforgettable. I prayed I would never offend her again.

I joined the congregation for the evening service, my guilt still hovering in the air. Glorious singing filled the Chapel which was packed to the doors with people from surrounding villages. The women were mostly in new hats and gloves, the younger ones dressed in spring outfits, made by the Misses Bowen. Mam was look-ing forward to hearing her favourite *baswr*, a red-headed young man from Tonypandy. He stood, feet apart, firmly planted, like a boxer taking on all comers. Then he raised his head and his rich, com-pelling voice flowed over us, moving many to tears. It was hard to believe that such a sound could come from a lean and lanky lad.

The *Parchedig* Noah Harris, a gaunt, white-bearded figure in Sunday black, rose in the pulpit to thank God we were such a musi-cal nation. He admired our Chapel, praising the magnificent pitch pine of the gallery. Our beautiful, tranquil valley was a gift from the Blessed Lord Himself. We must tend it with reverence and devotion, living in harmony with nature according to God's Law. The land and its bounty was held in stewardship for the Lord and the generations to come. In this remote place, we understood the value of friendship and community, keeping alive our language and traditions, respect-ing our history and the old ways. Not only did we live in God's Creation, we were part of it, body and soul. Anyone sullying the puri-ty of our endeavours should beware of the wrath of that God! The smallest sin casteth the longest shadow, stretching into the wider world beyond, swelling the realm of the Devil himself!

The *Parchedig* closed his eyes and held his arms aloft, looking like the painting of God in Nain's brass bound Bible. I knew when those burning eyes opened, they would look directly at me, the sinner of the hour! I slid frantically along the seat to hold my mother's hand. Only her reassuring smile kept me from taking flight, to hide forev-er in my secret place!

Apprehension drifted around the village with all the talk on Saturday nights centred on the war. When Ianto's Samson said we were going to be invaded by a lot of pagans, drop dead, I was glad the village was hidden from any boats out at sea. I'd never heard of the countries mentioned in the shop and my mind was full of other things. The hot weather made our trips with Mamgu Poli even more enjoyable and Rhodri and I spent more time together. He was bigger now, well able to look after himself. We sat on his Dadcu Siencyn's steps, listening to stories of the old days, ate Nain's cakes, played by the river and listened to the *Ladi Llwyd*'s sweet music. The postponement of Ita's wedding was a great disappointment but spring would soon come! She knew of a ruined house where dark-red roses grew, where blue-black plums ripened in the old orchard and clouds of butterflies fed on fallen pears. We watched foxes playing in the sunlight below the bank, and we saw thousands of grasshoppers in a glittering cloud over Cnwc field. I wandered about in my private world with Pedro and Dan, unaware that away from the house, my mother relied on Col as my keeper.

In the evenings we rehearsed for the missionary fund concert. The girls in my Sunday school class were chosen as fairies, dressed in pretty, gauze costumes. While they floated and flounced in their petal skirts, Mrs Emrys and Mrs Olwen Guto tried to find one to fit me. I sat in my flannel, trying not to look glum. I was too fat to be a fairy!

'Too fat to be a fairy indeed,' Mamgu fumed to her tearful granddaughter, 'I'll give them too fat to be a fairy. *My'n jawch i*, who wants to be a soppy old fairy anyway? Come on, *bach*, I'll show you something better than being a daft old fairy.'

Marching like a general into the barn, she called, 'Col, where's that Bomber? Damn bird, is he still lurking out there? Go and make sure, there's a pal.'

In the cockerel free yard, she removed her hat, throwing it in the hedge like an abandoned piece of regalia.

'Right then, up-a-Derry Dando into this trap and we'll give them fairies. You're Boadicea now, my girl, a great, Celtic Queen of high renown, not a quivering fairy. It's time to frighten the Romans to death. They've been nasty to you and your family and you're out to save your tribe. Col, you're the charioteer and no whipping the horses mind. I'm the Queen's assistant-in-chief and up you come, Pedro, you magnificent, royal hound. Right then, kid, let's hear the clattering of hoofs, pell-mell into battle we go. Listen to the wind whistling in your helmets, *boyos*, the horns blowing and the stirring shouts of your people. Put some *hwyl* into it now. Show a leg, up and over the top and to hell with the Romans and the fairies.'

A phone call from Martha Mortymer put everything in a turmoil. She was staying with her married daughter in Kidwelly at the time. Martha had recently become an ardent follower of the Evangelists, attending meetings in the Valleys, Cardiff, Swansea and Llanelli.

'The preacher's wonderful, Poli, outstanding,' she said on the phone. 'It's in English, of course, but powerful all the same. I'm adamant you shouldn't miss one of his sermons. Caerfyrddin is their last port of call before shutting up shop. Everyone north of there don't need converting, do they? They all go to Chapel already. It's not far from you and I can meet you there. My son-in-law will take me on his motorbike and sidecar. Come on, girl, you'll really enjoy it. Bring Blodwen and Margaret with you.'

Mamgu Poli's eyes sparkled as she persuaded my mother to join her.

'We'll take a picnic and have a lovely day out! I've heard about those Evangelists, full of religious fervour they are, just like our open-air prayer meetings in the old days. It'll give us a boost with all this dreadful worry about a war. I'd like to go and you must come too, Blodwen.'

'I don't know, I'm sure. There's more than enough work to do and it's a long way. Trefor won't be too keen traipsing all over the place, and it'll take hours if we have to get out of the car every five minutes. All that traffic will give him a fit.'

'We're going to Caerfyrddin, Blodwen, not Timbuktu. You leave

Trefor to me. Right then, the Evangelist meeting it is!'

'What's an Evangelist, Mam?'

'Someone who has a good time in Chapel.'

A cloudless, Saturday morning saw us on our way, three passengers, Trefor counted out. We were to picnic with Martha before the meeting at two o'clock sharp. The first surprise happened not long after reaching the Henllan road. Mamgu announced that Trefor had promised to let us remain in the car, except for the steepest of hills. We would make good time, have a cup of tea at the Ivy Bush Hotel and arrive as fresh as daisies.

'Amen to that,' my mother declared.

Trefor was as good as his word, but he didn't look very happy to me. Frowning heavily, he concentrated on the road. Could I please keep still and stop chattering until he got his bearings. Not like Trefor at all, and he was driving faster than usual.

At Caerfyrddin, Mamgu insisted on driving down Priory Street to see Merlin's Oak. The tree's presence protected Myrddin the Wizard's birthplace from harm. Its demise or removal was unthinkable, bringing certain disaster to the town. Fortunately, it was still standing, bound about with hoops of iron. Much relieved, Mamgu informed us that Caerfyrddin had always been a very important place. It was once a prominent Roman town on the Sarn Elen, the famous road running from north to south. According to Giraldus Cambrensis that is, a very distant relative of Dadcu Jono's!

'Anyone would think he was your second cousin the way you talk about that man, Mamgu Poli!'

'History is just over the shoulder, Blodwen, and we'd be wise to remember that. Our own Owain Glyndŵr fought here, capturing the castle from the English in 1403. Now there's a dazzler for you! The genuine article! Very handsome he was, and clever enough to be a Druid or a magician. Many thought so at the time. You'll be interested to know that his wife was called Margaret too. When he started the Rebellion against the English, people joined him in droves. His standard was a gold dragon, and he always wore a flamingo's feather in his helmet. The country was free for the first time since the death of Llywelyn ap Gruffydd. Marvellous times they were, full of promise, but it wasn't long before the old *Sais* poked their noses in. Owain was never defeated, he just disappeared on Saint Matthew's Day in Harvest, never to be seen again. But we all know he'll return when needed most. Oh yes, this place is loaded with history. Rhys ap Thomas and his men left here to help Henry Tudor on Bosworth Field. They killed Richard the Third, to make a Tudor King of England!'

The next surprise was a huge tent in a field outside the town. A tent for a chapel, never heard of that before. This was going to be different, I thought to myself. And another thing! It wasn't quiet inside. People walked about talking and laughing and shaking hands. Music came from a stage at the far end, where one man played the piano and another the accordion. What would Mr Rhys make of this?

We sat on wooden benches near the back, Mamgu Poli on the aisle to accommodate her hat. As usual, Martha was indifferently dressed, her hat and coat having seen better days. A choir appeared on the stage wearing long, white gowns. They started singing in a very lively way, clapping their hands and smiling broadly. After the lesson and prayers, collection boxes were brought into the packed marquee. As they passed from hand to hand, the choir sang,

'*Hear the pennies dropping,*
Listen how they fall,
Every one for Jesus,
He shall have them all.'

It was the only part of the proceedings I really understood.

Then the big moment arrived. Complete silence fell and the tension mounted. The curtains at the back of the stage parted and a tall, dark-haired man with a commanding presence stood surveying the congregation. It was a challenging look, holding us to account. You could hear a pin drop. After several moments, the preacher stepped forward to the lectern and spoke in a deep, melodious voice. He went on for ages, sometimes raising his voice to a shout, then lowering it to a whisper. Moving around the stage, he held his head or wrung his hands dramatically. The people were spellbound, hanging on his every word. It wasn't new to me, I'd witnessed many such sermons in our own Chapel when the minister went into a real *hwyl*. But what followed made me jump in my seat! The preacher gave a resounding hosanna and the congregation joined in, mixing the Welsh *gogoniant* with the English "Praise be!" Most unusual for Caerfyrddin, Mam said.

Suddenly, Martha rose from her seat with her arms in the air. Stepping into the aisle, she called out, 'I'm coming to you, Jesus, I'm coming.' To our amazement she joined many others moving towards the imposing figure on the stage. Mamgu Poli's piercing whisper rippled through the row.

'Shame on you, Martha Mortymer! Going to your Maker with the hem of your coat unravelled, straggling down around your ankles. There are limits!'

Martha stopped dead in her tracks, lowered her arms and said,

'I'm coming to you, Jesus, I'm still coming – later!'

Heavy rain fell on the sloping roof of the *gegin fach*. I was playing tea parties with Blanco and my dolls, silently using Mam's best china with birds on it, banished for Mamgu Poli's visit. Pedro, prowling about the eaves, would surely give away my hiding place one day. Mam and Mamgu were making bread while having a good *clonc* about Olwen and Guto.

'You'll never guess what's happened in a million years! There's been ructions up at Olwen's. Guto's mother came to see them on the hop last Sunday afternoon, it being such a lovely day, I expect. She got a lift up with that chap Jones from Dyffryn. Don't ask me why she came, she hasn't been this long time. Guto sees to that, doesn't want her to know what's going on. Perhaps she smelt a rat or heard some *clecs*. Anyway, she couldn't make anyone hear at the house, so up the stairs she went, in case Olwen was bad. *Uffern dân,* if she did, she found Guto in bed with Miss Davies! It was real Top C up there, the old lady went off her rocker, shouting to bring down the plaster. And on a Sunday, mind you. She's over eighty but she can hold her own any day of the week, yes indeed! They got the length of her tongue in no uncertain terms. What she didn't call them! Before you could blink an eye, Guto caught hold of her and put her out on the road. Fuming she was, fit to bust, wonder she didn't collapse at her age. Then back he went into the house, cool as a cucumber, if you please and shut the door.

'The old lady went to Mrs Rhys, they know each other well, their mothers lived close by when they were girls. She calmed down after a cup of tea and getting it off her chest like. Why hadn't she been told, she wanted to know, and how long had these disgusting antics been going on? Mrs Rhys kept her mouth shut. You never know with families, she said. You can take sides, to find yourself out in the cold all round. But the old lady is never going to speak to Guto again, full stop.'

'Blodwen *fach*, I don't believe it. He threw his mother out of the house?'

'Yes, indeed he did, he's been the talk of the place ever since. His mam said she didn't know, but I doubt it myself. You can't keep a thing like that quiet, can you? Mind you, he's been very cute about it, always going to see his mam, stopping her coming here, but she must have known. It's not as though she lives on the moon, is it? Came to see for herself she did. And, *pechod mawr*, see she did, with a vengeance. Couldn't have asked for better proof now, could she? It must have been a terrible shock, mind you, especially on a Sunday afternoon.'

'Where was Olwen then?'

'Helping for the concert in Sunday School. We've all known what's been going on since he brought her back from Aberteifi that night, bold as brass. *Duw Mawr*, when we heard she was a teacher, we almost dropped dead. What on earth did a teacher see in Guto? No telling, is there? A teacher! Haydn said he'd have been less surprised if he'd brought home a gorilla. Mind you, we hardly ever see her, only now and again and never in Chapel. Not yet anyway! When we do see her, she's all dressed up like a t'penny ham bone! He's built her a *gegin* of her own now and she's got a piece of garden to herself. Marvellous cook I've heard, by all accounts.

'I don't know how Olwen's put up with him all these years. He was the bottom of the pile to start off with, worse now. And the way he shows off that leg of his! He's carved more flowers on it and his name, daft old devil. Haydn says it's a work of art, mind you. He's touched if you ask me, always so biggity and chopsy with it. He thinks himself above others, prancing about in that brown bowler hat of his. But Olwen will never hear a word against him, you know. Can't understand it myself, makes you think, two women in the one house. Wouldn't suit me and that's a fact, but sharing the work is a good idea, come to think of it. He's a man with nasty ways is Guto, no getting away from it. Most people can't bear him. Never mind, his day will come, God is not asleep.'

'Poor Olwen, such a nice girl, heart of gold. From a good family too.'

'They treat her as if she's *twp* and she's taking it, daft thing. I know for a fact they've only got one room upstairs. The box-room's no bigger than a cupboard. The other day in the shop, Olwen was very quiet, you could tell by her face she wasn't her usual self. "What's the matter, Olwen?" I said. "You don't look yourself today." She started crying. Poor *dab*, I thought, you've got something to cry about, for sure. A cup of tea and she told me all about it. She'd been sleeping in the little bed since Miss Davies came, she said, but it broke and Guto didn't have time to mend it. Oh yes, I thought, I'm sure he hasn't, dirty old *hwrgi*. You'll never believe what she said next, Mamgu Poli. I could hardly credit it! Yes, they're sleeping three in a bed! "*Uffern dân*, Olwen," I said, "it's not possible in this day and age, I can't believe it. Why do you stand for it? It's disgusting, that's what it is, disgusting! Pack your bags, girl, go back home, you don't have to put up with that from any man. Anyway Olwen," I said, "your bed isn't big enough for three." And do you know what she said then? "Oh no, Blodwen," she said, "there's plenty of room, that's not the trouble. There's plenty of room, Guto takes off his wooden leg." Mamgu Poli, don't laugh like that, it's not funny.'

Looking between the floorboards, I saw Mam and Mamgu Poli hanging on to each other, shaking with laughter, tears rolling down their cheeks.

Sunday

F'annwyl Miriam,

What do you make of the news, very upsetting isn't it? Haydn's splashed out and bought a wireless, four valves, glued to it every night he is. And he's ordered the Daily Express, wants to be in the know, he says. Nain and Mr Hopcyn said the last war was supposed to end all wars. Just shows you! Surely this won't come to anything, but Haydn doesn't like the sound of this Hitler chap at all. He reckons Chamberlain's had the wool pulled over his eyes, good and proper. God help us all. I don't know what to think, we'll be caught on the hop anyway. We're not prepared for war, that's a fact. Plenty of men the right age for conscription around here, but Haydn will never pass, I know that. He'll be no good for fighting, Miriam. My brothers will get their calling up papers early, no reserved occupation for carpenters. Our Mam and Dat are not coming down to Haulfre this summer, everything so uncertain like. I feel for our Mam, three sons to worry about. Who's to know what's in front of them? This old world's changing fast, Miriam fach.

Mamgu Poli's leaving early because of the news and I'm thinking of going back with her to see everyone, just in case. It's been grand having her here. Margaret loves her Mamgu Poli. It's stories, stories, nothing but stories when she's about ...

Love from,
Blodwen.

After the trip to Caerfyrddin, Trefor no longer made his passengers alight at the foot of steep hills. He'd somehow unravelled the mystery of the combustion engine, and Mamgu Poli refused to walk anyway. Inspired by Trefor's new-found confidence, she stopped insisting on travelling in groups of three. Our journeys became shorter and more comfortable, but much less exciting.

Although Mam was quiet and preoccupied on our way to the South, I was full of high expectations. We stopped in Lampeter for *tê deg* at the Lion Hotel, and while Mam went to say a quick hello to her aunties in College Road, Mamgu gave me a history lesson. We strolled around the quadrangle of my father's old school, Saint David's College, founded by Bishop Burgess in 1822. It was the oldest degree granting institution in Wales. The Old Building stood partly on the site of the castle where Owain Glyndŵr fought another mighty battle against the English, and a manuscript in the library was still spattered with the blood of the monks of Bangor Is Coed, massacred by the heathen Saxons! Could I see it? Not today!

'After studying here for a few years your father decided he didn't want to be a minister of the Anglican Church, so he went to Llandovery College instead.'

'I didn't know Dad wanted to be a minister. He never goes to Chapel now.'

'That's all in the past, *cariad.* Llandovery is a very good school. Over the entrance it says that learning is better than gold. Quite right, too. Your father liked it there. When I came to see him, I used to stay at the Castle Hotel. And guess what? Once, I slept in Lord Nelson's four-poster bed!'

'Who's Lord Nelson?'

'He was a famous Englishman with very long feet. Come on, here's your Mam. Shall I tell you a story in the car? What about the Lady of the Lake? I know you like that and we'll be passing very close to Llyn-y-Fan-Fach later on.'

I loved Mamgu's dramatic version of the legend about a young man who lived in the Black Mountains. Long ago, he was tending his mother's cattle on the shore of Llyn-y-Fan-Fach. One day, to his astonishment, he saw a beautiful lady sitting on the water, combing her hair. He visited the lake every day, hoping to see her again. When she reappeared, he called out to her and to his delight, she smiled and spoke to him. She was the daughter of the King of the Lake where she lived with her people. They fell in love and the farmer asked the King for his daughter's hand in marriage. He gave his consent, on the strict condition that the young man would never strike his wife with anything made of iron. Even an impatient touch with a mailed glove could mean her return to the Lake, taking her large dowry of cattle, horses, sheep, goats and oxen with her. After a solemn promise from the young man, the couple were married and lived happily on a farm called Esgair Llaethdy, near Myddfai. The farmer kept his word and they had three fine sons. But alas, in time, the third careless touch befell, and his wife disappeared into the lake taking all her stock. Even the little black calf, slaughtered that morning, came back to life and obeyed her call.

> '*A'r llo du bach,*
> *Sydd ar y bach,*
> *Dere dithau yn iach adre'.*'

A team of grey oxen, ploughing in a nearby field, also followed their mistress, making a deep furrow into the lake, where it still remains.

To his great distress, the farmer never saw his wife again but she often appeared to her sons, teaching her eldest, Rhiwallon, great gifts of healing and medicine. He became a renowned physician and the tradition stayed in the family for generations. The fame of the physicians of Myddfai spread throughout Wales and is remembered to this day.

Mamgu explained the significance of being touched by iron. The ancient people feared the coming of the Celts with their superior strength, their horses and their lethal weapons. Iron became a sign of terror for them and they fled to remote places for sanctuary, especially dense forests. That's why we still touch wood for luck! The story with all its details lasted almost to Sennybridge, our stop for dinner.

We drove over the Brecon Beacons, all shifting patterns and colours, with Pen y Fan rising like a gigantic emerald wave. From the top you could look out over fourteen counties! Sheep and ponies grazed on the high moorlands near Ystradfellte and the great standing stones of Madog and Llia. Past Sarn Elen, the Roman road, through Penderyn, down to Hirwaun and Aberdare where the traffic began. I'd never seen so many cars, lorries and big buses. And the noise! Loud clatterings of machinery, trains and hooters, and the constant humming and rumbling from the Deep Duffryn Colliery. The valley floor narrowed at Mountain Ash, leaving little room for the road, railway and river, black as pitch. Mountains rose sharply on either side, slag heaps piling up the slopes. Grey, stone houses perched up high, some streets so steep they ended in steps. Coal dust descended on washing, windows, every nook and cranny but the women took great pride in their homes. Doorsteps and semi-circles of pavement were scoured white with sandstone, and doorknobs and knockers shone with Brasso. It took strength, spirit and humour to live in the Valleys.

We couldn't pass Martha's house without calling to say hello. It was a proper treat, with a cup of tea and a pikelet ready on the hob. Martha, who took in washing to bring in extra money, was wearing a mackintosh apron over her robust figure, her rolled up sleeves showing a hefty pair of forearms. The weather governed the layout of her *gegin fawr*. When it rained, more often than not, four lines around the ceiling dripped with wet clothes. All the furniture was crammed within the waterfall, the table in the centre and look out if you were wearing your best hat! Martha's welcome came from the heart, enough to beat the old drips any day. The table was seldom clear of dishes and delicious pikelets were plonked on any plate devoid of gravy.

'It's only a bit of jam left on this plate, *cariad*, and here's more to go with it. Eat up, there's plenty for a little one. Clean cups for you, ladies, mine's here somewhere. Well, there's lovely to see you. Down tools for a quiet five minutes, is it?'

The talk flowed, giving news of mutual friends and acquaintances. Martha began a vivid description of a recent laying out. She had my undivided attention.

'I think you knew him, Poli. Stan Clock we called him, he had one hand smaller than the other. Eighty-nine he was, big *butties* with

Zac's father, down the pit. Stan's father was killed in the Lancaster in Senghennydd, leaving a house-full of children, remember? Old Stan's always been an awkward customer, gave his wife a hell of a dance he did. Anyway, Mrs Potter and me, we gave him a good wash and put him in his best suit with his watch and chain, all tidy like. But we just couldn't shut his eyes. As soon as we took off the pennies, they kept popping open. It's not very nice, mind, washing a dead man with his eyes open. No indeed! I hope I don't have to go through that again. And his teeth! No hope whatsoever there, we just had to leave them out. But he looked lovely when we finished, all clean and peaceful, even if his eyes were open.

'Then, just as we were leaving the room, he sat up, if you please. Yes, honest to God he did, bolt upright, upsetting everything. We had a devil of a job to get him to lie flat again. As soon as Mrs Potter put his head down, his legs lifted up and vice versa. In the end I said, "Now look here, Stan Clock, we've had enough of this. Awkward to the end you are, but do us a favour now and lie flat for God's sake or we'll be here all day at this rate, playing see-saw!" And do you know, we had no trouble after that. It's the God's honest truth I'm telling you. Lay down like a lamb he did, no bother at all. I don't know what Mr Potter did about the eyes, but closed they were in the coffin. Grand funeral, people came from all over, everyone knew Stan Clock.'

Uncle Zac came home from his shift, black as ink, bringing the smell of the pit and a block of firewood under his arm. A big smile for the visitors, and "Hello, Dewdrop, how's my girl?" before he dragged a round-wooden tub from the scullery to the fire. Martha set up a clothes-horse draped with towels as a screen, and while taking a bath, Zac joined in the conversation. Before leaving, Martha asked us to join her in a prayer for Zac's conversion to the Chapel way of life. This had taken place for many years but she particularly wanted him to stop drinking in the Club on a Sunday morning. As she began her prayer, Zac interrupted with a great belly-laugh.

'Give over, old girl, it's a lost cause. You'll never catch me looking all sanctimonious in the Big Seat. Too late for that, my love, much too late for an old scallywag like me!'

When we arrived at Mamgu Poli's house on the main road, it was time for another cup of tea. Dadcu Jono was out and I could see Mam was relieved. They didn't like each other. There was always frost in the air when they were together. I thought he was a jolly man, full of jokes and laughter, but there were feelings between him and my mother hard for a child to fathom.

Megan, Mamgu's maid, brought tea to the upstairs parlour, where slanting sunlight caught the crystal lampshades, making rainbows. Mamgu had electric light in her house, upstairs and down! A large, ebony sideboard along one wall displayed pretty china dishes, its looking glass reflecting the crystal rainbows in another, over the fireplace. Sitting at the Pembroke table pouring tea from a silver pot, Mamgu Poli was surrounded by dancing, coloured lights. Never a tea drinker, I was delighted with a glass of orange Tizer pop, an unusual treat. The women laughed, heads close together in the dazzling room.

Mamgu Davies and my Aunties, May and Eluned were waiting at their door in Thomas Street with Shotty, the grey and white spaniel. The women, very happy to be together, had a good cry to get it over with before the men came home. My grandmother had a special welcome for me, her only grandchild. She was a reserved, compassionate woman with warm brown eyes and dark hair drawn into a low bun. I thought she and my mother looked very alike, except for Mam's deep hazel eyes. Seeing it was summer, Mamgu Davies wore a navy-blue frock with white piping. In winter, she favoured black and cream. There couldn't have been a greater contrast between my two grandmothers, in character and appearance. My Aunties, their dark hair Marcel waved, were wearing fashionable clothes, pale stockings and high-heels like Ceri. Aunty May was noted for buying quality clothes. Took her shopping very seriously, my Aunty May.

A feeling of peace and order filled the house, from the polished passage with its brown Lincrusta dado, to the spotless kitchen. The hushed parlour contained a piano, seldom played, and a much-used quilting frame. Mamgu and the Aunties were accomplished needlewomen. Their handiwork could be seen everywhere; embroidered linens, delicate crochet, fine lace, and satin cushions and eiderdowns, worked in Italian quilting. I liked the pictures of crinoline ladies framed with passe-partout. In the middle room, the dresser's glass-fronted cupboards displayed six tea-sets, the cups and saucers balanced one on top of the other. Nine painted jugs hung from the centre shelves which held three large willow pattern plates. Two Staffordshire dogs shared the board with family photographs. Dadcu had built a lean-too scullery between his house and his neighbour's, very modern, with running water, a bosh, or sink and a copper for washing clothes. Always referrred to as the glass-house, the slate floor was snow-white, scrubbed and slagged on Monday, newspapers down until Tuesday!

We prepared tea with fresh butter, cheese, ham and eggs brought from the farm. The tomatoes Mamgu and I picked from the tall, glass box on the back wall were tastier than usual, due to the prolonged hot weather. Although Dadcu's work-shed took up most of the space, Mamgu kept a very pretty garden.

'I still miss our garden in Llain-Goch. My sister Hannah and I grew flowers in a small patch by the gate. I've always liked growing things, ever since I was a little girl your age.'

'Did you really want to come to the South, Mamgu?'

'Your Dadcu and I wanted a family and a home of our own. There was very little chance of that down the country when we were young. Dadcu had a good job here building houses, and it seemed an exciting thing to do at the time.'

'Did you like it when you first came?'

'It was a big shock, *merch fach*, I couldn't believe it. All that noise! And the dust! Everything you touched was covered in it! Sticky, black dust! I got used to it in time, but I missed my family more than I can say. It was easier when I learnt English. Never been comfortable with it, mind you. We were very lucky to have such good neighbours, the Berrys first and now the Jameses. Other families came from Llambed, many of them old friends. That made things a lot better. We used to meet in each other's houses for Sunday services. When the numbers grew, we started collecting for our own chapel. Eventually, we had enough money to build Bethel Chapel in Glyngwyn Street. Your Dadcu was one of the carpenters. I'll never forget that first Sunday. A chapel of our own at last. We were all very proud, I can tell you, all friends together.'

'I don't think I'd like to live here all the time. We've got a really big garden at home. Why don't you come and see it, then we could grow things together?'

'I'll come one day.'

'Soon?'

'Perhaps.'

Dadcu and my Uncles arrived home from work in their dark blue carpenter's overalls, each with a fat pencil behind one ear. Laughter and greetings filled the house as we sat at the table. The eldest son, Ifor, quiet like his mother, shared his dark colouring with his youngest brother, Teify. Glyn was the only child to inherit Dadcu's grey eyes. They teased their sisters and me throughout the good-humoured meal. Teify, the favourite in the family, always laughed the most. As everyone talked nineteen to the dozen, Mamgu and Dadcu exchanged understanding looks. They were a loving couple, devoted to their home and family. Bringing the old, rural values with them to the South, they remained faithful to the language and the Chapel.

The conversation soon turned to the war. Uncle Ifor and Glyn were expecting their call-up papers from the Army, any day. I was encouraged to go over the fence to visit Mr and Mrs James and their children, little Eluned and David, old friends and neighbours. Mrs James was warm-hearted and cheerful, refusing to be daunted by Mr James' debilitating illness. He suffered from silicosis through working down the pit, and some days he couldn't move from his chair. Whatever the hardships, there was always a good welcome in Number Seven.

On Saturday, the Aunties and Uncles took my mother to Cardiff for a day out and I joined Dadcu in his shed at the end of the garden. It was a friendly place with the warm smell of sawdust, a glue-pot on the stove and rows of gleaming tools along the walls. Dadcu, being a good listener, had many visitors dropping in for a chat during the day. In later years I spent hours there myself, asking his advice and taking comfort from his understanding words. He was a wise, considerate man, seldom ruffled, and I loved him dearly.

Eluned next door and Catherine Berry appeared after dinner to play in the street. We tried to persuade Shotty to join us, but he rarely left Mamgu's side. The girls and I were much of an age and although my English was poor, we readily understood our own world. Come on, off to see the sights. Up Thomas Street and Llanwonno Road to the mountain, down Rocky Road to the Trip, Pengeulan School steps, Penrhiwceiber Road and the Co-op. They dragged me away from the window displays to go to the Miskin, up Mount Pleasant Terrace to the park and the swings. Then, hide and seek in the *gwlies* behind the houses, before playing hopscotch on the rare piece of flat ground outside Mamgu's back door.

'Ask your Mam if you can stay longer and we'll go to the Fish's Tail, and Llanwanno Church to see Guto Nyth Brân's grave.'

'Did he have two wives?'

'No, but he could run faster than any horse.'

'He ran all the way to Ponty and back while the kettle was boiling!'

'His mother clapped him on the back to say good boy, and he dropped dead through lack of breath.'

'He was a proper champion was Guto Nyth Brân.'

At Catherine's house in Mount Pleasant Terrace, Mrs Berry made us the best toast, on a fork in front of the fire with lashings of butter. We shared it with Ernie and Jean, Catherine's elder brother and sister. Mrs Berry was spirited and courageous, one of a special band of women found in the Valleys. She and her husband were trusted friends, and my father was particularly fond of Ike Berry. He often told vivid stories about his work underground. I liked the one about his horse, Apple, and how Mr Berry knew he was trouble the first time he set eyes on him.

'Strong devil he was, new to underground. Wicked in the eye. I thought I'd have a word like, let him know who was boss. Soon as I was close enough, the bugger bit me through my ear, blood all over the place. Right, I said, if it's a fight you want, here goes, and I bit a chunk out of his ear for starters! Stood there he did, and looked me straight in the eye for minutes on end. We understood each other after that, not a scrap of bother between us since. He's my best *butty*, is Apple. That horse is a miracle, I can tell you, knows when there's trouble, quick as lightening. If Apple lays his ears back and starts clicking his nashers, it's time to move, *boyos*. Saved me more than once he has. Couldn't be without him, old Apple. We do look after each other see. When it's time for him to go up top, I tell him about it, prepare him. It's like this, I tell him, you'll be going out of the dark soon so don't go mad like some do when they see the light, you could do yourself some damage. Be steady, old *butty*. I put the lamp closer and closer to his face, right up to his eyes for about a week before. He knows, and when he goes up, cool as a cucumber he is. Got a good brain on him that horse, cleverer than most people I know!'

I'd had a grand time, as black as your hat and tired out, pavements being much harder than fields. Back at the house, there were lovely presents from Cardiff, a leather shoulder bag and a green autograph book with gilt-edged pages. We had to start it at once! The Uncles drew a Wall of Friendship on a double page and we spent the evening signing our names with special verses and messages.

May your life be like a snowflake,
Leave a mark but not a stain!

For supper, Aunty Eluned and I took our basins to buy fish and chips from the shop on the corner. I was amazed at the vast, gleaming fryer, the loud hissing as the potatoes hit smoking fat, just like an explosion! The street outside still teemed with life. Miners, past and present, leant against the railings chewing twist, spitting with deadly accuracy into the gutter. Some were on their way to work, their eyes permanently ringed with smudged, black circles. Gangs of children played whip and top near the closed down furniture shop, and hob-nailed boots rang on hopscotch pavements. Several men sang in harmony as they walked up the Trip, arms around each other's shoulders. Outside the grocer's, a woman scrubbed the step while another cleaned the upstairs window, sitting precariously on the outside sill. Others stood in their doorways, arms folded, having a good *clonc*. Half a dozen children screamed in the *gwli* behind the houses, no shoes to their feet! Never go near that scabby lot, said Aunty, they live in Hellfire Farm! Hooters sounded, wheels hummed and a train rattled down the

Lower Level. Didn't anyone ever go to sleep around here?

Before leaving for Chapel on Sunday morning, the women pre-pared dinner, putting a joint of meat in the oven along with an enormous, delicious, rice pudding. The polished table was laid in the middle room, the leaves pulled out to their full extent.

Ten of us, including Eluned next door, walked down the Miskin, Mamgu in navy-blue, the sisters in linen suits and pretty blouses, Eluned and I in floral dresses and halo hats. The four men in the rear were brushed and polished fit for the King. We were joined by Mrs Berry and her children, Joan and the Wilson family and Margaret Evans, who received a big wink from my uncle Teify. On we marched, a formidable group, all carrying black hymn-books under the arm!

A large congregation sang with *hwyl* and verve to the rich tones of a pipe organ. Thank goodness the sermon was short, as Mam spent ages after the service talking to old friends. Finally, '*dewch 'nawr, ferched*', from Dadcu, 'the dinner will be burnt.' After Sunday school in the afternoon and Chapel again in the evening, family friends gathered for supper in Mamgu's *gegin fawr*. I enjoyed the remains of the rice pudding with the top of the milk, sitting under the wall clock, by the pantry door. The clock once had a carved eagle on the top, removed by Dadcu on his return from the Great War. The only time I ever saw Dadcu angry was when he spoke of his hatred for the war and being away from his family. A law-abiding man, the Military Police had to escort him back to the barracks at the end of every leave.

As the evening wore on, the atmosphere became subdued. Goodbyes were near. Mam was very quiet when we went to bed. No stories tonight, *cariad*.

Love from Blodwen

F'annwyl Miriam,

... Seth and Ita are getting married after all, things being as they are. The bans are up already. He'll be called up soon, no doubt, and Ita will be in Cnwc by herself then. Can't see her being happy on her own when her family leave as well. She's used to company and travelling different places. But 'ware teg, she wants to be in one place for Seth to come home to. God help, what's in front of us, I don't know. Anyway, the wedding will be their happy day, they've waited long enough.

Haydn and I are taking her to the registry office, and Seth's going with Evan Pritchard in his new lorry. They've got to have a marriage certificate, see, but Ita says the proper wedding will be on the rhos in the evening. Everyone's welcome, she said, but I can't see many going. It's a bit awkward, between you and me, they thought Seth would be married in Chapel. There's talk about it. Anyway, our Margaret can't wait. Dressing up every day she is, full of it, like a cat on hot bricks. Ita's persuaded Col to go, she and Col are big butties. Should be an eye opener, mind you, never been to a gypsy wedding before. Don't know what to expect quite, do you? Very exciting really, isn't it?

There's heavy this old weather is, Miriam, too hot for me anyway, I'm fagged out. I hope it will stay fine for the wedding though...

Love from,
Blodwen.

M am woke me early on the day of the wedding. There was plenty to do before nine o'clock, all hands on deck, if you please. A row of polished shoes stood under the window and the *gegin fawr* was as clean as a new pin. Dad and Col were sprucing up the van, draping floral curtains over the worn seats and tying white ribbons on the front. I helped Mam carry mountains of food to the table, giving Mrs Morris' beautiful iced cake pride of place. Everything was covered in a white, muslin cloth, to be unveiled as a little treat on their return from Aberteifi. My father bought sherry for the occasion and Nain provided glittering glasses.

My mother was all flustered when the time came to dress up in her best navy edge to edge coat and powder-blue, crepe-de-chine frock. With her matching hat, marcasite brooch and earrings, she was a proper sight for sore eyes, according to Dad. Hear! Hear! from Col and me, saying nothing for the silk stockings and high-heeled shoes, borrowed from Ceri for the day. Dad was well up to scratch too, in his black jacket, pin-stripe trousers, stiff white collar and Anthony Eden hat. They looked so posh, it could have been their wedding. I wished I could go, but everyone knew a registry office was no place for a child. Col and I were told to hold the fort until they came back, making sure the kettle was on the boil.

We followed the van up the school hill and stood watching from the twmp. It was a tender, cloudless morning, the sun shining along the valley making the river sparkle behind the *vardos*. Overnight, spiderlings had woven sheets of gossamer in the reeds, stretching to the bend beyond the trees. Gold and silver, a perfect day for a wedding.

The gypsy family, dressed in dark clothes, stood in the clearing waiting for the bride. Ita stepped out of the *vardo*, slim as a flower in a simple, cream frock, her black hair drawn into a knot beneath a Juliet cap. Intricate, silver jewellery adorned her neck and wrist, and she carried a posy from Mr Hopcyn's garden. She was beautiful. They all walked slowly up the track towards us and by the gate, Ita kissed her mother and Dado placed her hand on my father's arm. The bride was escorted to the van and, waving, they drove away. When the family returned to the camp, Col and I were left alone. His eyes were full of tears. Hand-in-hand, we walked back home.

Most of the village women gathered in front of the shop to throw confetti and make a big fuss of the bride and groom. They both looked very shy, so it was a cup of tea and food to bolster the spirit! Ita and Seth were delighted with the wedding breakfast, and Dad and Mr Morris made short speeches of congratulations. Seth said a lovely thank you before leaving to join Ita's family. We watched them cross the bridge, arms linked.

'God be with them,' said Nain quietly.

'And keep them safe in these troubled times,' added Mr Hopcyn.

A wistfulness fell over the gathering and Mrs Davies and Mrs Thomas dabbed their eyes.

'Come on now, no room for gloomy thoughts today,' said Mam, 'it's a wedding we're celebrating here. Plenty to eat inside, I can't be left with all that food on the table. In we go, and I'll tell you about the ceremony. It was very nice, but a bit on the dry side. We'll make up for that tonight, I'm sure!'

In the early evening, an exciting tempo of violins, accordions and pipes came from the *rhos*. We crossed the bridge, Col trailing behind. At the *twmp*, I couldn't believe my eyes! During the day, many brightly painted vardos had arrived on the back road, to form a large circle by the river. Horses grazed nearby and crowds of children and dogs ran around the fires, tables, stools, cushions and quilts. Young Romany women in long, bright skirts and embroidered blouses, wore coloured ribbons in their glossy hair and flashing jewellery on their necks and wrists. Most of the men were dressed in black, their short jackets sewn about with silver.

I was captivated, entranced. Below me lay everything my imagination craved from the exotic, colourful land of our dream-play on the rock. I ran headlong down the slope to be swept high into the air by Seth. Ita gave us a fine, warm welcome, placing garlands of flowers around our necks as she led us to sit beside her *vardo*. We weren't quite sure of ourselves in the company of these strong, reserved people but Ita, looking lovelier than ever in her silken, gypsy clothes, just laughed and kissed my mother.

'I told you it would be a special day, my little *rakli*. Come on, let's dance.'

She whirled me about in my swishy, gypsy skirt and I was in seventh heaven. Children and dogs joined in as we spun and jumped, intoxicated by the music and the joyous sense of freedom. Dilys and Ceri were having a good time, dancing with Seth's friends from the high farms, but there was nobody else from the village. When Ita and Seth danced together, we stood aside, feeling their happiness spreading through us.

The gypsy wedding had taken place in the late afternoon, witnessed only by the Romany families. Ita had described it to me many times. During the morning, her brothers made a large broom of sticks and twigs, placing it on the ground within the circle of caravans. For the ceremony, Ita's parents stood on one side, the bride and groom on the other. Ma and Dado sprinkled salt and breadcrumbs over Ita and Seth, who held hands and jumped over the broom three times. A great shout went up from the crowd and the music began. They were married! Ita and Seth were together at last.

When a generous feast of meat, fish, fruit, cakes, beer and wine was laid out on the tables, Mam's eyes were like saucers. Ita teased her saying the meat was baked *hitchiwotchi* – hedgehog! Anything as long as it wasn't rabbit, I thought to myself.

At sunset, glorious colours spread across the sky, out towards the sea. Flaming reds, deep indigos and gold added to the magic of that rare evening. It was a good omen. The music quickened and the dancing began once more, with everyone joining in, young and old. Even Mam and Dad had a few twirls and when Dad had to sit down, Seth took over, making Mam blush. Col was nowhere to be seen as I sat with my parents watching the party swirl about us.

'I wish Mamgu Poli was here.'

'Yes, *bach,* she'd be in her oils. Loves dancing she does. Her father used to have big parties when she was a girl, two or three times a year. You'll have to ask her about it. She didn't want to miss this wedding, but it can't be helped. We can't see into the future, can we?'

'Ita can.'

'Yes, I know that, but she can't see everything, can she? Things don't always go pat, you know, just as you want them. We can write to Mamgu, you'll have plenty to tell her about tonight. We'll never forget it, will we? A night to remember, yes indeed. *Diwedd mawr,* look at Ceri, I don't know where she gets her energy. Been dancing for hours she has, and Dilys. Never seen her so lively! Looks really pretty she does, all pink in the face. Should do this more often, jolly the place up a bit. I don't know what they'd make of it in the village though. I said not many would come, didn't I, Haydn?'

'I don't think they've missed it completely. I'm sure I saw Ifor Thomas, Siencyn and Rhodri on the *twmp* a while ago. Look, there's Wil Morris and Dai Davies strolling along there now. I bet the women aren't far away.'

Lamps were lit outside the *vardos* and candles in jam jars hung from the low branches of nearby trees. The moon came up and strong, thrilling voices started singing in Romany. A man sang to a lonely violin with a longing almost too sad to bear. When the story telling began, Dad went to find Col. He returned swiftly, whispering urgently to my mother. I heard every word.

'I found Col down by the river. There's something wrong, Blodwen, he's in a sort of trance, flinging himself about and spinning in circles. He fell and when I tried to help him, he pushed me away, very roughly. Not like him at all. I can't do anything with him. He'll listen to you, I'll take you down, but prepare yourself, it's a disturbing sight. Margaret, you stay here. No, you stay here until we come back and not a word to anyone. We don't want to spoil the party. You understand, don't you?'

I understood well enough, but I disobeyed. Creeping behind the caravans, I followed them to the river. In the firelight, a wild figure spun and tumbled, in and out of the shadows, running, falling, rolling on the ground. It was strange and horrible, like a demon in the night. I felt sick. What was happening to my dear friend? Come back, Col, come back! Don't leave me!

My mother started running, but we weren't alone. Ita's Ma was watching. Best to leave him alone, she told my parents calmly. A man so full of sorrow and pain needed to be in a world of his own. When it was over, she would give him a drink to make him sleep and then he'd be with us again. It happened just as she predicted. After a while, Col fell to the ground, Ma brought him a drink, covered him with a quilt and soon he was fast asleep.

Mam found me in a fearful state. Too concerned to chastise, she assured me Col was fine after his bit of a fit, I wasn't to worry. Dad sat with him until he woke, with no outward sign of his strange behaviour. But the magic was gone. It was time to go home. We walked down the road, narrow with late summer flowers and grasses. I could smell the sun-baked grain behind the hedges and the mist gathering on the river. Mam and I waited at the bottom of the hill, near the gate to Cnwc. The music was wilder and quicker, now the gypsies were on their own, the singing unfamiliar and haunting, from a distant, ancient time. Dad emerged from the deep shadow into the moonlight with Col holding his hand like a child. I felt a shock run through my mother. Without a word, we joined them, all holding hands as we walked over the bridge to the house. In the blink of an eye, something had changed.

Dad and I were late up the following morning. We entered the *gegin fawr* to find Mam standing stockstill, staring into space, her hand pressed to her lips.

'Blodwen, what's wrong?'

'I thought you all needed a lie in, but something's just struck me. Col didn't make a sound last night!'

A cold fear filled our minds. Col's strange behaviour had a legacy after all. My heart lurched and a metallic taste filled my mouth. *'Iesu Grist, aros gyda ni,'* Mam's prayer filled the dreadful silence.

The rattle of wooden rings made us jump! Col came down the stairs still dressed in his best suit, his cap firmly in place, the garland of flowers around his neck, brown and crushed. He crossed the room to my mother, took her hand and kissed it. And then he spoke!

'Thank you very much for looking after me all this time' he said, in English!

We stared at him in complete disbelief. Col could speak? After years of silence, Col could speak? Mam sat down suddenly, tears streaming, saying 'Col *bach*,' over and over. Dad was the first to recover, I'd never seen him make a cup of tea so fast. We sat at the table marvelling at the sound of Col's voice, low and gruff.

Not much was done that Sunday and Mam and I didn't go to Chapel once. We even had sandwiches for dinner! Mam was wanged

out, she said, fit for nothing. An anxious Mrs Thomas knew something exceptional was happening, not to be asked over the doorstep.
We sat around the fire and Col told us his story. It wasn't very long,
he said, he wanted to forget most of it. He spoke haltingly, in short
sentences, still using his hands in the old, expressive way.

His name was Stanley Collins, born in Wexford, Ireland, about
fifty-six years before, the youngest son of a large family. When he
was six or seven, his mother died. The family was split up and he
went with his two elder brothers, who were perhaps fourteen and
fifteen. They moved from place to place looking for work, sometimes begging, hungry all the time. Hundreds were in the same
state, slowly starving to death. His brothers desperately wanted to
earn enough money to go to America. Failing to do so, they became
human ballast on a collier ship returning to Barry, South Wales. His
brothers worked for Ocean Coal on the docks and railways, then the
canals, the buildings, any work they could find.

It was a harsh, unrelenting life, but they had each other, and they
looked after their small brother until he could join them in work. For
some time, they lived around Ethel Street and Saint Paul's in Cardiff,
along with hundreds of their countrymen. Work became harder to
find, and finally, they travelled to the Valleys, with the pits the only
option. All three had a horror of being underground, especially Col,
who, at about ten, was old enough to earn his living. He worked deep
down, mostly alone and terrified.

'Hated underground, I did. Yes, I did. No place for man or beast.
Didn't like the dark and the stink. On my own, working the doors.
Glad to see a rat for company, too many though. Awful noises.
Rumblings. Water dripping. Cracking props. Spooky for us kids, see.
Wanted to run. Stay put, my brothers said. Do as you're told. That's
what I did. Didn't have to like it, did I? Some nice men, some nasty.
Plenty of fetchers from them! Got trapped down there once. Had a
bad pull after that. Dreams. Long time ago now. Never get me down
there again. No. Never.'

They lived in a derelict house on the Merthyr Mountain. Col was
eleven or twelve when diphtheria swept through the Aberdare Valley,
leaving both his brothers dead. He wanted to forget all that, he said.

Away from the dreaded pits, he headed for the country. During those early years, he learnt he was somehow different, attracting ridicule and abuse. He chose not to speak, and silence became a protection, a way of making life tolerable. For a time, he lived with the gypsies on the Usk, near Abergavenny. Further west, he worked on the farms where he began to understand Welsh.

Many years later, Col passed through the Aberdare Valley once more, and in Mamgu Poli's shop, he heard Mrs Berry lamenting her friend's departure for Sîr Aberteifi. She spoke warmly of my mother's kindness and how she never turned anyone away in need of help. Listening to the chorus of agreement, he decided to find Blodwen. It didn't take long. He met two tramps on the road, Twm Aberdâr and old John McGrae. They told him to look for the chalk circles which indicated a generous house. They soon led to our house. It wasn't by chance he found Mam milking in the yard.

Col told his sad story impassively, almost indifferently, with few details and even fewer explanations. Mam and I were crying like the rain and Dad was swallowing hard. It was the longest speech Col ever made in our hearing. Our old habit of communication didn't alter much over the years, and he never spoke Welsh to anyone except me. We grew even closer as his child-like nature became more apparent. Dad taught him how to read and write and he and I spent hours, laboriously practising joined-up writing between four spaced lines. Col took great pleasure in the task, proudly keeping his pages in the big desk. Gradually, after the remarkable events of those few days, our family life took on its familiar rhythms, with one exception. Col no longer cried out in the night.

Love from Blodwen

F'annwyl Miriam,

I just don't know where to start, fy hen ffrind, it's hard to believe what's happened here. I'm sure you must have heard by now that Col can speak. What a shock, Miriam fach. All these years with not a gec, and then to talk, and in English too. It gave us a turn, I can tell you. Won't get over it in a hurry either.

What a few days we've had, my head is still spinning like a top. The wedding was lovely, like a picture book, but I'll have to tell you face to face about the rest. Col bach, he was cut in two. I've guessed this long time, mind you.

Love from,

Blodwen.

Part Two

September 1939 to April 1943

Chapter Seven

Sunday
September 3rd, 1939

F'annwyl Miriam,

What a dreadful day, a day the world will regret for sure. But too late now. We heard Chamberlain on the wireless at a quarter past eleven this morning. There's news on the hour, every hour until midnight. The King will be speaking at six o'clock. My dear brothers will be called up straight away. I'm so glad I went up to see them. Miriam fach, I can't get them off my mind, especially our Mam. Very quiet here today, nobody about. Mr Emrys is calling a special prayer meeting in Chapel tonight for guidance for the government. See you on Thursday.

Love from,
Blodwen.

On Saturday nights, the men gathered in the shop for the nine o'clock news. Their worst fears were realised on September the first, when Hitler invaded Poland. Britain and France declared war on Germany on September the third. The outside world had come to the village. My first days at school were overshadowed by preparations for an invasion by the enemy, probably by parachute. Who was the enemy anyway? Ianto called them the Hun. Was that the name of Mamgu Poli's hordes from the sea? It became compulsory to carry a gas mask at all times, an ugly thing in a cardboard box with a green, rainproof cover. Hanging on a strap across the chest, it bounced clumsily, always in the way. When we practised wearing it every morning at school, Rhodri almost fainted from the heavy smell of rubber, they could keep the gas. Left to our own devices, we frightened each other to death, leaping out from unlikely places, prancing about like demented, miniature elephants.

Several times a week, we took cover from pretend air raids. After being alerted by telephone, Dad sounded the siren and the school and village made for the dugouts. Mr Llywelyn and Miss Jones kept us in strict order and after struggling with our gas masks, we marched up the hill behind the building, class by class. Unfortunately, the see-through panel in the masks quickly steamed over, resulting in complete chaos. We made the most of it, generally behaving in a witless fashion, until, after weeks of uninterrupted calm, the routine was abandoned. In the event of imminent occupation, each child unable to reach his home was to be billeted in the village. The big boys made raucous comments. Who wanted to end up with the sanctimonious Elias Rhys or the starchy Misses Bowen? Perhaps Guto was looking for another wife? Not in front of Mr Llywelyn, of course, one eye on the *jini fedw* on the mantlepiece!

My father was recruited as Head Air Raid Warden before the outbreak of war. It seemed a sensible idea, in spite of his health, seeing nobody else wanted to answer the telephone. He received a white tin hat, a silver badge, an armband, a siren and a stirrup pump, which was very useful for watering the garden. Our shop became the information centre of the village, with Dad as interpreter, form filler, accountant and owner of the best wireless. Gas masks, ration books and petrol coupons arrived for distribution and in October, everyone was issued with an Identity Card. Inspectors arrived to check the dugouts, the wearing of gas masks and the blackout. Strangers told independent, self-reliant people how to run their lives and officials from the Ministry of Agriculture, the *War Ags,* interfered with age-old farming practices and customs. Voices were raised in anger on Saturday nights. Samson, said Ianto, predicted the end of life as we knew it. Samson wasn't far from the truth.

'I remember farmers being let down by the Government after the First World War. Young men left the land in droves. Talk about depression, we could hardly keep body and soul together. Same old promises now. *Jawl erioed,* how can we trust them again?'

'I had some jumped up chap in shoes traipsing around my farm yesterday, saying I had to plough up my best grass for potatoes. Not suitable I said. Dig for Victory is one thing, but planting the wrong crop in the wrong place is another. Might as well talk to the wall!'

'I don't want to reduce my herd, spent years building it up, and now all they want is cereals, cereals, cereals! Where will it end?'

'Look at the price of feed! And we'll have to pay through the nose for this artificial fertiliser stuff.'

Arguments raged, the younger men praising the introduction of good subsidies and guaranteed markets. Evan Pritchard was getting a Ford tractor.

'Think it over, it could be a lot worse. At least the Ministry officials are farmers from the locality. They know the land and they'll see sense. We'll make a few bob, labourers' wages will go up and machinery will mean more production. I'm all for modernisation and this is our chance.'

'It's all right for you, *boyo*. You've got a few bob already and more land than anyone in this room. You can talk! Not so good for the rest of us.'

'Is this artificial insemination idea modern enough for you, Evan? Cut down the use of your prize bull, that will.'

Dad said it was my bedtime, Mam was calling.

Good weather meant farm work was well in hand, leaving time to organise the Local Defence Volunteers. Men between fifteen and sixty-five, not eligible for the Forces, had already enrolled. Evan Pritchard was elected leader, in a meeting in the shop. Right and proper, being Nain's son and the owner of a good lorry. Dad became Communications Officer with Ifor Thomas as Second-in-Command, Wil Morris as Supplies Officer, Dai Davies as Weapons Officer and Mr Llywelyn in charge of administration.

The first marshalling of the troops took place on a lovely Saturday evening, in front of the shop. Women sauntered casually on false errands to watch the turn out, and Col and I sat on the gate to see which way the wind blew. About thirty men turned up carrying pitch-forks and pick handles. The promised uniforms and weapons never did arrive, leaving only tin hats, armbands and goggle-eyed gas masks. Instant suffocation prevented Dad wearing his but in spite of steaming up, the others persevered. In the ensuing confusion, Samson and Pedro circled the staggering men, barking loudly. The women, showing very little tact, started laughing. Mr Elias Rhys gave an icy glare as muffled oaths left the lips of the most respectable of men. A good thing Mr Emrys wasn't present to witness his flock's fall from grace. Refusing to be ridiculed by the women, the younger men started drifting away.

'Won't be any time for fighting with you old stagers falling about. We'll be too busy putting you lot back on your feet. You're not supposed to be here if you're over sixty-five. Have some mercy on the rest of us,' said Mic from Brynfa. 'Old Haw-Haw would love to see our magnificent, fighting force.'

Ianto lost his rag, throwing down his mask. 'And what the hell do you lot know about fighting the Hun? Get the cradle marks off your backsides before criticising your elders. Clear off, before I set my dog on you and don't come back. We can do without your sort. We'll get the police out if you're not careful. They'll give cheeky louts like you short shrift. Clear out of it.'

They mooched off, laughing and mocking. Then the women started! Nain was the first.

'We'll all be dead in our beds before you lot get your clogs on.'

'Like a bit of help there, boys? Jemima Nichols to the rescue-girls, show your red petticoats!'

'What was that you said, Mr Rhys? Can't hear you preaching behind your gas mask.'

'We'll never hear the siren in our house anyway, Dat snores like a horse.'

'Who's going to help Guto when it comes to running then? Any volunteers, ladies?'

'Come on, we'll have a nice cup of tea, then we'll show them a thing or two.'

'Can you wait a bit for a few lessons, or shall we start straight away? Speak up.'

Siencyn was rattled beyond endurance. Not well disposed towards women at the best of times, he took shelter in his shed as fast as his short legs could carry him. Mr Hopcyn enjoyed the spectacle, but it was the first and last Local Defence Volunteers parade in the village. They either trained in secret or gave up altogether.

The teaching of First Aid was more popular and for the purpose, a pretty, plump woman came from Aberteifi. Besi didn't think much of her, but Guto leapt on the table in a flash to demonstrate putting splints on a broken leg! One afternoon, we listened patiently to a perfect stranger, earnestly explaining how to convert our *cwch* under the stairs into a bomb shelter.

My father expected the code-word for an invasion at any hour. Unfortunately, the telephone could only be heard downstairs. Col volunteered to sleep in the *gegin fawr,* knowing that Dad would never survive a night on the *sgiw.* Two intervening doors to the phone room were left open, but the third, to the barn, was in poor repair. We were regularly disturbed by Col and Pedro chasing rats in the small hours. Mam was not pleased.

'*Uffern dân*, Col, an air raid would be less trouble than you clumping about! You're making enough noise to wake the countryside. Shut those doors and come upstairs to bed. If they're not dropping bombs anywhere else, why should they choose our village?'

'We have to be on alert in case the code-word comes. That's orders!' said my father.

'What's the code-word, Dad?'

'Never you mind, bat ears, that's top secret.'

The phone never rang, the doors were closed and Col returned to his bed.

War became a distant threat and Rhodri and I were preoccupied with our first days at school. I wasn't very enthusiastic as, brushed and polished, we crossed the bridge, escorted by Pedro. The room was filled with children between six and twelve years of age, seated at double wooden desks. I knew most of them from Chapel and Mam's school dinners. Miss Jones, the infants' teacher, showed the new pupils to their places, small boys on the left, girls in the centre and big boys on the right. I sat next to Nesta, a pretty, cheerful girl from a large family in Tan y Groes. We became good friends, and she often stayed at our house during term time. I learnt a great deal from Nesta, her calm, patient ways showing up my fits of selfish bossiness. She and Rhodri bore my numerous lapses with grace and good humour.

Mr Llywelyn ap Llywelyn addressed the school, welcoming newcomers and outlining his expectations for the future. He insisted on high standards of honesty and courtesy, glancing significantly at the cane on the mantelpiece, although I never once saw it used. Mr Llywelyn's appearance was enough to keep order, with his powerful build, intense gaze, and eloquent eyebrows. Educated and cultured, he was highly respected in the village, and in school, his word was law. On weekdays, he wore a hairy, ginger, tweed suit and waistcoat with highly polished, brown boots.

After assembly, the room was divided by a partly glazed partition on runners; junior classes with Miss Jones on one side, seniors and Mr Llywelyn on the other. The fire behind the brass and wire guard was stoked to a good blaze, slates were distributed and my formal education began.

My school days were undistinguished. I sat in the middle row and received middling marks. I already knew how to read and write but I had great difficulty with arithmetic. Figures always remained unfathomable to me, except for long division. My sums were rarely correct but I liked the pattern on the slate. I earned the reputation of being a dreamer, sometimes *mitching* off to my river hide-out after dinner. However, I was always present on the afternoons Mr Llywelyn taught Welsh history and literature. His skill lay in story telling, from the ancient tales of the Celts and the high Kings of the *Mabinogion* to those of our latter-day kings and princes, Llywelyn Mawr, Hywel Dda and Owain Glyndŵr. Mamgu Poli said he was a real Welsh patriot, on fire for the language and the culture. That's how I always thought of Mr Llywelyn. On fire, deep down! As he prowled around the room, dramatizing his stories, his face glowed, his eyes flashed and his ginger suit bristled and glinted. I was spellbound. Spellbound by the pageantry, the colour, the texture of his words. Even though education opened many doors, he beseeched us never to forsake our rich, poetic language for the thinness of English. As he spoke, I had a feeling that many things taught in that room would be a mystery to me, but never Llywelyn ap Llywelyn's stories!

Another highlight was a visit from our sturdy, exuberant school nurse. After inspecting each head for nits, she stood before the fire delivering a lecture on personal hygiene. Struggling not to laugh, we waited with bated breath. Sure enough, a few minutes later, she raised the back of her skirt to warm her bottom. Our interest in handwashing and teeth brushing waned at the sight of her voluminous, pink, fleecy-lined bloomers!

Throughout the autumn, the changes in our daily lives continued, not all of them for the worse. Food and petrol rationing promised more trade for the shop, recently depleted by the use of the Friday bus. The compulsory registration of ration books with a retailer was in our favour, ours being the only shop for miles! We didn't exactly suffer a shortage of food but margarine appeared on the counter for the first time. *Ach a fi!* Dad and Col spent ages sharpening razor blades inside jam jars. Blackout rules were enforced with the onset of winter with no light showing from sunset to sunrise. Although firmly shuttered against the dark and the cold, Dad and Col patrolled the village for a while, to be on the safe side. Hoods were placed on headlamps, torches were masked with tissue paper and everyone moaned about the price of candles. Evening service was taken in the vestry but low lighting was allowed for Christmas, in chapels, churches and shops.

That winter was the coldest we ever experienced in the village.

One morning, waking to a brilliant world, I felt I was breathing light inside a vast ball of shimmering, magical colour. Snow had drifted over the windows and long, glittering icicles hung from the shootings. It was completely silent with no wind, no bird-song, no river sounds.

The men took days to dig out the houses and clear a path to Besi's, the School House and Cnwc. Food was plentiful and melted snow provided water. Ita was alone, Seth being one of the first to be called up to the Army. Col uncovered the front of her little house which had almost disappeared under heavy drifts. He stacked extra wood near her door and brought Asia down to join Dan in our barn. It was Col's domain that winter, a warm Noah's Ark crowded with ducks, chickens, horses and cows. There were birds in the rafters and farm cats, driven inside for food and shelter, kept away the rats. Dividing doors to the cow shed were left open and I helped Col feed the animals and spread clean straw. He kept a sharp eye on decreasing stocks, knowing feed prices would surely rise in the spring.

Our cows were fed dark-brown, sweet-smelling nuggets of linseed cake, kept in large barrels in the far corner. One evening, I found a cat asleep in the scoop. Picking it up by the scruff of the neck, I placed it gently on the ground. It made a strange sound. In the gloom, I saw I was inches away from a very big rat. Past advice ran through my head, never corner a rat, no sudden movements. Col's movements were sudden enough, sudden and deadly. Swinging me behind him, he brought down the sledgehammer. The horrible, crunching sound made me feel sick. I stayed away from the barn for a long time.

We listened to the wireless by firelight, to save candles. Mam and Dad enjoyed a programme called *Itma,* especially a character called Funf, and even Col cracked a smile. I learned more English words from a song called *We'll Meet Again.* When the batteries failed, we sewed, knitted, played games and practised writing and reading. We enjoyed Dad's stories about his schooldays, complete with extravagant facial expressions and gestures. He made a drama of the time he and his best friend, Ces, broke the headmaster's chair.

'Ces and I were having a smoke behind the chapel, out of bounds, of course. It started raining so we stepped inside. The Headmaster kept his gown draped over a handsome, carved chair in the pulpit. Ces put it on, creeping and flapping around the pews, playing ghosts, having a fine old time until the bell rang. We rushed up the pulpit steps to replace the gown, but Ces couldn't manage it. Both of us jumped on the seat and to our horror, [deep breath, staring eyes] it split in half from top to bottom. My God, what on earth could we do? Six of the very best loomed ahead, even expulsion! Second bell. We quickly put the chair back together, arranging the gown over it. It looked a bit odd, but passable. The pair of us were awake all night knowing our silence had compounded the crime. Nothing was said the next morning. Surely it must have been discovered? With pounding hearts, we filed into Chapel for assembly and prayers. As usual, the Headmaster gave the opening prayer, without his gown. Then, he sat down. I closed my eyes. There was a terrible crash as he disappeared below the lectern. Stunned silence! He stood up very slowly, drew himself to his full height, and raked the pews with smouldering eyes. After what seemed a lifetime, he pointed an accusing finger at Ces and me. "You two guilty wretches, in my study at once." Rooted to the spot, we were speedily ejected in quick march formation by the Deputy Head. We were finished! Pale as ghosts, we faced Doctor Jones, his control more frightening than his anger. No ultimatums, expulsion at once, not because of the deed itself but because of our subsequent behaviour. He fixed an eagle-eye on me in particular, saying he was convinced I was not the stuff a minister of the church was made of. My mother readily agreed and I was removed without further ado. Ces was given a reprieve and after a suitable period of suspension, he became a veritable pillar of the church. There's a lesson there, Snwny, what do you think it is?'

Don't be found out, sprang to mind, but after the little angel, I knew the answer.

'Own up straight away, you'll be better off in the end.'

'Quite right,' from Mam, 'and don't you forget it.'

The school remained closed and heavy snow kept the village isolated for weeks. Besi spent most of her time nursing Hen Mr Hopcyn, very ill with pleurisy, and my father, once more disabled by severe bouts of asthma. In bed with a heavy cold, Mrs Rhys was being tended by Dilys as though she were the Queen of Sheba. Olwen said she hadn't seen such beautiful lace pillow-slips since the death of the Misses Bowen's father! Mam and Col worked long hours in the freezing cold. When the milk lorry failed to reach the village, they made extra butter and cheese, feeding the surplus to the pigs. Besi's salve for chapped and bleeding hands was in great demand, but soaking them in your own pee still proved the most effective treatment.

The *Ladi Llwyd*'s house was empty for a long time that winter. When the post finally arrived, Nain received a letter to say she'd be home shortly. But we never saw her again. Nain said she was as lady-like as ever, leaving no debt but no explanations either, none at all. Now there's a funny thing, yes indeed. It was the topic in the shop for weeks. No more sweet, sad music for Rhodri and me, listening in the honeysuckle hedge.

In Chapel, the Aladdin lamps dispelled the morning gloom as the village faithful huddled down the front, near the big seat. When it became even colder, all meetings were held in the vestry, where Mr and Mrs Davies kept a blazing fire from early morning. Safe and cosy, we felt the solace of being together, the outside world far away. The women lingered having a little *clonc*, words of understanding, offers of help and support.

Spring came at last, bringing hot, brilliant weather! We revelled in the sunshine and the early introduction of Summer Time. Dad was better, his ear glued to the BBC Home Service, relaying the news to customers in the shop – Chamberlain had resigned with a nudge from David Lloyd George and the new prime minister was Winston Churchill. His speech, *Blood, toil, tears and sweat,* even stirred Mr Llywelyn into admitting that the English language could be impressive. On times!

The war was going badly, with the Germans invading Holland and Belgium, pushing our forces to the sea. Dad was asked to buy several wireless sets because people wanted to hear the news for themselves, whether they understood the language or not. Photographs of soldiers stranded on a beach near Dunkirk filled Dad's newspaper. Chapel was packed for the National Day of

Prayer, and again, when the troops were miraculously rescued. Mam gave thanks that her brothers and Seth were still in this country. On June the twenty-first, France signed an armistice with Germany, and Mamgu Poli rang to say she couldn't come at all that year, Uncle Dai was ill and she couldn't leave the shop. Only one wagon came to the *rhos* for haymaking. Ita's Ma and Dado were alone, the war had split up their family, too. We saw less and less of Ceri, and Dilys started work at Evan Pritchard's farm. Nesta went home for the holidays, Rhodri visited his aunty in Aberteifi and all signposts and milestones were removed.

One hot, drowsy afternoon an elderly lady came to the shop, wearing a black hat over a frilled, white cap, a shawl and a long, black skirt and apron. She lived miles beyond the *rhos* and she looked so weary, Mam invited her into the house for a cup of tea. We'd never seen her before although she was known in the village. Her son was in the Air Force, and after hearing about the Spitfire Fund on the wireless, she'd come to the Post Office to buy him an aeroplane. She produced bundles of notes from her apron pocket, her life's savings, she said. To my father's astonishment, it came to over two thousand pounds. Such an amount had never crossed his counter before, and never would again.

Far away, the Battle of Britain filled the sky.

Margaret Wyles

Sunday

F'annwyl Miriam,

Well, Haydn passed C4. He wanted to join the Air Force mind you, daft with him so ill. They asked the questions and then examined him. It was all right until they told him to run around the room a few times. He could only manage one round, couldn't he? His chest was so bad, he had to sit down. Sometimes he can't move from the chair for days, leave alone drive an aeroplane. I knew he would never pass, you didn't have to be a lawyer to guess that. But I felt so sorry for him when he came back, all disappointed and miserable he was. And to make things worse, I just couldn't get the fire to go. I'd been throwing sugar on it all day. So the cawl wasn't ready to cheer him up when he came in. Poor old Haydn, to cap it all, Bon, our best cow has died of milk fever. We've been drenching her for days but she suddenly got worse and died on us yesterday. A big blow, Miriam, she was our best milker, Haydn is beyond. We all loved her, she was so swci. Margaret and her were the best of pals, used to ride her sometimes. She came home just as they were dragging Bon across the yard to the lorry. She broke her heart, she's so upset now, she'll take days to get over it. I'm worried about her, yes indeed, I am. She's still pining for Col, that's the top and bottom of it. We haven't heard a word from him yet. I'm very worried about him, Miriam.

I can't leave the shop because Haydn has to go first thing to collect two cows to keep up with the milk. We'll never find another milker like Bon. It's been something all the time lately. Never mind, thousands worse off. What about those poor people in London, then? Dear me, it's terrible up there. Good thing your Gwen sent the children down before. When is she leaving? Soon I hope, but you can't just down tools if you've got a business, can you? They're going through hell up there with this old Blitz. We can't begin to imagine what it's like, can we? Those poor people, God help, who would have thought it, night after night, non-stop. Diolch i Dduw we're here, Miriam fach, with the children safe and sound. God has been merciful to us anyway, but what about those other poor dabs?

You've got a house-full now. How are the children settling down? It's a good job the weather's fine, they can be outside most of the time. They miss their mother I'm sure, but they couldn't be in a better place than yours.

166

Love from Blodwen

It's still very hot isn't it? I get up early to do the milking in the yard. It makes you think with all these awful things going on, drowned the world was last time, burnt the next...

Love from,
Blodwen.

In July, my parents were told our smallholding didn't merit the labour of two men and Col was needed on a large farm, many miles away. Mam and Dad were distraught. Mr Emrys and Mr Llywelyn pleaded with the authorities to allow him to work locally and live at home. Permission was refused and Col was expected to leave for St. Clears after the August Bank Holiday.

We rose early on that unbearable day. I was crying my eyes out by the time Dad brought the van to the door. Col kissed me goodbye and raised Mam's hand to his lips. She gave him a pack of clean clothes, a large basket of food and five stamped, addressed postcards, each with a message. Four said, I am well and doing fine. On the fifth was written, Please come at once, Col.

After Col's departure, the familiar patterns began to change. I pined for him and my Mamgu Poli, Mam was hard pressed and Dad looked ill again. With war a constant topic, the atmosphere in the village became depressed. As a diversion, Aunty Miriam persuaded many of us to attend a film show at the YMCA in her village. Moving pictures meant nothing to me until Dad explained. I was as keen as everyone else when we arrived at the hall. A large, white screen hung at the far end, and a complicated machine on a tripod stood near the door. Silence fell. The lamps were extinguished and a flickering image appeared on the screen. Excitement buzzed through the hall. Miraculous! Amazing! Never seen anything like it! The programme consisted mainly of Pathé Newsreels, but as a special treat, a Laurel and Hardy comedy was shown first. Whoever they might be! Within minutes, the fat one thumped the thin one with a rolling pin. I ran from the hall unable to understand why the others were laughing! It was shockingly real to me, and Dad could not persuade me to return.

August passed and still no cards from Col! Mam wrote to the farm and, receiving no reply, she became frantic. Beg, borrow or steal the petrol she said, we were going to St. Clears. We left early on the Sunday, making good time until, almost at our destination, we came to a steep hill. Less than half way down, the brake-cable snapped and only Dad's skilful driving prevented a serious accident. Badly shaken but still determined to see Col, we found the garage and its sympathetic owner. Obviously not a Chapel goer, he agreed to repair the van. By late afternoon, we arrived at a big, well-kept farm. A man working in the yard told us that the family was in Whitland for Big Meetings, and would not be back until late. When Dad asked about Col, he said he'd run away after a week and the boss had reported it to the police. Was he belonging to us? Funny cove, spent half the night screaming his head off. The others couldn't stand it, so he had to sleep in the barn with the tramps.

Mam was stricken all the way home, biting her nails to the quick.

'We'd better go to the police, Haydn.'

'He'll be taken back if we do.'

'He'll only run away again. I knew this would happen. I tried telling that daft chap, didn't I? He'll be in a terrible state, back to the way he was, having those nightmares and not talking. Where could he be? Wandering about somewhere, I can't bear to think of it. Poor old *dab*.'

'Don't upset yourself now, Blodwen. I'll speak to Evan Pritchard and see what we can do. We'll find him, don't worry.'

'What if he doesn't want to be found? He doesn't want to go back there again, does he?'

'Have we lost Col, Mam?'

'No *bach*, don't you fret, we'll find him. *Cwch* up by here now and try to have a sleep. It's very late, you're tired out, we all are. What a day!'

One of the new cows was a Guernsey, sleek and handsome, with a proud set to her head. She caught Dad's eye but she turned out to be trouble, just like Bomber. Seren was an incurable jumper, attacking any gate, fence or hedge in sight. Ianto brought a prop to place around her neck to show who was boss, but the heavy, cumbersome cross made a sad figure of the proud Seren. Dad couldn't allow it and he paid the price.

Two apple-trees grew inside the garden gate, noted for their lack of fruit, until that year. One in particular was a glory to behold, laden with perfect, russet-gold apples. Barren since the First World War, Besi saw it as a much-needed sign of good fortune. Then Seren arrived. It was her first victim, along with two rows of cabbages from Col's ample vegetable patch. Seren was banished to the top field, kept in by a high gate. She continued to escape with ease and most mornings it was my task to find her, reporting her whereabouts to Dad, knowing she'd only come home for him. Mam fumed about milking her separately, but her yield was good and sooner that than the prop.

Early in September, my mother asked her sisters to spend a few days with us, before starting work in the munitions factory in Trefforest. My Uncle Teify was about to join his brothers in the Army and everyone felt down in the dumps. Seeing we had a spare bed at present, a little holiday would do us all good. I slept in Col's room and mine was spruced up for the visitors. No flouring the sheets this time, everything had to be just so! Mam spent days scrubbing and polishing, no dust under the mats, no cobwebs on the beams. The Aunties had an eagle eye for such affronts!

The weather was perfect when they arrived from Henllan in Dad's van, looking very smart and different. Very modern, Mam said. Aunty Eluned's long, brown hair was cut short, curling into a roll around her head, with a deep wave on her forehead. Aunty May still wore hers in a bun but there was a hint of lipstick!

One evening, after spending a happy day with Aunty Miriam in Llangrannog, the conversation somehow focused on the inconvenience of our house, the damp, and the lack of electricity and water. The Aunties made comments on how hard my mother worked. She brushed it off, saying you couldn't have everything and being happy was better than any old electricity. Dad looked uncomfortable, and when they suggested Col's disappearance was for the best, he left the room.

'How could you bring yourself to give him a home in the first place, that's what I'd like to know, our Blod? You can't say he isn't really peculiar, now, can you?'

'Those noises in the night, and not speaking for all those years and that to-do with the gypsies. Not a very tidy way of carrying on, is it? It's a wonder anyone around here talks to you at all!'

'You're both quite right,' Mam answered, 'Col is different, but he's worth his weight in gold to us, and always will be. Peculiar or not, he's part of our family, and we can't wait for him to come home. That's an end to it, nice cup of tea now.'

The following day was not a success. Aunty Eluned was frightened out of her wits on an early morning visit to the lavatory. In the barn, she came face to face with Twm Aberdâr, a one-armed tramp who paid us several visits a year. Being of a nervous disposition, she almost fainted from the shock. After smelling salts and a calming cup of tea, it was decided we should stay at home, take a rest and do some washing. As we hung out summer dresses and pretty underwear, the lurking Bomber performed at his terrifying best. Diving from the barn roof, he landed on Aunty May's immaculate head. Pandemonium! Mam and Aunty Eluned trying valiantly to rescue her, screaming and shouting enough to raise the dead. Luckily, Dad was nearby to save the day but not before Mam stood on her spectacles in the rampage.

'I honestly don't know how you can live in such a place. *Ach a fi!* Tramps everywhere in the middle of the night, and that cockerel! It should be shot at dawn! You don't have to put up with this, our Blod, you must do something about it!'

'Too soft you are, without a doubt, always have been. It's no life at all, nothing but hard work and no prospects. Put your foot down, you let people walk all over you, you do!'

'Yes, well, you're not me, are you? You live your life, and I'll live mine. We're managing fine here, and I wouldn't think of leaving. Everyone to his taste, see.'

The clothes needed ironing, ready for our jaunt to civilised Aberteifi. Bomber was nowhere to be seen but neither, alas, was the washing. Our Seren was in the yard munching the last of the Aunties' dainties. Completely overcome by mad tramps, cockerels and cows, they decided to leave early the next morning. Dad spent the evening repairing Mam's spectacles. Patience itself he was, most uncharacteristic of my father.

★

Ma and Dado left the *rhos* after the harvest. With Ita lonely too, I often went to Cnwc between first and second breakfast. 'Mind you come back in time for a good wash before school,' from Mam. 'Don't forget.' By then the morning was silver and pearl, the moon fading, soft wings folding, far away dogs barking. Above the mist on the valley floor, shrouded alders and willows appeared like castles with Brân and Branwen, Llew and Blodeuwedd, Arthur and Gwenhwyfar sleeping within.

Down the stony track, I found Ita sitting with her back to the big tree by the house, lonely and longing, gentle Mara pressing close. A smile for me, no talking, we sat together waiting for the sun to come through the mist. I tried to leave Pedro behind but he always found us, disturbing our female solitude, bounding about, edgy and peppery, determined to take me home in time for school. Ita and Mara came to the bridge, the sun warm as we left the tunnel of hedges.

'Do you know where Col is, Ita?'

'He's with us, little *rakli*. He's hiding until it's safe.'

'Why doesn't he send one of Mam's cards?'

'He's got reasons.'

'Will he have to wait until the war's over?'

'Maybe.'

'Does Seth have to wait until the war's over before he comes home?'

'Yes.'

'When will that be?'

'I don't know.'

'Perhaps they'll come home together.'

'Yes, perhaps they will.'

As we looked over the bridge along the riverbank, I knew Col was somewhere in the valley. He would never go away and leave me. Clouds of thistledown drifted over the field like a summer snowstorm.

I was playing with my dolls in the slope. Below, in the *gegin fach*, Mam was making jam with plums from the orchard by the ruined house. Dad said he'd just been talking to Dadcu Jono on the phone. Jam jars rattled loudly. Although they spoke in English, I certainly caught the gist.

'My father thought it would be a good idea if...'

'You know what I think of your father's ideas when it comes to us, Haydn.'

'But it's a good plan this time, Blodwen, fail-safe. It sounds as if he really wants to help.'

'A good plan, I'll be damned. A good plan for him maybe but it'll be a loss for us, without the shadow of a doubt. I don't want to hear any of Jono's plans at all, thank you very much, and that's the close of it.'

'Blodwen, be reasonable, you know three more cows would give us a good milk cheque. It's just the thing to put us back on our feet. My father will provide the cows for a small percentage of the milk money, and when we're in profit, we'll pay off the capital outlay.'

'Haydn, listen to me. If it's anything to do with your father, failure will follow, like night after day. It's happened too many times before. You close your eyes to it, because you want to give him a chance more than anything. He might really mean to help but we won't come out of it on the right side, that I do know!'

'Well, it's like this, Blodwen, he's...'

'*Uffern dân!* He's already done it, hasn't he? The damn cows are waiting at Henllan, aren't they? Just like him, he's dropped us in it again!'

The jam jars jumped as she banged the big saucepan on the table. I could feel her fury through the ceiling. It would be a miracle if the jam survived.

'Ring him up this minute and tell him you're putting them back on the train to wherever they came from. No argument!'

'I understand how you feel but we're near the bread line and we need a boost. This is it.'

'I can see you'll do what you want but I'll tell you this for nothing. You better learn how to milk in double quick time, because those cows are yours, udders and all.'

Crash! A jam jar met its fate on the flags.

'Now look what you made me do! We'll talk about this later. You can give our Margaret her tea, and look after her until I get back. When I've finished this jam, I'm off to prayer meeting, to hell with it all!'

In the morning, there were six scrawny cows in the yard and Mam and Dad were having another ding-dong battle in the barn. This was getting a bit much, I wished Col was there to take the steam out of things. Presently, Dad went to ask Evan Pritchard if he knew anyone who wanted to buy three cows, at a reasonable price. His friend had bad news. Orders had come from the *War Ags* to plough our top fields, which we rented under a casual arrangement. This left barely enough pasture for our original five cows. As a special favour, Evan Pritchard bought the new arrivals for slightly below cost price. Goodbye to the bigger milk cheque and any possible profit. Dad was in deep trouble!

It was late October, too cold to stay long in my secret river place, watching squirrels sampling beechmast and acorns on the opposite bank. Rooks and starlings gathered into flocks and most of the swallows had already left. Leaves were falling and the pig man was somewhere in the valley, I could feel the far away screams. *Arglwydd Mawr*, let me be in Aunty Miriam's soon. Although she had a house full of relatives, she asked me to stay over pig killing. Aunty Gwen had arrived from London, coming to paradise from a hell on earth. Pale and jumpy, her eyes filled with tears every five minutes. A bag of nerves, Aunty Miriam explained, we'd be jumpy too if we'd spent every night in an air-raid shelter, wondering if our last hour had come! You three be kind and considerate to her and her children, and don't you forget it. We all have to do our best in these awful times. Yes, indeed.

Four of us girls slept head to toe in the big bed, with Bryn in the single, behind a curtain. Eira and her cousin Laura were disgusted, sharing with babies, but we fell asleep quickly enough, the sweet smell of apples pervading the house.

I returned home to find Pedro behaving strangely, barking in the yard like a mad thing and even attacking Bomber, who retreated in disbelief. Sitting in the old trap, he barked for hours, refusing to come in at night. He disappeared on the day the evacuees arrived from Henllan Station, calling in other villages on the way. I was very disappointed to learn there were only two older boys left on the bus when it reached the Manse. I'd been hoping for a sophisticated companion like Laura, Eira's cousin from London. I missed Nesta who was needed at home to help with the new baby.

Pedro's absence overshadowed everything. My imagination worked overtime. All those rabbit traps and snares! On the third morning, I mitched from school and without telling anyone, I searched everywhere, venturing to distant farms, asking if he'd been seen. When I arrived home on the verge of tears, Mam was biting her nails on the doorstep, too relieved to scold.

'Well, there's a miserable looking child, I've been wondering about you for hours. I think you're worrying too much, *cariad*. Pedro will be back soon, he's found a girlfriend further away than usual that's all.'

'But he's never done this before, Mam, something's wrong.'

'Come on now, tea's on the table, I bet you anything he'll be back in the morning.'

I didn't know then that Dad and Ita had been quietly searching the countryside for days. Mam was right. In the morning, Pedro was sitting on the gatepost as usual, ready to escort me to school. I almost strangled him in my relief but after a quick lick, he stood still, looking directly into my eyes. By the bridge he did the same, waiting for me to understand. Suddenly, I knew and we were off! Along the river, over the iron gate in the big field, past my secret place and a good way beyond the huge, hanging willows. I didn't usually venture onto Mr Pryce's land, he wasn't keen on trespassers but each time I hesitated, Pedro rounded me up. On steeper ground at the end of the valley, he entered a sheep cover. It was empty, but something had recently made a bed in the straw. After one sniff, Pedro rushed pellmell along the river, across our yard to the Dutch barn. I climbed the cemetery wall and jumped onto the hayrick. Col was lying on his back, his eyes closed, his breath shallow, his mottled face covered in sores. Lice crawled in his filthy, matted hair. He was a ghastly sight. My poor, dear Col looked near to death.

'*Iesu Grist, aros gyda ni!* Don't touch him whatever you do!'

My parents had seen our headlong dash across the yard. Mam's voice was sharp and anxious. Besides the fever, Col was suffering from impetigo. He must be taken to the house at once and given a sulphur bath. I was ready to fetch Besi.

'No, *cariad,* nobody must know Col's back, except Ita. We've already decided he can't go back to that farm. Yes, Margaret, we knew he was around somewhere because of Pedro's behaviour. Dad and Ita have been looking for Col for days. We didn't want to tell you in case it was a false alarm. This must be kept a dead secret until we know what to do for the best. Do you understand me now? Do you promise?'

'Yes, I promise.'

'Good girl, of course you do.'

My father's struggles to get Col into the house looked hopeless but mercifully, Col regained consciousness. Somehow they managed to stagger indoors where Col crawled onto the *sgiw*. Dad collapsed in the chair, his chest heaving. I burst into tears, and when Mam put her arms around me, I knew she was crying too.

'Come on now, this will never do. Col's home, that's the main thing. The next few weeks are going to be very hard, though. We'll have to be extra-special careful because those sores are very catching. If we all get them, the fat will be in the fire. Dad is the only one to go near Col from now on. I won't touch him at all, then I can carry on with the milking and look after the shop. I know Ita will help with the other work. You won't be able to go to school, or play with Rhodri, just in case. We'll have to keep to ourselves for a bit and say that you and Dad are not well. I'll sleep with you and we'll isolate Dad and Col as much as we can. No hugs and kisses for either of them, you understand? You mustn't touch them, or anything they've handled. Have you got that now? It's very, very important, *cariad. O Duw Mawr,* that poor *dab*'s been through hell, he's nothing but a bag of bones and pitiful to see. Right then, I'll prepare this bath, and you go and get the Jeyes Fluid and carbolic soap. And the *Family Doctor* from the desk. We'll beat this, if it's the last thing we do.'

It took over a week for the fever to subside with Dad's nursing and much advice from Ita. The reek of sulphur and disinfectant wafted into the shop and our lengthy absence prompted questions. Dai

Davies looked sceptical when Mam said we weren't well and Besi was offended.

During that time, Mam faced the man from the *War Ags* twice. Bold as brass, she stood in the yard like a warrior, saying Col hadn't put his feet under her kitchen table since August Bank Holiday, and if he really wanted to know, she could do with some help herself, with a husband only half well. What a performance! She didn't give him time to draw breath, but she was very shaky on her return to the barn.

'I wish you could come in for a cup of tea, Ita, I'm feeling like a wet rag. God forgive me, the words I said were true, but it was still a lie. And may He forgive me for the other whoppers I'm bound to tell before this is over.'

'I think He'll understand, Mrs Blodwen,' said Ita.

The strict medical regime continued. Sheets drenched in disinfectant hung over every door, and clothes from the sick room boiled endlessly in the outhouse. Dad wore white, cotton gloves, changing them when he left Col's room. They reeked of carbolic soap, putting him off his food. He had us in stitches when he went down on one knee to sing Al Jolsen's *Mammy*. We couldn't help laughing as he waved his gloved hands in the air, impetigo or no impetigo. The way he endured those weeks of nursing was a measure of his affection for Col. Being a fastidious man, it must have been an ordeal, especially stripping off the scabs with starched poultices.

Every morning, Dad and I lined up for the blister inspection and a dose of Ita's blood clearing medicine. On a freezing cold day in late November, the first signs appeared on Dad's arms and neck, and a few days later there were blisters on my hands and legs. It was only a matter of time before Mam became infected. The shop must close and the milk given to the pigs. Our gruelling routine had failed, the lonely fight was over.

Of course, Mr Dai Davies had already guessed what was going on in the house, together with the Thomases and the Morrises. When my mother finally explained, help came from everywhere. Ita continued the milking, Mr Thomas did the outside work, Mrs Thomas and Mrs Davies looked after the shop and Mrs Morris did the accounts. Besi took over the nursing and although Col was almost well, Dad and I suffered her sulphur, zinc, calamine lotions and powders, along with the cruel, starched poultices. However, we had grand news for Christmas! Mr Emrys and Mr Llywelyn had convinced the authorities that Col should work locally and live at home. To crown it all, Mam escaped the dreaded impetigo!

Rhodri and I were watching Mr Morris gilding his gravestones when Dad came into the workshop. A telegram had arrived for an address unknown to him or my mother. Wil Morris gave directions saying it was miles away and nobody'd lived there for years! Dai Davies, the postman, was busy but the telegram had to be delivered immediately. Even though my father still felt unwell, rules were rules! Rhodri and I begged to join him for a trip into the unknown.

Most of the journey was uphill with the road ending in a stony track. By the time we walked to the gate, Dad's chest sounded like a bellows. The house looked deserted as Wil Morris had described; little more than a wooden shack in poor repair. We ran up the steep steps, knocked on the door and swiftly rejoined my father and Pedro at the gate. A dog barked loudly before the door opened a crack. The man stayed in the shadows as he called out several times for his dog to stay back.

'Sorry I can't come down,' he said, 'my dog's very fierce. I daren't let him out. What can I do for you?'

When my father explained his errand, the stranger asked him to leave the telegram on the gate. He watched us walk away without a word.

'There wasn't a dog in there at all,' said Rhodri when we reached the van. 'For a start, that barking wasn't real. Pedro's fur would have been standing up to his ears if it was. He didn't look interested. The man was making that noise himself. Why would he do that?'

'You may well ask, Rhodri, it's a mystery to me,' answered my father.

Dai Davies delivered most of the subsequent telegrams which arrived up to Christmas week. Speculation was rife in the shop on Saturday nights.

Love from Blodwen

F'annwyl Miriam,

Thank you very much for your long letter with all the news. I miss not seeing you too, what with one thing and another. And now on top of everything, the weather is enough to freeze you to the bone.

I expect you've heard about the Spy by now. We're all talking about it here non-stop. Haydn and Dai Davies had been wondering for a while, those telegrams being in such funny Welsh, it didn't make any sense at all. Dai Davies said the bloke was a queer cove, only opened the door a crack, and never looked him in the eyes. Not a very clever way for a spy to behave, I must say, acting guilty from the start. We were talking about it in the shop when the police rang. They wanted to know if Haydn, as Postmaster, had noticed anything funny going on in these parts. Now you come to mention it, yes, he said. This chap, living in a lonely house up here, is getting some very funny telegrams, and nobody knows anything about him at all. Well, they were here in a flash and he was arrested as a German Spy. I don't know if he was a real German or not. Couldn't be a Welshman, anyway. There's excitement for you, isn't it? We're not completely out of it after all. I thought the police might have told Haydn a bit more, seeing he'd given them the gen about the telegrams. But no, they were very close indeed. Almost as exciting as that parachutist, isn't it? Dai Davies and Haydn were out on their bikes all day, that time. Haydn was half dead when he got back...

I'm sorry to hear Gwen is so upset. Far from home for Christmas and Huw due for embarkation, you can't wonder at it. She must be worried about her house as well with everything still being bombed to bits. The news tonight said it's like the second Great Fire of London up there. Poor old Coventry's almost been wiped out, and Bristol's getting it hot and heavy. Much nearer to home now, Miriam fach.

Haydn's chest is still bad, coughing day and night. I've made him a Thermogene waistcoat to wear under his vest. Between that and the goose grease he says he smells like a cross between a cooked dinner and a chemist's shop. And it's his birthday tomorrow too. He hasn't been right since that awful impetigo. Nursing Col took it out of him. Marvellous he was, never faltered. I take my hat off to him, indeed I do. Thanks to Besi, he and Margaret didn't have it as bad as Col. He's not too grand either, doesn't complain, but he's lost his strength somehow. That pneumonia almost put pay to him, mind you, tramping around afraid to come home. But he's stopped shouting in the night, it didn't last long. I expect they'll pick up when the weather gets better, but looking a bit frail at present.

We all had a good Christmas, considering. Margaret had lovely presents from the boys. It was very good of them to remember her, being so far from home. A silver fountain pen from Ifor, a gold cross and chain from Glyn, and a leather writing case from Teify. She was as pleased as Punch, made her feel very grown up.

One of Neli Thomas' family died in Aberteifi before Christmas. Have you heard? Only forty-three he was, with three children. I met him once, pleasant chap, very dark eyes, pinky cheeks and a beautiful skin. He was in London working in a dairy for years, but they got bombed out and came back home. Dead now, and for what reason? God works in mysterious ways. His wife was terrible in the funeral, could hardly stand. English girl, but very nice they say, a devoted couple. Neli said she was wearing a beautiful fur hat. They were going to stay the night, but the beds are not like ours, and very scanty with the bedclothes, Neli said.

We're all knitting like mad for the troops. Mrs Emrys brought bales of khaki wool and we're making balaclavas, socks, gloves, scarves and mittens. I'm still not too clever turning the heel, you'll have to show me again. The Misses Bowen made beautiful clothes for the evacuees for Christmas. They're a dab hand at make do and mend, they can turn a shirt collar in no time. But I've never seen a darner like Nesta's mother, best in the district. She can make things look brand new she can...

Love from,
Blodwen.

Chapter Eight

The tradition of several villages congregating for New Year's Eve came to an end with the blackout, but most of our community gathered in the vestry to welcome the start of 1941. Each family arrived in a blast of cold wind and icy breath, placing their baskets of food and dishes on the table near the door. A cup of tea brewed from steaming kettles on a roaring fire kept up the spirits. The horses snorted and stamped in the stable below.

For the occasion, Mr Emrys had prepared a modern entertainment of comical songs and poems from *Penill a Thonc* by W.R. Evans, Llanfyrnach. The words, set to popular English tunes, made light of the lesser trials of wartime. *Dim Heb Gwpon*, (Not Without Coupons) was set to *Where are you going to, my pretty maid?* and *Sigaret* to *Banjo on My Knee*. My recitation, *Betsi ar y Ffôn*, described an old lady who insisted on changing into her Sunday clothes to answer the phone. It touched a nerve in the audience but the warm applause did little to lessen my embarrassment. Besi had shaved a circle of hair on the crown of my head weeks before, to treat the impetigo. The new growth was a large, fat curl, at odds with my straight crop. Hoping to make it look less incongruous, Mam tied it down with an enormous bow of ribbon. Considering the size of the hateful thing that night, the audience must have been waiting for take off. The concert ended with a rousing chorus set to *Polly Wolly Doodle*.

'Y Blacowt, Y Blacowt,
Y blacowt mewn tref a llan,
Rhaid cael defnydd ar ffenestri,

Ar bob tŷ a thwlc a festri,
Byth na chyffrwy' mae mor dywyll ym mhob man.'

Tables drawn close to the fire were laid for supper, and after serving the men, the women sat on their own. As usual, the men talked politics, war and agriculture. Hen Mr Hopcyn was certain our independence was over, the government firmly in the driving seat. Samson and Ianto were very agitated.

'A subsidy of two pounds an acre of ploughed land doesn't make up for the ruination of the valley. This heavy machinery will pound the soil flat in no time. Then they'll plaster more and more of that artificial fertilizer all over the place. It doesn't take a genius to see it won't work in the long run. Samson and I are proper fed up we are. All these changes, we can't keep up. No indeed we can't! We'll have to sell the farm before those blasted *War Ags* take possession. My father must be turning in his grave!'

'Come on, Ianto,' from Mr Pryce, 'things are not that bad. A farm's got to be grade C before they can take over. Anyway, you'll have a couple of hefty land girls to help you soon!'

'God forbid! I don't want women on my farm. Samson and I would rather give it away. *Ach a fi!*'

'There's a war on and like it or not, it's a priority to grow all we can. We have to move forward. I'm getting a milking machine next week.'

Siencyn ap Siencyn pulled on his pipe.

'You're very hot for what you call progress, Evan Pritchard. But what do this lot care about us? Strangers they are.'

'Yes, and they've got very long noses, those blokes in shoes. They'll never leave us alone now.'

'If we come through this war in one piece that is.'

'Well, Ianto, you've got one thing to look forward to. It's Double Summer Time next month. There'll be more daylight to chase your land girl around the hayrick!'

'You show some respect, Wil Morris, or I'll set Samson on you, you see if I don't!'

Mari Pryce, Brynfa, tucked into her second plate of ham and

pickled onions. 'Listen to old Ianto. He does nothing but grizzle these days.'

'I think he's beginning to feel his age. It must be very lonely, up there all on his own,' said Mam.

Nain was on Ianto's side.

'He's quite right, you know, him and Madoc Hopcyn. Look at us here tonight! Celebrating on our own for the first time I can remember. You mark my words, this year coming, there'll be no picnic, no trip to the sea and machinery will take over the haymaking. We'll stop needing each other, and in no time, the heart will go out of the place.'

'And Chapel attendance is falling,' chimed in Mrs Rhys.

'*Diwedd mawr*, anyone would think we're here for a funeral. What's the matter with us? Time to cheer up.'

'Quite right, Teg. Let's have another cup of tea.'

'It was lovely to see your Anwen home for Christmas, Mari. Pity she had to go back so soon. She's not in London anymore, is she?'

'No, she's in Wiltshire, working in the NAAFI. Do you know Lowri Jones from Penrhiwpal? She's in charge there and they came back together. They couldn't stay long, they're on duty tonight.'

'Same as our Ceri then. It was touch and go whether she came home or not. The hospital's full to overflowing.'

'Yes, I bet she could tell us a thing or two. We don't know we're born here, I'm glad to say.'

'Where's Guto and company tonight? I thought they'd be here in full force.'

'Well, I for one am glad they're not! I couldn't stand one more look at that wooden leg,' said Dilys.

'Where are they then?'

'Haven't you heard? Guto's mother is very ill. They all went over yesterday morning.'

'Not that Miss Davis as well! She's got some cheek going over there after what happened.'

'Well Guto's mam is beyond hope they say. She won't know any different, will she?'

'She may not, but what will people think? It's not decent, no indeed, it's not decent!'

'Guto doesn't care two hoots about being decent. Gave that up years ago!'

'On the quiet, we've heard his mam's got a tidy bit put by. And she owns her own house. There's talk she's leaving that to Guto, the only son without a place of his own.'

'If that's the case, I expect they'll be moving soon.'

'Nain Pritchard, a little bird told me you've offered Olwen a house rent free, to get away from those two.'

'You always were partial to little birds, Siân Bowen! Yes indeed, it's quite right. I'm worried about Olwen. She's gone right into herself lately and I don't like to see it. I'm very fond of her, she's a nice girl from a good family and she deserves better.'

'I'll wager a shilling to a farthing she'll go with him in the end, daft thing. Resigned she is now, can't see the wood for the trees.'

'But you can't interfere between man and wife, can you?'

'Correction there, Neli, you should use the plural in this case.'

'It's no laughing matter! How do we know what Olwen thinks? She won't have a word said against Guto. Speaking out could make matters worse.'

'Go she will, for sure. You've seen it in the hand, haven't you Besi?' from Anni Bowen.

Besi gave a stern look.

'Another little bird, is it? What I see in the hand is between me and the person it belongs to. It's not for idle talk!'

'If you ask me,' said Neli Thomas, 'that big bully Guto needs a good thumping. Somebody ought to sneak up on him one dark night and show him what for. How about it, ladies?'

My father, Hen Mr Hopcyn and Siencyn ap Siencyn were having a smoke in the shop. They dreaded the rationing of cigarettes and tobacco, scarce enough already. You couldn't tell Dad was down in the dumps, but his heart wasn't in his story-telling, and he'd stopped talking about Arizona. Mam said the impetigo had left its mark. To make matters worse, Bomber had gone to his Maker, falling off his perch in the night. It must be said that only Dad lamented his passing. Determined to cheer him up, Col and I did some of his early morning jobs in the shop, polishing the copper scales, washing the counters and spreading fresh sawdust on the floor. Dad was touched and responded by keeping his fears to himself. He became preoccupied with the business and a serious lack of cash. Our stock had dwindled to three cows, four pigs, chickens and ducks. The shop faced competition from deliveries by a local baker, and a registered butcher's van from Castell Newydd Emlyn. The latter made a brisk trade due to a steep decline in the rabbit population. They no longer hung in doleful rows by the shop door. Post Office wages were small, almost everything was rationed, and coupons put an end to the catalogue commission.

Shortly after Siencyn's departure, Dad could be heard laughing loudly, an unusual sound at the time. It was provoked by a diabolical plan hatched by Mr Hopcyn. During the past few years, his neighbour, Mr Rhys, had taken to dumping garden rubbish on a piece of spare ground owned by the old gentleman. He'd complained repeatedly to Elias Rhys, to no avail. It seemed the latter's jealousy had finally got the better of him. Madoc Hopcyn's house was one of the few not owned by Nain Pritchard. He'd already bequeathed it to his nephew, Gareth, but he wanted my father's assistance to change his will. The spare piece of ground was now to be left to Elias Rhys. He, being of an obsessively tidy nature, would find it impossible to leave the ground uncleared!

At the end of January, word came that good money could be made carrying hardcore for an airstrip construction in Aberporth where the Ministry was hiring labour, paying by the load. Dad saw his opportunity. He bought a second-hand, tip-up lorry on weekly payments, prepared to make a small fortune! This essential war work released Col to crank the engine and operate the winding gear. Although Mam considered the work too heavy and the weather too cold after the trials of the previous weeks, Dad convinced her they could set their own pace. Anyway, beggars could not be choosers!

The plan went well until the first breakdown. They became good mechanics and Dad even began teaching Col to drive. Profits were within reach when my father's health failed again. Covered in boils and barely able to walk, he was forced to take to his bed. Besi, in daily attendance, looked through me with her silver eyes. She started calling me *crwydres fach*, little wanderer. What did she mean? Was the answer in the hand?

During my father's recovery, he read aloud extracts from a novel by John Cowper Powys, called *Owen Glendower*. One of them told the story of the Prince and his army marching to Bryn Glas to fight a battle against the Mortimers. One beautiful June evening, they camped in the grounds of a mansion-house at Pilleth on the banks of the river Lugg. There was tension in the air when they sat down to their meal under the walled terrace. Then, a great white owl came flapping over their heads, circling slowly. Could this ghostly bird be a bad omen? The Prince leapt from his seat forbidding anyone to draw a bow. The owl hovered lower, its huge eyes searching every face. Unease spread throughout the company until Broch-o'Meifod rose to his feet. He was Owen's close friend, a giant possessed of the ancient knowledge. The axe-blades at his waist gleamed in the strange light as he disappeared into the mist rising from the stream.

> *Suddenly from the river-mists there came a low prolonged owl-cry, a sound so startling after the silent flappings of their visitor that the spell-bound warriors stared at each other and some of them rose to their feet.*
>
> *Again came this unearthly sound, and after its third repetition, lo! the great bird above their heads whirled round with evident intention, and in an impetuous flight quite at variance with its former movements flung itself down the slope and was lost in the mist. Once more, but from higher up the valley and with perceptibly different accent, came the cry; but that was the end. None of the little army saw the bird again.*

Col loved this passage and asked my father to read it repeatedly. He borrowed the book to make several copies in his careful hand. He kept two; one he placed in the desk and the other he always carried in his wallet.

Love from Blodwen

F'annwyl Miriam,

They've had bombs on the mountain back home! Scared everyone to death. The planes were going back from Cardiff docks and emptied their load, hoping to hit the pits, I expect. I've asked Mam and Dat to come down here but they won't hear of it. And poor old Swansea's getting it hammer and tongs! We could see the fire in the sky from here. I couldn't believe it, it was really terrible. Teg and Wil Morris are worried sick about Ceri. And those poor dabs in London are getting it day and night. God keep Mr Churchill on the right path now for all our sakes.

Haydn's much better, thank you for asking. Beginning to sit up and take notice at last. Mamgu Poli and Martha came down to see him on Friday. We were worried about the journey, there's still snow on the Beacons. Trefor's very careful and they got through all right. They're all A1 except for being shaken up by the old bombing. Lucky it didn't do much damage although they'll never feel safe again. The windows rattled like mad but the tape kept most of them intact. They went back after dinner today. Trefor couldn't risk the petrol to come and see you this time, but I'll be over on Thursday.

You know how Haydn likes talking to stray people. Well, one night before he was ill, he brought this chap home from Aberporth. Something to do with the airfield. French he is. Yes indeed. He speaks English very well but not a word of Welsh. He's very nice, though, and after the first shock we got on champion. He's good looking like, dark hair with really twinkly eyes. He laughs a lot and throws his arms about. He loves his food he says, and he enjoyed his supper. He had some wine from somewhere and he was smoking cigarettes that smelt like the herbs Haydn burns for his chest. It did drewi, I must say. His name is Jack, but he says it soft, like in Siôn. We got it right after a bit. He was here when the war started and decided to stay and fight. He told us about a big French General in London now, but I can't remember the name. Jack's fighting to save his family he says. He showed us photos of his Mam and Dad and three sisters. Lovely family too. Bless his heart, I hope he'll see his dream come true, and that God will keep them safe until this is all over. Such terrible things happening. We must count our blessings.

Poli says it's really exotic to find a Frenchman in this out of the way place. She's exotic if you ask me. You ought to see the hat she wore to Chapel this morning! Hardly suitable for praying, Mrs Rhys said. And you'll never believe what happened last night! Mamgu Poli felt tired and went to bed early. We were just sitting down to a salad supper when we heard a thump from upstairs. The lamp spluttered and went out, leaving us in total darkness. Then Poli's voice came through the floorboards. "Whatever you do down there, don't eat the beetroot!"...

Love from,
Blodwen.

'**D**id I see Ceri at the tap now just?' asked Martha.

At last they were going to talk about something interesting! We were having our Sunday dinner before Mamgu Poli left for the South. The conversation so far had been about the war and the bombing, non-stop.

'Yes, she's home for a few days. Needs it by the look of her. They're worked off their feet with all the casualties.'

'*Ach a fi*, they gave Swansea an awful pasting. Gives you the shivers it does, when you think what might happen.'

'Come on, Martha don't get morbid. We've all got to keep cheerful.'

'Morbid! You can hardly call me morbid, Poli, but facts are facts.'

'Well,' said Mam, 'I've got a bit of *clonc* to keep us going. Ceri came into the shop yesterday when Jack the Frenchman was there. *Caton pawb*, as soon as he saw her, his eyes went as big as saucers. When Ceri gave him one of her big smiles, he blushed to the roots of his hair. Really smitten he is! After she left, he couldn't stop asking questions about her. This morning, he was here on his motorbike, long before second breakfast. Ceri's going back today and you can guess who's giving her a lift to the station.'

'A wartime romance, is it?' said Martha. 'I thought she was courting some chap working in the bank in Swansea, with prospects.'

'Yes, but that's not as romantic as keeping company with a Frenchman, is it?'

'Well, she'd better be careful if you ask me. I bet Teg Morris is sweating on the quiet.'

'Quite novel, being the mother-in-law of a Frenchman, don't you think?'

'Poli, you don't half say some daft things sometimes, honest to God you do. No girl from around here would marry a foreigner now, would she?'

'What about your Cati's daughter? She married an Italian, didn't she?'

'Yes, but that's different. He was born and bred in Wales. His father had a Bracchi's shop in Swansea for donkey's years. They're all interned now, you know. Disgusting, I call it, they're as Welsh as you or me. Fancy doing that to people who've been here all that time.

This war's got a lot to answer for, if you want to know. Talking of romance though, there was a big wedding back home the other day, Blodwen. You know the Robertses living by the Isolation Hospital, don't you? Their youngest daughter got married last week. Very posh, although they don't have two ha'pennies to rub together. Against the wedding, their brother-in-law painted the house from top to bottom with paint from his job. He's the painter and wallpaperer for Lewis and Son, Consort Street. When he'd finished, the furniture looked very shabby so Mrs Roberts went to the Co-op and got loads of stuff on the never. And what did she do after the wedding? Yes, she sent it all back, saying it wasn't quite what she wanted. Now that's what I call barefaced cheek of the first order. But she's like that, plenty of *swanc*, and nothing in the cupboard. She'd sooner have a showy hat for Chapel than a square meal on the table, any day. How some live is beyond me!

'Anyway, there was a really good spread in the vestry, I could hardly believe my eyes! Nobody could tell there was a war on! It was hot, sit down, with plenty of everything. Ten out of ten by anyone's standards. Where they got it from, God only knows. All their relations were there, and most of the street. The bride herself came to ask us. I nursed her father through pneumonia once. Dorothy's a nice girl, always pleasant. The bridegroom went off to the army this week, poor *dab*.

'Old Mrs Irving was there. Remember Arthur, the sweep? He wasn't quite sixteen ounces? His mother. She's belonging to the Robertses. She's Mrs Roberts' sister-in-law's cousin, on the mother's side. They've always been big pals. She's a good old thing, but she's some sort of maniac, you know, the sort that steals things. She can't help it, but when she's around you've got to see to your things. We all had a good look in her basket on the way out, in case she'd pinched anything with our mark on. You don't like to say anything to her. She's got a very kind heart and we wouldn't like to see the family in trouble.'

As we waved them a reluctant goodbye, I'd have felt much sadder had I known Mamgu would be gone for a long time.

In May, London suffered one of the worst nights of the blitz. The newscaster announced that the Germans were taking advantage of a 'Bomber's Moon'. Dad said it seemed as if everywhere was being bombed except Sîr Aberteify! Posters in the shop declared that 'Loose Talk Costs Lives' and 'Walls Have Ears'.

Preparations were taking place in Ceri's house for her afternoon out with Jack the Frenchman. Ceri sat at the table, soaking her hands in a bowl of lavender-scented water. Dilys was helping out by sewing a clean collar and cuffs on Ceri's best dress.

'You're not starting to get keen on him, are you?' asked Dilys.

'He's very nice.'

'But he's a foreigner! Surely you wouldn't go and live in France, would you?'

'How do I know? There's a war on and anything might happen. Anyway, you've got a short memory, Dilys *fach*.'

'That was different.'

'No, it wasn't. You were ready to leave everything yourself once.'

'I don't want to talk about it!'

'Sorry. I didn't mean to upset you. It's been ages now, I thought you might have got over it a bit. Perhaps the time has come to think of the future.'

'I'll never get over it, and I don't want to think about the future.'

'Get over what, Dilys?'

'*Duw Mawr,* I'd forgotten about Miss Big Ears sitting here, quiet as a mouse. Nothing *bach,* it's all in the past. Anyway, we were talking about Ceri, not me. Are you serious about this Jack, that was my question?'

'I haven't known him long enough yet.'

'Have you given up that bank clerk in Swansea?'

'Of course I have! I don't go out with two men at once, thank you very much!'

'I thought you were smitten with him before Christmas.'

'Well I like this one more, and he's much better looking', said Ceri, buffing her nails vigorously. 'I wonder if Dat'll notice pink varnish? Better not, he's feeling rattled as it is.'

'I'm trying to be serious here, Ceri.'

'I'll talk to you later. We can't let Miss Big Ears know all our secrets, can we? I'm off upstairs to get changed, Jack's due in half an hour.'

'Are Ceri and Jack the Frenchman going to get married, Dilys?'

'I don't know, *bach*, who can tell?'

'Will you get married one day?'

She gave me a long look before saying, 'Let me do your nails while we're waiting. Put your hands in here, the water's still warm. Mam says you've got lucky finger-nails and you should look after them.'

Mrs Rhys had noticed my finger-nails? Never!

'What are lucky finger-nails?'

'Don't ask me.'

As Dilys gently pushed back my cuticles, we heard Jack the Frenchman's motor-bike roaring down the school hill. Ceri rushed into the room, her eyes shining and the seams of her stockings as straight as a die.

'Come on you two. Walk me to the bridge. Jack will be waiting.'

On my way home from school, I was surprised to see a strange car near the gate. As it drew alongside, Dadcu Jono opened the door! He looked an imposing figure in his fur-collared coat and Thurso hat, his silver-handled canes by his side. Inviting me to hop in, he explained he'd called to discuss business with my father, and he was glad to see me before leaving. He gave me four, shiny half-crowns for being a good girl! My expression made him laugh, his eyes a very bright blue. Did I have a hug for my old Dadcu then? Right you are, keep smiling. Mamgu sends her love. Cheerio until the next time. He was gone before I could say a proper thank you.

A smell of burnt Welsh cakes filled the house, and Mam and Dad were shouting at each other in the *gegin fach*. An uneasy atmosphere had developed between my parents lately, but this was different! It was about money, and Mam was off top C.

'I know Jono's been cooking up some plot but the pigs are staying put, thank you very much. I'm tamping mad you could even consider such a thing. It's against the law and you might be caught. How can you risk everything like that? You might have a superior brainbox but I've got more common sense in my little toenail. I can tell you that for nothing! If that's what education does for you, you can keep it!'

'For God's sake, Blodwen, please stop shouting! I'm trying to find a way out of our financial difficulties, and all you can do is nag on about things you don't understand.'

'Oh yes, is that so? And what don't I understand this time, if you please? I understand a lot more that you think, *boyo bach*, and if it means dealings with Jono, you can take me to Henllan station this minute.'

I didn't like the sound of this, I wasn't used to my parents behaving like enemies. Pedro and I went to the crossroads to wait for Col and tell him my tale of woe. He gave me a hug, making a sign that it would soon blow over. When I showed him my present from Dadcu Jono, a knowing look crossed his face. Tea would be late for sure, we'd better go to Ita's.

The only room in the cottage was bright and welcoming, like the inside of a *vardo*. Patchwork curtains and cushions shared their multi-colours with rag rugs and an embroidered coverlet on the box bed. Blue, red and gold dishes, a wedding present from Ma and Dado, lined the shelves of Mrs Morgan's dresser. I sat in the rocking chair by the fire and over tea and spice cake, Ita showed us a photograph of Seth in his army uniform. He wasn't smiling and his quiet eyes looked more patient than ever. Ita stared at it for a long time. Col brought out the dominos and we played until we thought it safe to go home.

It was almost dark when Ita and Mara walked us down the hill. Col stopped, pointing to the gateway where two handsome foxes stood facing each other on their hind legs, pawing the air. Col placed a quiet hand on my head. I was aware of the utter stillness of my companions, their ability to withdraw their presence. We watched until the foxes, regarding us with glowing eyes, walked unhurriedly towards the river.

'Very lucky that,' said Ita 'the sight of foxes dancing.'

Mam greeted us all cool and collected.

'Where have you two been then? Tea's been on the table for ages. Dad's not feeling too good, having a bit of a pull. You'll feel better after a nice cup of tea, won't you, Haydn *bach?*'

She laid a gentle hand on his shoulder and Col gave a shrug and a wink. Peace was restored. But not for long!

Sunday

F'annwyl Miriam,

I've got something weighing terrible on my mind, and I must tell someone. I can trust you, I know. Don't tell a soul what I'm going to tell you now, as Haydn would be arrested, as sure as eggs, and Col with him. It's that flaming Jono's fault, always sticking his nose in where he's not wanted. He asked Haydn to kill a pig on the sly, and take it up to him for bacon. I said, now don't be daft, it's not worth it. He wouldn't help you if you were on your knees. He's nothing but trouble for us, always has been. But Haydn said we badly needed the cash to tide us over. Yes, I said, but that old devil won't pay you anyway, after all the risks you'll be taking. Might as well have talked to the wall. But they didn't get away with it, no indeed!

They were going over the Beacons in the pitch dark, Col in the back with the pig. Not a soul to be seen, black as bola buwch. Then out of nowhere jumped some soldiers with lights and rifles. Haydn almost had a heart attack then and there. Halt! Who goes there, they shouted. Oh God! What the hell is going on? Col was making that noise in his throat, trying to get out the back, and shouting everywhere. Haydn thought like wildfire. He put his foot down and drove hell for leather, sweat running down his face so he could hardly see. Then the guns went off! Col jumping up and down like a mad thing, bullets all over the place! You can see two holes in the back doors now! Lucky they were, God was with them that night, I can tell you. Just think what could have happened for the sake of a bit of bacon. Dead, or jailed for black market. I just can't believe it, I can't bear to think of it. They didn't breathe properly until they got to Hirwaun. Haydn can't breathe properly even now, hunched in his chair day and night. It'll take him days to get over it, and Col's in the falen, he hates to see Haydn ill. The wrath of God has come down on them with a vengeance, it looks like. They were very lucky, mind you, very lucky indeed. The only bullet found was in the pig ...

Love from,
Blodwen.

An eerie light filled the valley. Summer thunder rumbled out at sea where black clouds gathered on the horizon. I stood on the *twmp* in the sultry stillness, longing to see Mamgu Poli. When the car appeared on the top road, silhouetted against sheets of silver rain, I ran home for the welcome. Standing with the others at the gate, I watched Mamgu step from the car. Thin and pale, almost too frail to smile, she leant heavily on Trefor's arm. Beneath her straw hat, her hair was as white as snow! Although I knew she was unwell, the change in her appearance shocked me deeply. My Mamgu Poli looked very ill!

Dad and Trefor ushered her gently into the house, passing into the coolness of the *gegin fach,* darker than ever as the storm broke. Exchanging anxious glances, my mother and Martha settled a breathless Mamgu in the high-backed chair. She closed her eyes. Trefor sat nearby and I huddled on the bench in the corner, trying to control my feelings. Dad lit the lamp and the women prepared tea. A white cloth billowed above the table, floating slowly, very slowly downwards. In the silence, Mamgu shimmered against the shadows in her pale, silken dress. Time stopped as in a dream. Only I saw Col enter by the back door, watching in his special stillness. Removing his cap, he faced Mamgu. She opened her eyes and something passed between them. What was it? I felt lonely and uncertain. Col sat beside me, Mamgu smiled and the moment passed.

Those summer months became known in the family as *Amser Poli,* Poli's time. We were governed by the pace of her recovery, and at first, the change in her subdued us all. My bedroom was transformed into what Mamgu called her boudoir, where Besi arrived every morning for washing and dressing. Afterwards, I gently brushed Mamgu's long hair one hundred times. It was silkier and more manageable now, easier to secure into a knot with tortoise-shell pins. Any hair on the brush, along with nail trimmings, were entrusted to Besi for immediate burning. Nothing must be left for the unscrupulous to use against the person! When Mamgu was comfortably settled in an embroidered nightgown and swansdown bed jacket, it became my pleasure to choose clothes and jewellery for her afternoon downstairs. She indulged my fancies, encouraging me to flounce about in her lace and velvet, watching like the queen from our never-ending story. Looking through her jewel box was a special treat, prinking and preening before the looking glass. Mamgu said that most of it would belong to me one day, especially the amber beads, my favourites.

Dadcu Jono visited every Saturday at first. Mam, very starchy, walked to Aunty Miriam's after dinner, shop or no shop! Trefor saved petrol to come as often as possible, sometimes accompanied by Martha, Big Zac and Uncle Dai, Dadcu's brother. Trefor never drove Dadcu Jono.

By mid-August, Mamgu and I were taking daily walks around the village, relishing the interest shown in her outlandish hats. Her love of clothes was undiminished, and the Misses Bowen were busily engaged in alterations for her thinner figure. I made sure I was present for the fuss and flutter of frequent fittings, listening to talk of scalloping, appliqué, feather and stem stitch, needle-made-lace and broderie Anglaise. Miss Anni and Miss Siân were in their oils, displaying their skills to someone in the know. Make-do and mend took a back seat for the time being!

We spent languid afternoons with Ita, sitting under the tree by her house-drinking lemon barley water, kept cold in river crannies. The moment I wandered off, the two women became absorbed in Mamgu's outstretched hand. Sometimes, they didn't see me edging closer listening to whispers of a vision, a dream, preparations for things to come. There was a secret, a mystery I couldn't fathom. Something in the wind!

Nain's predictions came true. There was no Women's Picnic, no outing to the seaside, prices were sky high and everything was in short supply, from sago to soap. Tea with saccharine was disgusting, wraparound aprons were hard to find and nobody wanted Utility goods. Forty-eight coupons a year wouldn't clothe a scarecrow, according to Mamgu and while they were at it, had anyone taken hats into consideration? Mercifully, bread and tobacco were still unrationed.

Every Saturday night, maps were laid out on the *gegin fawr* table with Mr Llywelyn pointing out where the Russians were fighting with all their might against the Germans. In Europe, the Americans had joined us in the nick of time. Surely the tide would turn in our favour, at last? Mam was interested in North Africa, where General Monty had the honour of serving in the Eighth Army with her brother, Ifor! Everyone in the village was full fuss about two Italian prisoners of war, helping on the farms. They were brought to the village, every weekday, in army trucks. To make them conspicious, they wore brown uniforms dotted with yellow discs. After several weeks without any attempt to escape, two were billeted with Ianto, who had plenty of room to spare.

'Good boys they are,' said Mr Evans, Gilfach. 'Hard workers and they've settled down marvellous, considering. They go back to Henllan at the weekend, helping to make a church out of a Nissan hut, by all accounts. Beautiful, they say, with paintings all over the walls. Catholic, of course, most Italians are Catholic as far as I can make out. Is that right, Mr Llywelyn? Only we're having a bit of a job with the language at present. Mind you, they're picking up the Welsh like wildfire. Surprised me, I must say. One's called Carlo, but I couldn't get my teeth around the other chap's name, so we call him Llew. Made him laugh that did!'

'He's a good cook, that one,' said Ianto. 'He can make a tasty meal out of next to nothing. Samson really enjoys his food these days, we haven't been looked after so well in a long time. Cheers the old place up, it does, puts a bit of life into things, having those two around.'

'I'll tell you something,' said Wil Morris, 'that Carlo can sing like an angel. I've heard him in the fields. Lovely tenor he is. *Duw Mawr,* he could give Caruso a run for his money, without a word of a lie. Outstanding! If we're still in one piece next Easter, Mr Emrys should ask him to sing in the Cymanfa. I'd consider it a privilege to sing a duet with such a voice. Yes indeed. I wonder how he'd take to *pennillion*? I'll ask him when I see him. Can Llew sing?'

'No, but he's a *dab* hand with the football,' said Eben Pryce, Brynfa. 'Our boys say he's a real champion. He plays with Mic and Huw for hours.

'Pity we don't play the *Pêl Ddu* nowadays. With those three on our team we could make a good contribution, for once,' said Mr Hopcyn.

'Now there's a game and a half, if you like,' said Siencyn ap Siencyn. 'Never had so much fun in all my life! Mind you, it was past its hayday by then. I remember old Dafydd Pritchard talking about it before they replaced it with the Sunday School singing festival. In those days people came from all over, didn't they?'

'It was the drunkenness that brought it to an end! And not before time,' from Elias Rhys. 'We're supposed to be a God-fearing nation, resisting the Devil's kingdom on earth.'

'Give it a rest, Elias Rhys. You're a proper Howel Harris, Trefeca, you are. The old Devil's round the corner day and night for you. Anyway, your father and the preachers got their way in the end, didn't they? No more *Pêl Ddu* for us!'

'What was this game, then?'

'Well, Haydn, it was a game of football played on Old New Year's Day. A set of goalposts were put up in Llandysul and the other in Llanwenog, eight miles away. We played until the first goal was scored, or until we dropped. Weather permitting, we left early in the morning on horseback, coming back all hours! Remember when we got stuck in that ditch, Madoc, us, and Emrys Bowen? Covered in mud from head to foot, looking like monsters from the deep. Dafydd Pritchard and the boys pulled us out, remember? Freezing cold we were, and Dafydd gave us a nip from his flask to keep us going. Carried on regardless after that. But they put a stop on it for good a few years later. Marvellous times they were, say what you like!'

Siencyn was in his *hwyl*, the old stories coming out in a flood. I sat close to Col, by the door, hoping Mam would forget my bedtime.

Sunday

F'annwyl Miriam,

It's a very sad house here, my friend. Pedro was killed by the milk lorry the day before yesterday. I can't understand how it could have happened. He's never gone anywhere near it in all these years. He was sitting on the gate post waiting for our Margaret. As the lorry drew in by the churns, he jumped down right under the wheels. I was brushing our Margaret's hair by the window and she saw it happen. She didn't make a sound. She went as cold as ice and fainted clean away. Miriam fach, it broke my heart to see her.

Col made a little box yesterday and we buried him in the garden by the apple tree. Rhodri was there, very upset he was. We all shed a tear, I can tell you, except our Margaret. She hasn't cried once or said a word. She's been in bed ever since, asleep most of the time, or pretending to be. I wish she'd have a good cry and let it out, more natural than bottling it up at her age. Mamgu Poli says to give her time to get over it in her own way. I don't know so much, Haydn and I can't help worrying. Col thinks the old boy had a bad turn and fell off the gate post. He was too clever to jump just at that minute. Well, it's done now and Margaret's world is upside down. We'd only just sent Dan back to Mr Pryce, the feed is too much for us now. I hope my next letter is more cheerful. We're a bit in the falen as you can imagine.

Miriam fach, I can't come over for a week or two, but if you've got time I'd love to see you.

Love from,
Blodwen.

Towards the end of August, Mamgu announced we were taking a special trip.

'I feel so much better, I'd like to visit my brother Henry before I go home. I haven't seen him for years and I want to put things right. He'll be pleased to see you, Haydn, and he's never even met Blodwen and Margaret! We'll go together and have a grand time. I'll telephone and make arrangements straight away. Trefor will have a job getting petrol, but we'll manage somehow.'

'You've got a surprise in store for you, Margaret,' said Mam.

'What surprise?'

'Well, your Great-Uncle Henry lives in big house outside Whitland, set in its own grounds. It's very posh, with lots of rooms.'

'Will I have to sleep on my own? I'm not going if I have to sleep on my own.'

'No, no, we're not sleeping there, *cariad*,' said Mamgu. 'Henry couldn't cope with that, he's lived alone for too long. Proper recluse he is now. We'll be calling in to see Didi on the way back and we'll sleep together in the box bed, as usual.'

In the event, only three of us set off for Whitland, Trefor counted out. It was a cloudless morning, with everything spic and span, the car shining like a new sixpence and Trefor looking his very best. Dad's slouch hat was set at a jaunty angle, his check jacket sponged and pressed, the creases in his grey flannels sharp enough to cut butter. Mamgu looked truly magnificent! The Misses Bowen had surpassed themselves with the alterations to the tussah silk frock and linen coat, and her huge straw hat displayed flowers the size of teacups. I was decked out in my best florals, the bow in my hair adding six inches to my height. Mam said we looked like royalty, no doubt about it! Leaving the village in grand style, Trefor bowled along at a brisk pace, in such full command, we were not once requested to alight.

At mid-morning, we drove through tall iron gates, along a tree-lined drive into a gravelled semi-circle. Before us stood a large, granite house with too many windows to count! The front door opened, and an elderly couple in black stood in the pillared porch at the top of the steps. After exchanging warm greetings, Dad introduced me to Mr and Mrs Jenkins, Uncle Henry's butler and house-keeper! I heard Trefor's footsteps crunching around the side of the house. Mr Jenkins solemnly informed Mamgu that the master await-ed us in the drawing room. In the large hallway, a round table held a silver bowl of white flowers and a wide staircase curved upwards. Creamy walls above the panelling were covered in paintings like the *Ladi Llwyd*'s, only bigger. Why hadn't Mamgu ever told me about this grand house? Why hadn't I been here before?

Mr Jenkins opened double doors into a room full of sunlight.

'Miss Poli, Mr Haydn and Miss Margaret, Sir,' said Mr Jenkins.

The doors closed behind us. Nobody moved. Then Mamgu crossed the room to kiss a tall, thin man, standing against the light.

'Henry, my dear, it's good to see you again. You remember Haydn, of course, and this is his daughter.'

We shook hands and Uncle Henry invited us to be seated. With Mamgu unusually subdued and the atmosphere stiff and uneasy, I was glad to be swallowed up by an armchair the size of my bed. During the polite English conversation, I saw Uncle Henry's face clearly for the first time. He wore a close cut, grey beard and mous-tache, and tinges of red showed in his curly hair. Although he seemed more reserved, there was something of my father about his manner.

Mrs Jenkins entered, carrying coffee and biscuits on a silver tray. As she placed a glass of lemonade on a small table beside me, I almost jumped out of my skin! Two enormous dogs appeared behind her, the size of donkeys, with rough, grey coats and sad, bony heads. They walked over to my chair and gazed down into my face. I went rigid, inches away from two huge, black noses.

'Don't be frightened,' Uncle Henry said in Welsh, 'they're very gentle, and they love children. They're called Max and Smoky. Perhaps you and your father would like to take them for a walk before luncheon?'

I wasn't at all sure, but Dad was obviously pleased with the sug-gestion. Quickly drinking his coffee, he escorted me from the room, the dogs following on a command from Uncle Henry.

'Thank God for that,' Dad said with feeling. 'They need time to break the ice.'

'What do you mean?'

'Never you mind, let's play with the dogs. They're Irish wolfhounds. Splendid, aren't they? Uncle Henry's kept two ever since I can remember, always with the same names. I used to play with them when I was your age.'

'You came here when you were my age? You never told me about that.'

'It was a long time ago. Mamgu and I visited every summer until I went away to school. I loved it here. Mr and Mrs Jenkins had a son my age and we got up to all sorts of pranks together. Sometimes your Great-Uncle Nicholas and his family came too, and we went fishing and camping in the woods. It was ideal and I've never forgotten it. When I started coming on my own...'

'Why did you start coming on your own?'

'Well, when I was about twelve, there was a big family quarrel. It was between your Dadcu Jono and Uncle Henry really. They never did like each other. It was a real rumpus and Mamgu and Uncle Henry haven't seen each other since. Must be over twenty years now.'

'Is that why they have to break the ice?'

'Yes, Snwny.'

'Why did they quarrel?'

'You don't need to know that, little bat-ears.'

'Why did we come here today, Dad? Is it something to do with Mamgu's vision?'

He gave me a sharp look.

'What vision? What do you mean?'

'I've heard Mamgu and Ita talking about a vision. How quarrels and bitterness must be laid to rest and promises made for the future.'

'Have you indeed? Well, let me tell you something, you've heard too much for your own good. It wasn't meant for children and you must stop eavesdropping on grown-ups. Now then, let's play with these dogs and say no more about it.'

The sound of a gong came from the house! Dad explained that luncheon was served. There was a change of mood when we returned, and I heard Dad breathe a sigh of relief as Mamgu and Uncle Henry stood in the hallway, arm in arm. I saw how much they resembled each other with their hooded, dark-brown eyes, strong noses and curly hair.

They even laughed in the same way, tilting back their heads.

In the dining room, I sat at a large, oval table laid with dozens of knives and forks, silver dishes, glasses and bottles of wine! Uncle Henry was kind and considerate and I enjoyed my food, although I recognised very little except the roast potatoes. What a story I had to tell back home! Uncle Henry and my father retired to the library after lunch, and Mamgu sent for Trefor. She touched his arm, looking into his eyes.

'Take her to the ridge and show her the farm. I wanted to show her myself, but I'm tired, I need a nap before we set off. Tell her how much we loved the place, Trefor. No questions now, *bach*, we can talk on the way home.'

When I saw the rose gardens, the ornamental pond and the summerhouse, I understood why my father enjoyed visiting this beautiful place. Followed by the dogs, we passed through a small wood to rising ground overlooking a long valley.

'See that house down by the river? That belonged to your great-grandfather, Mr Edward. Your Mamgu and her brothers were born there. It was a big farm in those days, best dairy pasture in the country. Mr Edward was a first-class farmer, ran the place like clockwork he did. A better man never walked the face of the earth. God-fearing he was, fair and square in his dealings. My family worked for him, and we lived on the farm. I looked after the horses with my father and brothers, and my sisters worked in the house and dairy. Your Mamgu and I were born in the same year, 1868 that was. We grew up together, always in the stables we were. She loved the horses. She could tell a good horse a mile off, no bother at all. When she was eighteen, Mr Edward let her take over the stockbreeding. She chose me to help and we worked together for almost twenty years. Even had a race-horse once. You can see the cups and medals we won in the library. Grand times they were. In the holidays when the boys came home from school, we had dances in the barn and everyone from the district came, especially at Christmas. Martha was a good dancer in those days. Yes, her family lived close by. We've known each other since we were children.'

Trefor had a far away look in his eyes. I kept quiet, knowing I'd learn more if I didn't interrupt.

'Your Mamgu was a good looker, I can tell you. Turned everyone's head she did. That blazing red hair made her stand out a mile. Nobody to beat her on a horse either, she could ride as well as any man. Horses were her life, and mine, come to that. Miss Poli was the apple of her father's eye. She broke her heart when he passed away, and her mother didn't last long. The spirit went out of the place when Mr Edward died. A big man he was in every way. Hard to fill the gap, like. But Mr Henry did a good job of picking up the reins, mind you, seeing he wasn't a real farmer, too bookish for that. The other three were gone, married with families of their own. None of them wanted to be farmers. Miss Poli ran the business then, always had a good head for business, like her father. One day, your Dadcu Jono came to work on the farm. Handsome chap he was with a good education. It was obvious they were keen on each other from the start. We all missed her terrible when they got married and moved to the South.'

He pulled his cap low over his eyes.

'Big changes came not long after. The Great War. A calamity for everyone that was. Young Mr James was killed in France, along with one of my brothers, and dozens of others in the district. Nothing was the same after that. Mr Nicholas went to live in England and when Mr Henry won his fortune on the Irish Sweepstake, it came as no surprise that he wanted to sell the farm.

'I remember the day of the sale as if it were yesterday. The house had a spring clean from top to bottom, my sister Lotti giving the orders. Buildings were whitewashed inside and out and the yards cleaned and swept. All the animals were washed and brushed before being penned up on clean straw. We plaited and ribboned the horses' manes and tails, their coats shining like velvet! There were tears in my father's eyes, and mine weren't dry either. Plenty more felt the same! The place looked just the way the old master liked it, but he was turning in his grave that day, I know. I'll never forget it, your Mamgu and the boys standing there like statues, hardly believing their eyes. But they'd all agreed to the sale, no argument. In the end, the farm went to strangers and that was that, gone from the family for good. Mr Henry bought this house and I worked here until Miss Poli asked me to look after her horses in the South. I went like a shot, but I always think of that place down there as home. Your Mamgu feels the same, yes indeed.'

He fell silent, looking down the valley.

'Why did Mamgu and Uncle Henry quarrel, Trefor?'

'What do you know about that?'

'Dad said they had a quarrel and they hadn't spoken for twenty years.'

'I speak nothing of quarrels, *bach*, not for me to say. It's in the past, long gone and best forgotten. Come on, time to go, the dogs are fed up now. I was sorry to hear about your Pedro, Margaret *fach*. He meant such a lot to you, I know. Are you going to have another one?'

'No, I'd rather not. Mrs Davies' corgi's just had a new litter and she's offered me the cheeky one. He's always jumping onto her lap, nibbling holes in her apron pocket, looking for Welsh cakes. He's lovely, but he's not like Pedro.'

After saying our goodbyes to Uncle Henry, we sat in the car while he and Mamgu lingered on the steps, talking and holding hands. It was a silent journey, the mood sad and gentle, all three deep in thought.

A warm welcome awaited us at Didi's with supper on the table and Gwyn's place laid as usual. Moses was perched by the door, looking less proud and menacing nowadays. We sat in the cosy room, recounting the exciting events of the day until the men left to sleep in the village. Didi declared that Mamgu looked tired enough to have the box bed to herself. I slept on the *sgiw* opposite Didi Fawr, content to be together. The lamp was still lit when I woke to see Didi sitting on the bed, holding Mamgu in her arms. In my drowsiness, I thought I heard the sound of crying.

Love from Blodwen

F'annwyl Miriam,

...A solicitor named Baines came to see Poli on Friday. He's helping Mr Howard these days, by all accounts. There were papers to sign, and he called on the way to Aberteifi. Good looking chap, with a smart car, very polite and very nice, but I didn't like him. When you look him in the eye, he's cute enough not to look away, but a shutter comes down as if he's got a secret. Haydn didn't take to him either. He told his mother to be careful, but she said not to worry, old Mr Howard is definitely in charge of her affairs. Now there's a proper gentleman, you could trust him with your life. But I, for one, hope we never have dealings with Mr Baines...

Love from,
Blodwen.

There was something wrong if Aunty Miriam came to our house in the morning.

'I'm glad you're on your own, Blod, I came as soon as I could. I don't want to worry Mamgu Poli, but I thought you and Haydn ought to know. When I read your letter, the name of that solicitor clicked, but I couldn't place it for the life of me. It's been nagging at the back of my mind for a couple of days. Well, last night I rang our Alwyn in Ponty and he knew Baines straight away. He was in some scandal years ago, but he managed to keep it hush-hush. A big business pal of his was sent to Cardiff jail for forging money. I remembered then! About twenty years ago it was. This chap, a proper toff he was, got all dressed up in a top hat and a morning suit with a flower in the buttonhole. He went to the Mint in Llantrisant saying he was an inspector and he wanted to be shown around. He got away with it! Drop dead! They say he came out with the thing for making half-crowns in his pocket. He used it for years, so the story goes, and he was only caught when he made too many at once to buy a car. When you said you didn't like the look of this Baines, I thought you ought to know about his past. Our Alwyn says nobody's got much looks on him up there and he's surprised at Mr Howard having anything to do with him. What do you think?'

'You were quite right to tell us, Miriam. I smelt a rat the minute I saw him. Haydn must tell his mother as soon as he comes back. She says he's only a messenger, but you never know these days. Thank you for coming over, we really appreciate it. Poli's very anxious for her wishes to be carried out to the letter. Jono wants to retire, he can hardly move for rheumatism now, and there's plenty of money to keep him in a bungalow with all mod cons. The house and the business are supposed to go to Haydn, with a substantial sum to bring things up to scratch. After the war, he can sell it as a first-class going concern, and we can live by the sea. Poli's convinced Haydn's chest will get better there, and he can study his books without financial worries. She's got it all planned, but Jono's the one to watch. I've never had any looks on that man, as you know. Baulked Haydn at every turn has Jono. I might be wrong and I hope I am, but I can't see it being any different this time either. That's why this Baines chap makes me wonder. Birds of a feather, Miriam *fach*. Perhaps everything will work out fine, but what if it doesn't? We'll be high and dry, that's what we'll be, high and dry!'

'What do you think you ought to do then, Blodwen?'

'Sometimes, I've got a good mind to tell Mamgu Poli I won't leave here, but Haydn's health is getting worse, that's a fact. Besi says it's living so close to the river, much too damp. The shop is going downhill with all these changes and it's getting too much for him. On the quiet, I know he wants to go. Well, who wouldn't, with the picture that's being painted for us? He thinks, if we stay here, we'll be staring failure in the face before long. But I'll miss the village terrible, we're part of it now, almost as if we were born here. And our Margaret, how is she going to manage? She'll break her heart, for sure. I'm afraid for her, yes indeed I am. I'll be near my family, that's one good thing, and our Mam will be glad to see us. The house feels empty, she says, the boys away and the girls in the factory on shift work, day and night. And that's another thing. It's obvious there's a war on up there, air raid warnings and everything. Mam says they spend many a night in the *cwch* under the stairs with black pats crawling underfoot. But not our Dat, he'd sooner die in the open, he says.'

'That's what I was thinking. With this old war, you'll be better off down here, and God forbid, what if there's an invasion? Has Poli thought of that?'

'That's exactly what I said to her. What if there's an invasion, I said? She looked at me as if I was *twp*, and do you know what she said? Didn't I know that Brân Bendigeidfran's head is buried under the Tower of London, keeping us from harm? It faces east, looking down the Thames, so no invasion will ever come from there. Well, that's a new one on me, I must say. According to Mamgu Poli, the Germans were doomed from the start, they just don't know it yet!'

'She's one on her own, she is, an answer for everything. How is she then, is she still going back at the end of the month?'

'Yes, we'll miss her, I can tell you, especially our Margaret, we've had such a lovely time together. She's marvellous, considering, as full of fun as ever but she tires quite quickly and needs to rest more and more. There's no doubt about it, Miriam *fach*, her heart is very weak.

We've begged her to stay with us. Haydn's half out of his mind with worry. But she's as calm as anything, no fuss and bother and she won't let us be downcast. She says she's seen it all in her vision, she's going to die peacefully with no pain. Everything's arranged, cast iron, right down to the funeral. Martha's moving in when she goes home and she and Megan will look after her well, nobody better. The horses are being sold, except for Prince, he's going to Trefor. Poor Trefor, he seems to have aged all of a sudden. Funny thing, I've never thought of Trefor as old before. He'll come to live in Hafod with Lotti, I expect.

'It's a funny old world, Miriam, the one thing Poli wants now is to be with Jono. There you are, that's how it is. After everything he's done, there's nobody like him for Poli. The sun rises and sets with him and she'll forgive him anything. It's always been like that, you know, she's always thought the world of him and she won't hear a word against him from anyone else. I can't understand it myself. He's never realized how lucky he is to have a wife like her. I could cry my eyes out thinking about it.'

'Blodwen *fach*, don't upset yourself. Poli's lived her life to the full, as she saw it. A case on her own she is and we'll never meet her like again. Come on now, I'll make us a nice cup of tea and we'll change the subject. Did I see the back of Eben Pryce on the crossroads? What was he doing in the village at this time of day?'

'He came to ask us to phone for the doctor. Mrs Gwilym, Bwlch, is fading fast. Besi's been there since the day before yesterday. I don't know much about Mrs Gwilym, don't think I've seen her more than half a dozen times since we've been here. She doesn't come to Chapel, does she?'

'No, she's Methodist. She walked miles to a chapel up the top until her rheumatics got the better of her. She never liked interference, wouldn't have anyone to help her when her husband died. Carried on by herself until she dropped with pleurisy a few years back. It was Mari Pryce who found her that time too. The old lady was in an awful state with the house closing in on top of her, cats everywhere. She'd been in bed, God knows how long. Her hair was straggling down her back and her finger and toenails were like claws.

She looked like a witch from the back of beyond! Mari sent for Besi straight away. They cleaned up the place and made the old lady comfortable. The cats were put outside, but there was one big, ginger tom who wouldn't leave her side, fought like a tiger when they went near. Turned out he was Mrs Gwilym's favourite, inseparable they were. She was very upset when he died a few years later. She got Eben to make a coffin for him, and it's been locked in a tin trunk ever since, waiting to be buried with her. Besi knows the arrangements. She's been marvellous to Mrs Gwilym over the years, her and Mari Pryce. Kept a keen eye on the old lady and seen to it she was never in want. Besi and Mari are two of a kind, hearts of gold.'

'You mean to say they'll put the cat in the grave with Mrs Gwilym?'

'Besi will keep her promise, you can bet your life on that.'

Mamgu came to meet me from school on that fine day in late September, crossing the bridge in her pale dress, her large hat floating in the shadow of her parasol. The other children stopped for a good look, the ones who knew her crowding around to be noticed. They waved their way up the school hill, walking backwards until they were out of sight.

'We'll go for a little walk before tea, shall we? You know I'm leaving soon, don't you, *cariad?*'

'Can't you stay longer, Mamgu, we don't want you to go.'

'I know that, but there are things to be seen to. Important things.'

'What things?'

'Let's go down to the river and I'll tell you my plans. Very exciting they are, I'm sure you'll like them. *Caton pawb!* It's warm enough for a paddle. We'll sit here on the bank and dangle our feet in the water, shall we? Help me unbutton my boots, there's a good girl. There's lovely! It's grand to feel the water between your toes. I've always liked that, especially when it's clear and sparkly like this.'

'What are the exciting plans then, Mamgu?'

'Well, let's talk about you first. Have you ever thought what you'd like to do when you grow up?'

'I want to help Dad in the shop.'

'I've got a feeling you'll be ready to see the Big World before long.'

'Like Ceri?'

'Yes, like Ceri and Rhodri's brothers, and like them, it's essential to have a good education. Learning opens many doors and makes life all the richer. Isn't that what Mr Llywelyn tells you?'

'Yes, but he says this valley is much better than the Big World.'

'I know you love it here, *cariad*, it's your home after all, but nothing stands still, you know. In another year you'll be old enough to go to school in Aberteifi.'

Iesu Grist aros gyda ni! I hadn't thought of that! Leaving the village and sleeping on my own in Aberteifi in the dark! I wasn't going to do that, for sure.

'Tell me more about your plans, Mamgu.'

'Instead of going to school in Aberteifi, I thought it might be a good idea if you all lived in my house in the Miskin, and you could go to the County School in Mountain Ash. It's not so far away and it's still in Wales, that's the most important thing.'

'Will I have to sleep somewhere else?'

'No, of course not, you'll be at home in your own bed. I think you'll like the school, I know some of the teachers. Miss Peters, Mrs Hughes, Mrs Lewis and Mr Jenkins, and very good they are too. You'll get on fine, pass your Higher and go to College for your qualifications. That's what I wanted for your father, but it wasn't to be. With qualifications you can earn your own living and make your own choices, *merch fach*. There's nothing like making your own choices, you believe me.'

'I'm not very clever in school.'

'Of course you are. In the South you can have special lessons in English and lots of other exciting things. Just imagine, you can learn how to play the piano and how to sing and dance. You won't know yourself, you'll have such a wonderful time. And when this old war's over, your Daddy can sell the shop and you'll live by the sea. His chest will be much better there, I'm sure. You'd like a nice house by the sea, wouldn't you?'

'In Llangrannog?'

'Yes, perhaps in Llangrannog.'

'Will you come and live with us?'

'*Cariad fach*, I'm old now and...'

'You're not as old as Nain!'

'Quite right there. She must have insides made of boot leather the way she goes on, year after year. But my turn will come before Nain's, Margaret *fach*. Do you remember, a long time ago, when you and Trefor talked about Gwyn on Didi's mountain? How hard it is to find the right words to explain difficult things? Remember we talked about it afterwards?'

'I remember.'

Very carefully, she retied my straggling hair ribbon. As she put her arms around me and kissed my cheeks, I saw the tears in her eyes. I knew what she wanted to say.

'Are you going to die, Mamgu?'

'Yes, *cariad,* that's what I'm trying to tell you, right enough. As you know, we must all die sometime, but I shall go soon. I wanted to tell you myself because I want you to know how much I love you. You are so very precious to me, Margaret *fach*, my one and only grand-child. I'll always be with you, your very own, extra-special Guardian Angel. You need as many of those as you can get, you believe me. I'll be the best, you can be sure, watching over you day and night. Don't be sad, *cariad*, listen to me now. Whenever you think about me, I'll be there in your mind's eye, quick as a flash, just as you see me now. We mustn't cry because one day, a long way off, we'll be together again. You believe that, don't you? Look at me, *cariad,* we all know it's true because it says so in the Bible, doesn't it? Come on, sit on my lap, we'll dry our eyes and I'll tell you any story you like.'

We were still sitting under the trees when Mam came looking for us at teatime.

'*Duw Mawr*, I've been looking for you everywhere! Didn't you hear me calling? Look at the pair of you, soaking wet asking for pneumonia. I can't let you out of my sight for five minutes before you do something daft. I'm surprised at you, Mamgu Poli, you should know better!'

Mam wiped our feet in her apron and buttoned up Mamgu's boots.

'Home now, quick march, and change those clothes. I don't know what I'm going to do with you two scallywags. Look, Dad and Col are on the bridge, waiting for their tea, no doubt.'

Mamgu smiled at me over Mam's head. I was part of our special secret, Mam, Mamgu and me, the lucky three.

Chapter Nine

F'annwyl Miriam,

... I haven't seen a funeral like it since the old days. Hundreds of people lined the pavements to pay their respects. The curtains were drawn in every house in the street, and all the shops were closed. It was a bitter cold day, but the Chapel was full to overflowing, dozens standing on the steps, out to the street. The singing was beautiful, you've never heard anything like it, all the old hymns, Mamgu's favourites. There wasn't a dry eye in the place.

Our Margaret was supposed to stay with Mam, but she wanted to see the funeral, she was quite certain on that. Although I know it isn't done, I almost took her to the Chapel service. I was worried about her, she was so quiet somehow. In the end she stayed with Megan in the shop until I got back. We were together when the coffin passed on the cart covered in spring flowers. Trefor was leading Prince, Mamgu's favourite horse. He looked his very best, Trefor saw to that. His coat was like new silk with the black plumes on his head and his hoofs muffled. Everything was just as Mamgu Poli wanted it. We watched them to the end of the street, and then our Margaret waved goodbye. Dear me, it broke my heart to see her little face, I won't forget it in a hurry. She's taken it very hard, only to be expected with the two of them so close, and her being a knowing child.

It was gentlemen only to the cemetery, a long walk with Trefor and Prince moving so slowly. Jono and Haydn were in the only car. Poor Haydn, he was really bad, I didn't think he'd be able to carry on. Jono looked ill too, he can hardly walk nowadays, much worse than when I last saw him. I almost felt sorry for him on times. It was so cold in the cemetery

215

they both had to stay in the car. Uncle Henry and Uncle Nicholas were there, but they left after the service at the graveside. They had a good talk to Haydn, but only exchanged a few words with Jono. Mr Howard wasn't there, he's very ill indeed.

The food was in the vestry, of course, far too many people for the house. I couldn't leave our Margaret again, so I took her with me. She was as good as gold. I think it helped her being with the women, seeing everything going on. Nobody said a word about it being no place for a child. Martha was in charge, a real stalwart as usual. Glad of plenty to do she said, or she'd be in the falen good and proper. There was a marvellous spread, sit down, hot, with plenty of everything. No expense spared, as you'd expect, and no sign of rationing. It was very welcome, the weather being so perishing. Uncle Dai almost broke down once or twice, poor old dab. He and Poli were big pals to the end, and he was always there in time of need. We'll all miss her terrible, what we're going to do without her I don't know. She was a true blue friend to so many.

Haydn's been ill ever since, and Margaret's quiet beyond, spends hours with Col in the barn. He didn't come to the funeral after all, said he'd stay at home to look after everything. He picked a big bunch of snowdrops to put on the grave. Thought the world of Mamgu he did, just like the rest of us.

Well, everything is set in motion now, Miriam fach, it's bant a'r cart and no looking back. We've handed in our notice to Nain. She was very nice about it, said she was sad to see us go and she'd give us a goodbye tea party. Jono's moving to a bungalow in a fortnight's time, and Uncle Dai will keep the business going until we get there. Time to start packing up, I suppose, but I haven't got the heart for it somehow. Thank you for offering to help, it will be grand to have you here. Remember the day we came and the lovely welcome you gave us? March, ten years ago that was, almost to the day ...

Love from,
Blodwen.

Spring was late with the weather still very cold for my trip to Llangrannog on Asia's back. Mam refused me little during those last weeks, and Ita and Col thought the outing would blow away the cobwebs. We promised to be home by three o'clock, no argument.

Ita was wrapped up in heavy shawls and long skirts and as for me, I could hardly move for clothes. If I fell off Asia's back I wouldn't feel a thing! Swamped by his big coat, cap and balaclava, Col carried a mysterious, brown-paper parcel on his back. Dad laughed when he saw us in the yard, looking like something straight from Russia!

There wasn't a soul to be seen when we left the village, climbing between the tall hedges to the top road. Free as skylarks in the high, silver light, the day was ours alone, Ita's, Col's and mine. I was thrilled to be on our promised journey, playing once more the lords and ladies of our stories.

Two young men appeared on bicycles, shouting as they passed, 'Clear off out of it! We don't want your sort around here. Go back where you belong, gypos!'

The clicking noise in Col's throat meant trouble, but Ita was there before him. Shrieking something in Romany, she chased them down the road, shaking her fist. I couldn't help laughing and Ita was very glad to hear it.

I dismounted before the hairpin bend on the steep descent to the deserted beach, where Carreg Bica stood, black against the water. A few curtains twitched as we passed through the narrow street, and a man in the pub doorway gave us a hard, second look. Col wandered off while Asia drank from the stream flowing into the bay. We knew what to expect, and sure enough, a low howling came from a nearby cave. Col was playing ghosts again! On cue and out of earshot, Ita and I rushed along the sand, shouting and screaming with fright, Mara at our heels. The three of us behaved like mad things on holiday until, freezing cold and starving hungry, we found a sheltered spot to empty Ita's picnic basket.

Col unwrapped his parcel to reveal a red, home-made kite with streamers. Our surprise and delight almost made him smile. We climbed the steep slope to the cliff top where he released the kite into the wind. It soared for several minutes before diving like an arrow to the ground. Col tried everything to make it fly again, running and leaping about, refusing to give Ita a turn. Finally, he walked slowly towards the poor, bedraggled thing and jumped on it repeatedly with all his might. In the midst of his fury, a sharp gust of wind snatched his cap, taking it high over the cliff. Ita and I, helpless with laughter, watched his disbelieving face as it soared and dipped out to sea. The last of the spice cake and warm tea did little to cheer him up. He was in a real *pwdi* until Ita sang her gypsy love-song, the one that made us think of Seth, far away, goodness knows where.

For a keepsake, she told us a favourite story about her grand-mother, from ten ages before, who watched the peacock fly to catch a snake at dusk. Bought by a wealthy man and clothed in garments of silk and gold, she was his heart's desire. They lived in a richly orna-mented house, standing in lush gardens cooled by fountains. But her sadness so touched his heart, he set her free to find her people in the land of Sara, the saint with the silver face.

It was time to leave. Col went to saddle Asia and as we waited, huddled under Ita's shawls, she gave me a small box. Inside lay a beautiful, carved, silver ring.

'This is for remembrance, my little *rakli*. May you always be with those who love you.'

Mam and Aunty Miriam were scrubbing out the dairy while Rhodri and Bryn piled rubbish on Col's bonfire in the yard. Boxes of books littered the *gegin fawr* and dog-eared copies of Zane Grey stood on the table.

'What are qualifications, Dad?'

'Certificates to show you're properly trained for your chosen pro-fession or trade.'

'Do you need qualifications to live in Arizona?'

'No, just a big hat.'

'Why a big hat?'

'The sun's very hot in Arizona.'

'Is it by the sea?'

'No, but there's plenty of sand.'

'Would your chest get better in Arizona?'

'I think it might.'

'Why don't we go and live there then?'

'It's a very inviting idea, my Snwny, but I think the time has come to say goodbye to Arizona and cowboys and Indians. I'm nearly forty now, too old for daydreams.'

'Did you want to live there when you were my age?'

'I was a little older, about fourteen, I suppose. I was ill for a long time and I started reading about America. It seemed a very exciting place to me, especially the Wild West, as they called it. Imagine riding a horse all day and sleeping under the stars, far away from the rain and the noise of the pits.'

'Why were you ill, Dad?'

'I had rheumatic fever when I was thirteen and it left me with a weak chest. I didn't go to school for almost a year.'

'But you went to college, didn't you?'

'Yes, and afterwards I trained as a master grocer in a big shop in Brecon.'

'Was that you own choice, Dad?'

'I think I hear Mamgu Poli's voice here. Very keen on qualifications was your Mamgu Poli. She wanted me to go to Oxford University and be the Prime Minister, at least. Yes, *cariad*, it was my choice to go into trade but I don't think it's exactly my line. I find making money very difficult, and it must be said, I haven't been a huge success so far. My farming skills are pretty limited too, but one must keep a sense of perspective. Nothing's wasted and every experience teaches you something. I hope I've learnt enough to make a good job of returning to the South.'

'I want to stay here.'

'I know you do. It's very hard for you but I think it's for the best and Mamgu left us enough money to do really nice things.'

'We do really nice things here.'

'Yes, but our future's tied up with Mamgu Poli's shop, and I'm afraid that means moving to the Miskin. I'm sorry you're so upset. Mam and I love you all the world and we'll do everything we can to make it easier for you. Shall we count the good points? You know lots of people there already and it's not as if you're going to a strange place. We'll be near Dadcu and Mamgu Davies, the Aunties, Martha and Big Zac and Catherine and Little Eluned. And there's one thing I know you'll enjoy, for sure.'

'What's that?'

'The pictures! There are three cinemas up the road in Mountain Ash, showing different pictures every week!'

'I don't want to see that fat man hitting the thin one again.'

'No, there are lots of pictures besides Laurel and Hardy and what's more, some are about cowboys and Indians! What do you think of that then? We can go first house every Thursday night and maybe on Saturdays too. Doesn't that sound good? Mam and I used to love the pictures. It was a new thing in those days, all the rage, especially when the talkies came along.'

'Where did you meet Mam?'

'In the Miskin. I was helping in the shop and one day I delivered some goods to Mamgu Davies' house. Your mother opened the door and I thought she was the prettiest girl I'd ever seen. I made sure I saw her every time I went home, until I finally plucked up enough courage to ask her to go to the pictures with me. Before long, we were courting and after a couple of years we decided to get married. Marrying your mother is the best thing that's ever happened to me in my whole life. She's an absolute gem, but if I haven't finished here by teatime, she'll go up like a rocket! You can help me, if you like.'

'Do you have horrible dreams, Dad?'

'Sometimes. Do you?'

'Yes.'

'I know you do, Margaret *fach*. I think you ought to tell Mam and me about them, then they'll go away.'

'No. If I tell, they'll come true.'

'Don't look so sad, my little Snwny, come here and sit on my lap. Perhaps you could just give me a hint of what's really bothering you?'

'Have you ever had a Vision, Dad?'

'No, I haven't, and neither has your mother. That was something unique to Mamgu Poli and hardly likely to happen to us lesser mortals. There's no need to worry about that, your Mam and I'll be

220

around for ages, probably until you're as old as Nain Pritchard! You'll
have a grand time when we've settled down. We're going to wallpaper your new bedroom, and the Aunties are making you a special
quilt, so I'm told. We'll buy posh clothes when the war's over and go
to Cardiff every Thursday afternoon on the train. I know you're
going to enjoy it once you get used to it. Come on now, cheer up and
let's get on with this packing. On second thoughts, I don't think I'll
burn these Zane Grey books after all.'

During our last days in the village, Nesta, Rhodri and I pledged our
everlasting friendship. I received many gifts, including a photograph
of Ceri and Jack taken on their engagement day. As we were leaving
Nain's tea-party, she and Miss Eirlys gave me a hand-painted cup
and saucer from the china cabinet!

Everyone showed me great kindness, knowing how I missed my
Mamgu and how I dreaded leaving. But nothing prepared me for the
news that Col was not going with us to the South. Mam tried to soft-
en the blow, explaining it was best for Col to stay where everyone
knew him. Evan Pritchard had offered him a home on his farm. He'd
be well cared for, never fear, young Mrs Pritchard was kindness
itself. Most important of all, he'd be close to Ita. Ita would always
look after Col, we all knew that, didn't we? I couldn't listen. I could-
n't leave without Col. I stayed in bed all day, pulling the blankets over
my head, deaf to the pleadings of my parents and Ita. When Col
came to see me, I wanted to shout in his face that I hated him forev-
er, but I stayed silent under the bedclothes. That night, Mam sat on
my bed as usual, but I told her I didn't want her. Her hurt face almost
melted my resolve to wait alone for the dreaded darkness to drift
deep, deep inside and kill me.

I was astonished to find myself still alive at daybreak. I left the
house to hide in my river place where the powerful outside darkness
of the coming night would surely do its work, keeping me in the valley always. Nursing my misery all day long, I finally fell asleep. It was
dusk when I woke to the sound of footsteps on the bank. Col climbed
into my most secret place and sat beside me.

'How did you know where I was?'

'I knew.'

'Have you always known about this place?'

'Yes.'

'Have you ever told anyone?'

'No.'

'I don't want to go to the South. I want to die here in the dark. Do I have to go, Col?'

'Yes.'

'Why?'

'Dad's ill.'

'He'll get better, he always does.'

'Worse now. Mamgu Poli left money for doctors.'

'If we must go, why won't you come too?'

'Can't.'

'Don't say that. You can if you really want to. Why not?'

'Afraid.'

'Afraid! What are you afraid of in the South?'

'Everything.'

'But Col, you'll have me to look after you.'

'Can't come, Margaret *fach*.'

'You won't come, not even for me?'

'No!'

'Don't say no. Please, please, don't say no.'

'Don't cry, *cariad,* don't cry.'

'I'm cold, Col.'

He took me under his coat, my head under his chin.

'I love you for ever and ever, Col.'

'I love you for ever and ever, Margaret.'

Oakland Street,
Miskin,
Mountain Ash,
Glamorgan.

Sunday

F'annwyl Miriam,

Tonight I'm so full of hiraeth, I'm writing to you with a heavy heart. It's not good here at present. Haydn has no part in the business, no house and not one penny piece. Jono is adamant that Mamgu Poli did not leave a will and he's broken his promise, as I knew he would. God forbid, he wants us to live in the house with him, and run the business for wages! We couldn't spend one single night under his roof. I was lucky enough to find these two rooms in Oakland Street, which will do until we can rent a place of our own. Haydn's looking for work, and I'm starting in a factory the week after next. That will help a lot. Margaret is trying to be brave, but she's not herself. School is difficult because of the language, and she's pining for Col and Ita and her friends. My family and everyone here are kindness itself, but I can't tell you how I miss you all.

Remember us in your prayers, Miriam fach, as I remember you.

Love from,
Blodwen.

The Author

Margaret Wyles was born in the industrial valleys of south Wales but brought up in the rural west of the country. Having spent much of her life in England, she now lives in southern France with her husband, the artist Walter Wyles, and her family.